War and Nature

War and Nature combines discussion of technology, nature, and warfare to explain the impact of war on nature and vice versa. While cultural and scholarly traditions have led us to think of war and control of nature as separate, this book uses the history of chemical warfare and pest control as a case study to show that war and control of nature coevolved. Ideologically, institutionally, and technologically, the paths of chemical warfare and pest control intersected repeatedly in the twentieth century. These intersections help us understand the development of total war and the rise of the modern environmental movement.

Edmund Russell is Associate Professor of Technology, Culture, and Communication at the University of Virginia. He has published in *Journal of American History, Environmental History, Technology and Culture, American Entomologist,* and *Environmental Entomology.* This book is based on his doctoral dissertation, which won the Rachel Carson Prize from the American Society for Environmental History.

STUDIES IN ENVIRONMENT AND HISTORY

Editors

Donald Worster, University of Kansas
Alfred W. Crosby, University of Texas at Austin

Other books in the series

War and Nature

Fighting Humans and Insects with Chemicals from World War I to *Silent Spring*

EDMUND RUSSELL

University of Virginia

CAMBRIDGE
UNIVERSITY PRESS

PUBLISHED BY THE PRESS SYNDICATE OF THE UNIVERSITY OF CAMBRIDGE
The Pitt Building, Trumpington Street, Cambridge, United Kingdom

CAMBRIDGE UNIVERSITY PRESS
The Edinburgh Building, Cambridge CB2 2RU, UK
40 West 20th Street, New York, NY 10011-4211, USA
10 Stamford Road, Oakleigh, VIC 3166, Australia
Ruiz de Alarcón 13, 28014, Madrid, Spain
Dock House, The Waterfront, Cape Town 8001, South Africa

http://www.cambridge.org

© Edmund Russell 2001

Cover credits: Soldier provided from RG407 CW1, USGPO, Still Pictures Branch,
NARA. Picture of mosquito from Leonard Munstermann, Mosquito Genomics,
WWW server (http://klab.agsci.colostate.edu/aegypti/aegypti.html) 1995, reprinted by
permission.

First published 2001

Printed in the United States of America

Typeface Sabon 10.5/15 pt.   *System* QuarkXPress™   [HT]

A catalog record for this book is available from the British Library.

Library of Congress Cataloging in Publication Data

Russell, Edmund, 1957–
    War and nature: fighting humans and insects with chemicals from World War I
to Silent Spring / Edmund Russell.
        p. cm – (Studies in environment and history)
    Includes bibliographical references.
    ISBN 0-521-79003-4
    1. Chemical warfare – Environmental aspects – History. 2. Insect
pests – Control – Environmental aspects – History. 3. Chemical warfare –
Effect of technological innovations on – History. 4. Insect pests – Control – Effect
of technological innovations on – History. I. Title. II. Series
    QH545.C48 R87 2001
    577.27 – dc21   00-040323

ISBN 0 521 79003 4 hardback
ISBN 0 521 79937 6 paperback

For Lucy

Contents

Illustrations

xi

Acknowledgments

One of the pleasures of this project has been its habit of bringing me into contact with delightful people. At the University of Michigan, Beverly Rathcke and John Vandermeer supported this foray across disciplinary boundaries in a multitude of key ways, and Gerald Linderman, Richard Tucker, Earl Werner, and Susan Wright gave valuable advice and comments. I conducted the bulk of the research and writing as a fellow at the Smithsonian Institution's National Museum of American History, where Pete Daniel, Paul Forman, Patricia Gossel, Pamela Henson, Louis Hutchins, Jeffrey Stine, and the fellows discussion group generously shared their ideas.

Brian Balogh, Amy Bentley, Nancy Bercaw, John Burnham, Pete Daniel, Thomas Dunlap, Brett Gary, Gabrielle Hecht, Margaret Humphreys, Linda J. Lear, Peter Norton, John Perkins, Anne C. Russell, Edmund P. Russell, Jr., Lucy Sankey Russell, G. Terry Sharrer, Linda Tucker, Donald Worster, and anonymous referees commented helpfully on various parts of the manuscript. I benefited from discussions with Paul Forman, Sharon Kingsland, and Stuart Leslie; from comments at meetings of the Organization of American Historians, Society for the History of Technology,

American Society for Environmental History, and Society for Agriculture and Human Values; and from seminar participants at the Beckman Center for the History of Chemistry, Johns Hopkins University, National Air and Space Museum, National Museum of American History, University of North Carolina Wilmington, Virginia Tech, University of Virginia, and Carnegie Mellon University.

Material in this book appeared in Edmund P. Russell III, "The Strange Career of DDT: Experts, Federal Capacity, and 'Environmentalism' in World War II," *Technology and Culture* 40 (Oct. 1999): 770–796; Edmund P. Russell III, "L. O. Howard Promoted War Metaphors as a Rallying Cry for Economic Entomology," *American Entomologist* 45 (summer 1999): 74–78; Edmund P. Russell III, "'Speaking of Annihilation': Mobilizing for War against Human and Insect Enemies, 1914–1945," *Journal of American History* 82 (Mar. 1996): 1505–1529; and Edmund P. Russell III, "Testing Insecticides and Repellents in World War II," in Merritt Roe Smith and Gregory Clancey (eds.), *Major Problems in the History of American Technology* (Boston: Houghton Mifflin, 1998), 399–409. As editors or referees for those publications, Paul Boyer, Alan Brinkley, Craig Cameron, J. E. McPherson, David Nord, John Perkins, Carol A. Sheppard, Michael Sherry, John Staudenmaier S. J., David Thelen, and anonymous reviewers advanced my ideas.

For help with research, I thank Paul Milazzo, Michelle Ierardi, Andrew Thompson, Peter Norton, and Justin Reich. James Roan at the National Museum of American History, Janice Goldblum at the National Academy of Sciences, Marjorie Ciarlante at the National Archives, Richard Boylan at the Washington National Records Center, Jeffrey Smart at the United States Army Chemical Research, Development, and Engineering Center, and librarians at the Truman Library, National Agricultural Library, National Library of Medicine, and Library of Congress helped me find materials. Randall Bond, Paul Boyer, Ian Gordon, Pamela Henson, Linda J. Lear, Peter Norton, Lynne Snyder, and Paul Sutter kindly passed along materials.

Many thanks go to Frank Smith of Cambridge University Press, series editor Donald Worster, and Larry Meyer of Hermitage Publishing Services for guiding this book to press.

I am grateful for funds from a National Science Foundation CAREER Award, a Smithsonian Institution predoctoral fellowship, a University of Michigan block grant, and the University of Virginia Alumni Board of Trustees Teaching Award research fund.

Too many scholars to count influenced my ideas. Some of the most important were Brian Balogh, Paul Boyer, Frederic Brown, William Cronon, Alfred Crosby, Pete Daniel, John Dower, Thomas Dunlap, William Durham, J. Glenn Gray, Daniel Jones, Linda Lear, Paolo Palladino, John Perkins, Julian Perry Robinson, James Scott, Chris Sellers, Michael Sherry, Ronald Spector, Russell Weigley, James Whorton, and Donald Worster.

Edmund P. Russell, Jr., Jean Sankey, Anna Russell, and Margaret Russell gave me the time needed to write. My wife, Lucy Sankey Russell, supported the project financially, enabled me to devote long hours to research and writing, and cheered on my work during even the most difficult times. She has my unbounded gratitude.

Charlottesville, Virginia
June 2000

Terms

This book uses "chemical weapons" and "chemical warfare" the same way as chemical officers in the U.S. Army did in the period under study. Those officers considered poison gases, incendiaries, and smokes to be chemical weapons. It uses "war" to mean all things military. This usage is consistent with current practice among British historians and historical practice in the U.S. government, where the army was part of the War Department in wartime and peacetime. It uses "pesticides" to mean chemicals used to kill several kinds of pests, mainly insects, fungi, and weeds. It uses "insecticides" to mean insect-killing chemicals. "Pest control" means the effort to control pests by any method, including, but not limited to, chemicals. Other methods included "biological control" (use of other living organisms) and "cultural control" (use of various cropping schemes). "Nature" refers to everything other than people and their creations.

Many of the organizations cited in this book underwent name changes. Most of the changes were irrelevant to this narrative, so the author selected the clearest name and used it throughout the narrative (e.g., Bureau of Entomology, air force). The exception was the Chemical Warfare Service, whose change to the Chemical Corps was relevant to the story.

COME, my tan-faced children,
Follow well in order, get your weapons ready;
Have you your pistols?
Have you your sharp edged axes?
Pioneers! O pioneers!

Walt Whitman

1

Introduction

It has been called "the nation's most ironic natural park." The Rocky Mountain Arsenal National Wildlife Refuge near Denver is one of the premier urban wildlife refuges in the nation. It is large (twenty-seven square miles), popular (50,000 people visit each year), and bountiful (some 300 species of wildlife, including candidates for the endangered species list, inhabit one of the largest tracts of shortgrass prairie in the West). At the same time, the refuge is one of the most toxic sites in the world. By-products of nerve gases, now-banned pesticides, and other lethal compounds contaminate the land and groundwater. A Superfund site, the refuge is the focus of a $2 billion cleanup effort expected to last well into the twenty-first century.[1]

The refuge seems ironic because, as a journalist wrote, it has "a lot more to do with nurturing life than with the arsenal's long mission of death."[2] Another word often used to describe the refuge (and other military sites hospitable to wildlife) is "paradoxical."[3] "Irony" and "paradox" are words we use when the world does not work the way we think it should. They are also arrows pointing to new ways of looking at familiar topics.

This book is an effort to rethink the relationship between war, nature, and human history. Long cultural traditions have given us little practice thinking about them at the same time. Since at least the days of the Old Testament, we have seen war and interactions with nature as separate, even opposite, endeavors. One of the most popular ways of expressing this idea came from Isaiah: "They shall beat their swords into plowshares, and their spears into pruning hooks: nation shall not lift up sword against nation, neither shall they learn war any more."[4] Military strategist Karl von Clausewitz defined war as "a form of *human* intercourse" and virtually ignored nature.[5] Similarly, we have often seen a distinction between war and the military, on the one hand, and peace and civilian life, on the other. As one observer put it, Americans in particular "are inclined to see peace and war as two totally separate quanta. War is abnormal and peace is normal and returns us to the status quo ante."[6]

With a few exceptions, even historians who have broken down other boundaries have left the war–nature divide intact. Military historians have pushed beyond studies of battles and armies to examine the impact of military institutions on civilian society – but rarely on nature. Environmental historians have emphasized the role of nature in many events of our past – but rarely in war. Historians of technology have analyzed the impact of military technology on society – but rarely on nature. Cultural historians have emphasized the impact of war on the way people interacted with each other – but rarely its impact on the way people interacted with the millions of other species on the planet.[7]

This book challenges these traditions. Its thesis is that war and control of nature coevolved: the control of nature expanded the scale of war, and war expanded the scale on which people controlled nature. More specifically, the control of nature formed one root of total war, and total war helped expand the control of nature to the scale rued by modern environmentalists. This book makes this argument through a case study, the interaction between chemical warfare and pest control in the twentieth century.

These might not seem the most obvious cases to study. Since 1945, nuclear weapons have stood as icons of military technology and the threat of war. And, probably because we think of insects as trivial or low-status creatures, pest control is not a glamorous field. But these images have obscured our vision. Although clearly significant, atomic weapons were not the only important weapons of mass destruction. Atomic bombs killed an estimated 100,000 people; chemical weapons killed about 90,000 people in World War I and 350,000 in World War II, plus the victims of Nazi gas chambers. Chemical weapons framed the century: a treaty designed to limit poison gas in warfare ushered in the twentieth century, and another treaty designed to eliminate chemical warfare ushered it out. In between, chemical weapons wrought profound changes in civilian life, science, and war. The seeming triviality of insects, on the other hand, was one of the reasons they were so important. Two examples from wartime are illustrative: commanders often ignored the potential of insects to transmit diseases, with disastrous results (in the Pacific in World War II, for example, malaria felled American soldiers eight times faster than Japanese soldiers did); and popular views of insects as trivial made them especially valuable to propagandists seeking to mold images of human enemies. Among experts, though, countering insect problems was seen as a Nobel-class issue: for discovering DDT's insecticidal properties, Paul Müller won the Nobel Prize for Medicine or Physiology in 1948.[8]

These two endeavors – chemical warfare and pest control – expanded each other on three levels. *Ideologically,* pest control created a set of values that warriors used to argue for combating and even annihilating human enemies. War created a powerful motive and rationale for a huge leap in the scale on which people controlled insects.[9] *Scientifically and technologically,* pest control and chemical warfare each created knowledge and tools that the other used to increase the scale on which it pursued its goals. *Organizationally,* war (and sometimes peace) stimulated the creation, growth, and linkage of military and civilian institutions devoted to pest control and chemical warfare, accelerating developments in both spheres.

Neither chemical warfare nor pest control was new in the twentieth century. The first recorded use of poison gas in war came in 428 B.C., when Spartans besieging Plataea tried to oust defenders by burning wood soaked in pitch and sulfur under city walls. Various succeeding armies used suffocating and incendiary mixtures to attack their enemies. One of the most famous, Greek Fire, burned and produced suffocating fumes while floating on water.[10] By the nineteenth century, however, poison chemicals had lost favor. In the Crimean War, British chemist Lyon Playfair proposed without success that naval shells be loaded with cacodyl cyanide (an arsenic compound) and fired into Russian ships. In the American Civil War, Union leaders rejected several proposals for gassing Confederate soldiers with chlorine, chloroform, and hydrogen chloride.[11]

The ideology of "civilized war" contributed to excluding gas from warfare. By the nineteenth century, professional soldiers had developed an unwritten code of behavior designed to limit harm to themselves and to civilians. The Hague Conventions of 1899 and 1907 advanced this common understanding by (among other things) defining and specifying the rights of combatants, noncombatants, neutrals, prisoners of war, journalists, and cities. One of the "declarations" of the 1899 conference banned the use of projectiles designed to spread "asphyxiating and deleterious gases." Twenty-seven nations ratified or adhered to the declaration, including France, Germany, Italy, Japan, Russia, and Great Britain.[12]

The United States rejected the gas declaration. Naval theorist and American delegate Alfred Thayer Mahan persuaded an initially divided delegation to take this stand. Poison gas might be more humane than existing weapons, Mahan argued, and could produce a decisive result.[13] Another delegate, Columbia University President Seth Low, agreed, reasoning that no such projectiles existed so their effect was "purely hypothetical." He said it was not "clear why shells which asphyxiate only should be forbidden, while shells which both explode and asphyxiate should be permitted."[14] The U.S. Senate followed suit and rejected the declaration banning asphyxiating gases.[15] Ironically, it ratified another "convention" from the Hague Conference that forbade use of "poison or poisoned weapons." The reason is unclear; perhaps the Senate overlooked the provision, which was only six words in a much longer convention on "laws and customs of war on land."[16]

Insecticides also had a long history. Over the centuries, various dusts and concoctions, many made from plants, found their way into farm fields and homes to control insects. Some two thousand years ago, Pliny urged the use of salt and ashes to keep worms away from fig trees, burning a plant product called galbanum to rid gardens of flies, and applying beaten larkspur to "kill vermin in the head."[17] In 1658, Thomas Moufet (also spelled Moffat and Muffet, and perhaps the father of the miss who met a spider while eating curds and whey) recommended fern root, penny royal, rue, and "the dregs of Mares-piss."[18] These recommendations likely grew out of informal experiments that formed the basis for folk knowledge. Pyrethrum was the most important botanical insecticide in the American market. Ground from the petals of several species of chrysanthemum, it achieved prominence as "insect powder" before 1800. First Persia, then Dalmatia (part of Austria-Hungary at the time), then France became major exporters in the eighteenth and nineteenth centuries.[19] Unfortunately, pyrethrum was too expensive to use widely in agriculture. Pyrethrum flowers were picked entirely by hand, which concentrated production in countries where labor was cheap.[20] These investments in land and labor made pyrethrum too costly to use profitably on any but the most valuable crops. It was employed primarily in households to kill flies, and even then the quantities were not large.[21]

In the nineteenth century, arsenic joined pyrethrum as a major active ingredient in insecticides, especially in agriculture. Although its first such uses are obscure, an arsenic powder called Paris green became popular in the United States in the 1860s for use on the Colorado potato beetle.[22] The success of Paris green against the potato beetle led apple raisers of the East Coast to try it against canker worm and codling moth in the 1870s. It worked again. By 1896, the United States consumed 2,000 tons of Paris green annually. In 1892–1893, a chemist working for the Massachusetts Gypsy Moth Commission developed a new arsenic insecticide, lead arsenate, which killed insects over long periods because it adhered to foliage. The well-publicized campaign against the gypsy moth doused lead arsenate on trees quite freely. Farmers and researchers soon found lead arsenate effective against elm leaf beetles, grape worms, and codling moths. The U.S. Patent Office denied the Gypsy Moth Commission's chemist a patent, turning the manufacture of lead arsenate into an open business. In 1907–1908, at least eighteen concerns manufactured about 2,500 tons of lead arsenate valued at more than half a million dollars.[23]

Pest control involved ideas as well as technology. The evolution of a word used by Americans for both human and insect enemies, "exterminate," suggests that the ideology of eradication appealed to long-standing values. The Latin root meant "to drive beyond the boundaries." Humans and insects that did not respect boundaries – of home, farm, or country – ought to be driven out, this term implied. By the fourth century, "exterminate" had taken on another connotation: "to destroy utterly" or annihilate.[24]

What set the twentieth century apart from earlier epochs was the *scale* on which people could annihilate human and natural enemies. Our narrative begins with World War I, when modern chemical warfare debuted. It ends with the publication of *Silent Spring*, the best-selling book by Rachel Carson that helped catalyze the modern environmental movement by characterizing pest control as a self-defeating form of warfare. Between these events, the United States gained unprecedented power over people and nature by mobilizing ideas, technology, institutions, and nature more efficiently than ever before. The result was wonderful and horrifying. Around the time of World War I, James J. Walsh published a book titled *The Thirteenth: Greatest of Centuries*.[25] Had Walsh lived to see the new millennium, what superlative title might he have attached to a book about the twentieth century? My nomination would be *The Twentieth: Most Ironic of Centuries*.

On the one hand, the quality of human life accelerated at an unheard-of rate. Simple survivorship was a good measure. In the last fifty years of the twentieth century, the human population nearly tripled. A drop in the death rate – not a rise in the birth rate – was the key to this rapid increase. As one expert put it, the human population did not surge because people "suddenly started breeding like rabbits: it is just that they stopped dying like flies."[26] This book tells part of that story: people stopped dying like flies because they got better at controlling nature, including flies and other insects that spread diseases and reduced crop yields.

On the other hand, the rate at which human beings killed each other also soared in the twentieth century. World War I killed more people than all nineteenth-century wars combined. World War II accounted for more than half the people killed in wars over the past two thousand years. Population growth contributed to the surge in numbers of deaths, but the *rate* at which people died also jumped. By one estimate, people in the twentieth century were fourteen times more likely to die in war than were people in the sixteenth century.[27] Here, too, this book tells part of that story: the main agent of civilian deaths in cities in World War II was fire, and chemical weapons (incendiaries) started most of those fires.

The irony of this combination grew not just out of coincidence in time; it grew out of causal interaction. Americans got better at saving lives partly *because* they got better at taking them. Americans got better at taking lives partly *because* they got better at saving them. Peace and war did not inhabit separate spheres. As one of the figures in this book said, Americans lived a world of "peaceful warfare."

To understand how and why, we have to think about war, nature, and politics at the same time. One of the most insightful analysts of American society, Alexis de Tocqueville, provides some guidance. Tocqueville thought the "chief circumstance" encouraging American democracy was nature. "Their ancestors gave [Americans] the love of equality and of freedom," Tocqueville wrote, "but God himself gave them the means of remaining equal and free, by placing them upon a boundless continent.... In the United States not only is legislation democratic, but Nature herself favors the cause of the people."[28] If Nature (so powerful it was capitalized) was the chief promoter of American democracy, war was its chief enemy. "All those who seek to destroy the liberties of a democratic nation ought to know," Tocqueville believed, "that war is the surest and the shortest means to accomplish it" by encouraging hierarchy and a strong central state.[29]

One could not separate these forces: Americans were democratic because they avoided war, and they avoided war because nature protected the country from external and internal threats. Nature shielded Americans from outside threats by placing the

country "in the midst of a wilderness." A "few thousand soldiers" sufficed. This was important because the army's hierarchi-
cal spirit and desire for power clashed with democratic values.
Nature protected the country from internal threats by supplying
bountiful natural resources. The availability of land created an
"innumerable multitude" of middle-class property owners, who
opposed revolution and war as threats to their property. Their
numbers enabled them to quell agitation for violent change by
the rich or the poor.[30]

So far so good in Tocqueville's land of Eden. But the garden
had its snakes. Ironically, Tocqueville believed, democracy made
war more severe as well as less frequent. Popular passion was one
reason. "There are two things that a democratic people will
always find very difficult," Tocqueville argued, "to begin a war
and to end it." So long as wars were struggles among the nobility,
the views of the people had little impact on leaders. But, in a
democracy, once war had "roused the whole community from
their peaceful occupations," the populace would throw toward
war "the same passions that made them attach so much importance to the maintenance of peace." Similarly, wars among the
nobility kept battles small by keeping armies small (because
nobles had to pay professional soldiers). But, as Napoleon had
shown in France, feudalism's downfall enabled nations to raise
gigantic armies from the citizenry and conquer capital cities in a
"single blow." Finally, the spread of democracy encouraged war
over a wider geographic scale. Democratic countries shared
"interests ... opinions, and wants" so closely that "none can
remain quiet when the others stir," Tocqueville argued. "Wars
therefore become more rare, but when they break out, they
spread over a larger field."[31]

Much of Tocqueville's analysis held true in the twentieth century. Democracies did find their interests intertwined, which
helped give birth to the first two *world* wars. Once in a war, popu-

lar passion did soar. Patriotism (and the wartime power of the state) did enable the country to raise a large army that aimed to overthrow the enemy's ability to wage war entirely. The United States did have a hard time ending a war without "total victory" and "unconditional surrender," as the nation showed at the end of both world wars.

But another aspect of Tocqueville's analysis did not hold true. He, like many others, saw the control of nature as a civilian occupation and war as a military occupation. It was America's focus on gaining power through conquest of nature, rather than conquest of other people, that set it apart from undemocratic Europe. He made this point by comparing the United States and Russia in a passage worth quoting at length: "The American struggles against the obstacles that nature opposes to him; the adversaries of the Russian are men. The former combats the wilderness and savage life; the latter, civilization with all its arms. The conquests of the American are therefore gained by the plowshare; those of the Russian by the sword. The Anglo-American relies upon personal interest to accomplish his ends and gives free scope to the unguided strength and common sense of the people; the Russian centers all the authority of society in a single arm. The principal instrument of the former is freedom; of the latter, servitude. Their starting-point is different and their courses are not the same; yet each of them seems marked out by the will of Heaven to sway the destinies of half the globe."[32]

What Tocqueville did not foresee was that control of nature, including by civilians, could increase military power. The Industrial Revolution transformed nature into useful products on an unheard-of scale with astounding efficiency. In the same way that industrialization increased productivity of laborers in factories, so it increased productivity of soldiers on battlefields. In an industrial world, one could not calculate, as Clausewitz had, military power almost solely as a function of the number of soldiers.

One had to include natural resources and technology in the equation. These inclusions meant that not just the army could benefit from (and agitate for) war, as Tocqueville believed. Now civilians could benefit as well. The citizens who stood to benefit most were not individual pioneers chopping down trees, but industrialists who could transform nature quickly on a large scale. Because political power grew (partly) out of economic power, war could undermine democracy by shifting power not just from individuals to a large state, but from individuals to large private institutions – especially if those institutions worked closely with the army to advance the interests of both. Along with technology and institutions, ideas developed to control nature were useful in war. The formalized set of ideas known as science contributed insights useful in developing technology. Informal ideas about the moral and practical importance of controlling nature provided a set of common values the state could mobilize in efforts to control human enemies. The American focus on transforming nature was not proof against war or its concomitant challenge to democracy.

Nor did Tocqueville foresee that war could increase control of nature. War, even in another country, increased demand for agricultural and industrial products. Civilians responded by intensifying their transformation of nature into those products. Increased demand increased the market for more efficient technology, which stimulated invention, development, and marketing of new tools. As appreciation for the importance of science and technology in war grew, so did government efforts to mobilize these resources. The federal government did not wait for market forces to change the civilian economy; it intervened by creating and linking institutions, by expanding industry, agriculture, and science through direct funding and tax subsidies, and by hastening technology transfer through changes in intellectual property rights. Recognizing that nature, in the form of disease, threatened troop strength (and manufacturing of war materiel) more than did combat, the federal government developed and applied new methods to control disease overseas and at home. It kept these methods secret so that disease would continue to cripple enemy soldiers, converting natural enemies into natural allies. It mobilized ideas about the moral and practical importance of war to encourage control of nature on a wider scale.

This book examines these processes, which helped transform the United States from the condition Tocqueville described in the nineteenth century to the one Dwight Eisenhower and Rachel Carson depicted in the early 1960s. (This is not to say that Tocqueville was precisely accurate at the time he was writing, nor that conditions had not changed by World War I. The United States waged wars in the nineteenth century too, and the United States did not have an even distribution of power among citizens. But Tocqueville's analysis was a reasonable rough description of the way Americans saw things on the eve of World War I.) By the time Eisenhower delivered his farewell address as president and Carson published *Silent Spring,* the United States had increased its industry, military, and civilian government to sizes that an Eisenhower Republican (Ike himself) and a Kennedy Democrat (Carson) both saw as threats to democracy and even survival.

The first two narrative chapters (2–3) of this book describe the impact of World War I on the United States. For the first couple years of the war, the United States participated without going to war by supplying the Allies with industrial and agricultural products. This participation changed the way Americans interacted with each other and with nature. The American chemical industry grew in size, expertise, profitability, and status. American scientists developed new chemicals to kill insect pests. Farmers applied more kinds of insecticides, in greater quantities, than ever before. Americans imbibed Allied propaganda, which drew on the American relationship with nature to frame American understanding of the war. When the United States declared war, the changes already underway spread more widely through the country. The need to wage gas warfare forced the country to marry science and the military. This marriage increased commitment of military and civilian chemists to poison gas and created a new institution within the army, the Chemical Warfare Service. Gas research stimulated research on war gases as insecticides and ties between entomologists and chemical officers; it also increased the profile and activities of federal entomologists. The federal government mobilized public opinion through a large propaganda program that, among other strategies, tapped into ideas about nature to frame understanding of the war.

The next two chapters (4–5) focus on the aftermath of World War I. Chemical warfare advocates thought they had proven the power, efficiency, and humanity of poison gas on the battlefield. But they returned home to find their ideas and technology rejected by the army and the public alike. The Chemical Warfare Service survived a series of threats between the world wars by enlisting allies and lobbying Congress effectively. Part of its strategy was to transform its image by developing and publicizing civilian uses of gas, one of the most important of which was using war gases as insecticides. Because agriculture had long been seen as a morally uncontroversial civilian endeavor, this campaign enabled the Chemical Warfare Service to describe itself as the Chemical Peace Service waging "peaceful warfare." It also reinforced the service's ability to redefine chemical warfare as pest control. Civilian entomologists also entered the world of "peaceful warfare," albeit for opposite reasons. Fighting the image of insects (and thus entomology) as trivial, entomologists promoted the idea that human beings were engaged in a war for survival with insects. In cooperation with the armed forces, they adapted military weapons, notably airplanes (and to some extent poison gases), to agriculture. Chemical companies capitalized on the capital and expertise gained in the war to grow and expand their work on insecticides, especially by searching for synthetic organic insecticides. American companies achieved limited success in this search by World War II. In the 1930s, some of these companies found themselves on the defensive when charged with profiting from (and even fomenting) warfare. Associations with chemical warfare reinforced the notion that these companies were "merchants of death."

The following four chapters (6–9) examine World War II and its aftermath. At home and overseas, the United States mobilized to wage "total war" on human and insect enemies. It linked military and civilian institutions, developed new chemical technology to control insects and people, and joined chemical warfare and pest control on rhetorical, institutional, and technological levels. These efforts paid off when the United States gained the ability to "annihilate" people and insects. Against civilians, the main weapons were incendiaries. Against insects, the main weapon was DDT. The stunning practical power of science demonstrated during the war led leaders to plan ways to apply the lessons of World War II to the postwar world. For academic scientists, this meant seeking to continue federal funding of science. For industrial scientists, it meant switching from military to civilian markets, including marketing the new wonder insecticide DDT. For government scientists, it meant trying safely to guide the blunt weapon that was DDT to civilian life. For military scientists, it meant maintaining links with civilian science and industry. At the end of the war, the ideas, technology, and institutional structures of the war entered civilian life roughly as planned. For the most part they were welcomed, though doubts swirled in some specialized circles.

Chapters 10–11 focus on the Cold War, an extended period of peaceful warfare punctuated by shooting wars. Against the Soviets and insects, the United States engaged in arms races by continually escalating the power of its chemical arsenals. For use against human enemies, the United States relied in battle on incendiaries.

It armed itself with a new nerve gas it had gained from Germany at the end of World War II, added a more powerful nerve gas (apparently derived from insecticide research) later in the decade, and researched psychochemicals that were to create bloodless warfare. Against insects, one family of insecticides after another lost their ability to kill insects as their targets evolved resistance. The army took the lead in trying to understand this process by organizing and funding research that civilian institutions would not otherwise have undertaken. Continued funding, sometimes with the help of intermediary institutions, accustomed civilian scientists to doing research for the armed forces while pursuing their own interests. Confident of the technology they had gained during and after World War II, chemical officers and federal entomologists promoted eradication of human and insect enemies to the American public in the latter 1950s. The strategy backfired as scientists and the public protested against chemical warfare and large pest eradication projects. The ability of scientific and technological elites in government and industry to develop and seemingly foist such measures on the public motivated two of the signal critiques of the Cold War distribution of power. Dwight Eisenhower left the presidency by criticizing the ideology, institutional relations, and technology of the "military-industrial complex." Rachel Carson catalyzed the modern environmental movement by making a parallel argument about chemical pest control.

The epilogue briefly describes events from 1962 to the end of the century, and it essays some lessons. The latter are not simple. We like to hear stories of progress or decline. An historian has termed them ascensionist and declensionist narratives, and dramatists call them comedies and tragedies.[33] In tales of progress, we learn of heroic individuals we can emulate and grand ideas we can follow. In tales of decline, we see cautionary tales that warn us off dangerous people and ideas. The narrative drive derives from our sense that we know where the tale is headed. Beware, for this tale is both. The events described here made the world both a better place and a worse one. For some people insecticides and chemical weapons were blessings, for others they were curses, and for some they were both. The world gets both better and worse, and we have yet to exterminate either good or evil.

2

The long reach of war (1914–1917)

Soon after Europe thundered into war in 1914, the head of an American chemical company looked across the sea and tried to grasp the scale of "the present, devastating struggle." He compared it to the Civil War, the Spanish-American War, and images in "our imaginations." Then he gave up. "It is simply impossible to forecast the results industrial, geographical or moral," he concluded. "The world has never seen anything like it before, and, therefore, reasoning from analogy is entirely out of the question."[1]

There was no denying the fantastic scale of the European War (as Americans then called it). Before the United States officially entered the war, the war changed the United States. The usefulness of nature to the new form of warfare in Europe gave Americans the best of both worlds: they profited from war without waging it. In doing so, they changed the way they interacted with each other and with nature alike.

For our story, one of the most important effects of the European War was its Cinderella-like transformation of the American chemical industry. On the eve of the war, the United States was hardly the belle of the chemical industry ball. Germany was. Germany had the best schools, best chemists, best factories, most sophisticated products, and largest output in the world. American chemists manufactured mainly low-profit bulk chemicals, had to buy intermediates for organic chemical processes (often called "coal tar" or "dye" chemistry at the time because they turned the former into the latter) from Germany, and resented their low international and domestic status. Orders trickled so slowly into American chemical factories before the war that some companies planned to forego dividends. Others faced "financial ruin."[2] Wall Street investors placed their money into other industries, leaving chemical companies strapped for cash.

War waved the magic wand that transformed this homely industry into a beauty. Charles E. Roth, secretary of the American Chemical Society, said in 1917 that American chemists had "accomplished within two years what it took Germany forty years to attain."[3]

Part of the transformation was quantitative: European demand, coupled with alert Wall Street investors, enabled companies to expand production as never before. Du Pont, Hercules, and other companies ran their plants to the limit.[4] The value of U.S. explosive exports rose over sixty times between 1914 and 1917.[5] Du Pont charged its desperate European customers so much that it financed plant expansion through sales rather than debt.[6] The river of money from Europe to the United States convinced Wall Street to open its floodgates too. In 1915, James Withrow noted that "business is awakened to the value of chemistry as a source of power and wealth as business has never had occasion or opportunity to be hitherto."[7]

The change was also qualitative. Before the war, eight German companies made almost 80 percent of the world's dyes, and the tiny American dye industry imported 90 percent of its intermediates from Germany.[8] When England blockaded Germany, the price of dyes and intermediates skyrocketed and American companies rushed to fill the void.[9]

An eager young chemist named James B. Conant exemplified the alacrity with which Americans entered the uncharted, dangerous, and potentially lucrative waters of organic chemistry. Armed with a fresh Ph.D. in chemistry from Harvard and visions of "vast profits" in his head, Conant joined two classmates to set up a plant in New York City to make chemicals no longer shipped from Germany. Conant designed a new procedure for making a chemical. When used in the firm's factory, the procedure caused an explosion that injured one partner and killed the other and a plumber. Conant later wrote, "the procedure had been formulated erroneously, which was no one's fault except my own."[10]

More skilled companies built a formidable organic chemical industry. Seventeen American companies joined the dye field in 1917 alone, with two – Du Pont and National Aniline and Chemical (later the core of Allied Chemical) – dominating the field for many years. These companies increased production so quickly that they cut the prices of some products by more than half.[11] A company did not have to be one of the two giants suddenly to become a powerful player. At the beginning of the war, the Hooker Company made two products: bleach and caustic soda. By November 1918, it made seventeen chemicals and was the world's largest producer of monochlorobenzol, a chemical used to make explosives, poison gases, and dyes.[12]

A war-stimulated tariff helped this expansion. Fearful that German companies would choke them after the war, chemical companies lobbied for a tariff on dyestuffs in 1914 and 1915. But this lobbying, which stressed the financial benefits of a tariff, failed. Then the companies shifted their tack. With support from the secretary of commerce, they emphasized the importance of the chemical industry for national defense. Germany had stifled the American dyestuff industry before the war, they argued, and dyestuff intermediates were used to make ammunition. This argument worked. Passage of the Emergency Tariff Act in September

1916, which protected American dyestuff makers for five years, helped solidify prospects for the future and increased the confidence with which manufacturers invested in dyestuff technology.[13]

Chemists welcomed the prestige conferred on them by the war. Chemist L. H. Baekeland noted that "since the beginning of the present war, even the most ignorant people have more or less become awakened to the fact that chemistry plays a big role in modern warfare. Through the newspapers the public knows pretty well, by this time, that modern explosives are made by intricate chemical process; the horrible use of asphyxiating gases also has played on the imagination."[14] Charles Herty of the American Chemical Society welcomed the "much more prominent place" of chemistry "in the thought of the nation" since the beginning of the war. He credited this rise to the press's "constant repetition of the phrase that 'modern war is largely a matter of chemistry and engineering.'"[15]

Less prominently, but important, the European War also made pest control more "a matter of chemistry" than before. It set the stage by increasing demand for, and price of, cotton. Belligerents imported vast quantities of cotton (among other farm products) to use in uniforms, tents, and bandages. Chemical companies, who used cotton to make explosives, also sent demand skyrocketing. Unfortunately, the boll weevil had continued its march from Mexico across the Southeast, devastating cotton fields from Texas to Georgia by 1914. As they had for two decades, entomologists urged farmers to combat this nemesis with "cultural control" methods, such as burning cotton stalks at the end of each season. And as they had for two decades, farmers resisted such labor-intensive methods because of expense and delayed benefits.[16]

The soaring price of cotton sent entomologists back to their laboratories to look for an insecticide that could save cotton as soon as possible. They decided to test a chemical called calcium arsenate, which they had tried a few years earlier on other crops and discarded because it burned foliage. But the original tests apparently had not included the boll weevil and cotton, so off the shelf calcium arsenate came for another audition. It succeeded. It was cheaper, easier, and faster than alternative methods. Entomologists recommended calcium arsenate to cotton farmers in 1917, and the latter snapped it up.[17]

The European War also introduced a different type of insecticide to American agriculture: a synthetic organic chemical. A key element in calcium arsenate, arsenic, had long been known to be poisonous. Other "arsenicals," lead arsenate and Paris green, had found wide use in orchards, forests, and potato fields. Pyrethrum, a chemical in chrysanthemum petals, joined the arsenicals as the stalwart among insecticides. But no one had yet developed a widely used synthetic organic insecticide. Explosives and gas warfare indirectly opened the door. Manufacturing of picric acid, an explosive in high demand in Europe, created large supplies of a hitherto obscure by-product called paradichlorobenzene, or PDB.[18] In 1915 and 1916, federal entomologists tested PDB and other volatile, toxic compounds (including war gases) and found them promising as insecticides. Follow-up research would later bring PDB to market.[19]

The European War shaped the rhetoric as well as the technology of pest control by encouraging use of military metaphors. Writers, entomologists, and farmers had long described humans as locked in a war with insects. According to Joel, God told his people that he would "restore to you the years which the swarming locust has eaten, the hopper, the destroyer, and the cutter, my great army, which I sent among you" (2: 25). But the war in Europe enhanced the appeal of such images. For writers and entomologists interested in reaching the public, linking struggles against insects to the European War provided a way to tie their subject to current events, express ideas in vivid language, and deploy humor. No doubt, writers were aware that their rhetoric was sometimes exaggerated.

But in other ways military metaphors expressed ideas of deadly seriousness. For entomologists, the discovery that insects transmitted diseases had transformed some nuisances into lethal threats. They chafed when the public and policy makers failed to respond with sufficient alacrity and thought escalating their rhetoric might produce better results. Shortly before the European War, L. O. Howard had proposed that the housefly be renamed the typhoid fly. His reasoning was simple: people "will fear and fight an insect bearing the name 'typhoid fly' when they will ignore one called the 'house fly,' which they have always considered a harmless insect."[20]

The scale of killing in Europe supplied a ready-made comparison for the scale of the insect threat. In August 1915, the popular magazine *Living Age* suggested that the outcome of the "war to the finish" between Man and Arthropod for "mastery of the planet" was "almost as much a toss-up at the present moment as is the result of this devastating War between Teuton, Kelt, Latin, Slav, and Turk which is now being waged in Europe, Asia and Africa." Insects transmitted a host of diseases, including plague, yellow fever, malaria, "possibly" cancer, sleeping sickness, and "almost all the diseases of cattle, sheep, swine, horses, camels, and poultry." It was "just conceivable" that insects would "depopulate" the earth.[21]

Along with conveying the scale of the insect menace, comparisons to the European War expressed the scale on which people might respond. Nothing less than extermination of insect enemies, some writers charged, would protect humanity. "We shall conquer if we realize in time the seriousness of this war against the Arthropod; as no doubt we shall get the better of the Teuton and the Magyar if we brush aside half measures," the *Living Age* article predicted. But conquest could be achieved only if "Man" applied "all his resources to the gigantic task of eliminating from the world the germ-conveying agents."[22]

Such rhetoric might be dismissed as the work of a hack in the employ of the popular press, but one of the most respected entomologists in the United States – Stephen A. Forbes – argued the same thing. As a young man, Forbes had enjoyed the excitement, patriotic spirit, and time he spent outdoors while a Civil War soldier. He credited his war experience with guiding him to a career in science. He joined the revolution in biological thinking that swept American universities in the 1870s, when Darwin, Agassiz, and Huxley kindled interest in evolution and competition in nature. Forbes served as professor of zoology and entomology and dean of the College of Science at the University of Illinois, state entomologist of Illinois, president of the Entomological Society of America, and member of the National Academy of Sciences. He was the only man twice elected president of the American Society of Economic Entomologists.[23]

The Civil War, scientific traditions, and entomological experience probably combined to influence Forbes's views. In an article published in a scientific journal in 1915, Forbes wrote what would become one of the most-quoted passages in entomology: "The struggle between man and insects began long before the dawn of civilization, has continued without cessation to the present time, and will continue, no doubt, as long as the human race endures.... Wherever their interests and ours are diametrically opposed, the war still goes on and neither side can claim a final victory."[24]

By framing pest control as war, Forbes hoped – as had L. O. Howard and the popular writer mentioned above – to convince Americans to mobilize against insects with as much fervor as they would against human enemies. Lamenting the public's inability to see that insects threatened the country's economy and health as much as did human foes, Forbes noted that Americans had hardly fought the San Jose scale, "a foreign enemy who had succeeded in completely overrunning" the country. He called the scale, which entered the United States from Japan, "a case of Japanese invasion far more successful, and probably more destructive also, than any which Japan could possibly make by means of dreadnoughts and armies of little brown men."[25]

In addition to helping frame views of insects, military metaphors helped Forbes frame views of entomologists. Given a strong tradition of respect for private property, federal and state governments rarely held legal authority to compel farmers to control pests. The United States would continue to suffer from insect foes, Forbes believed, until it organized war on insects the same way it organized war on human foes. Just as professional soldiers formed the skeleton of an army that could be expanded with recruits in wartime, so Forbes believed that entomologists should form officer corps in wars on insects. At peace, one could leave individuals to do what they wanted against insects. But in wartime, the United States needed "carefully planned campaigns by organized communities participated in by every one so situated as to be available, directed by experts and financed so far as necessary by the state."[26]

At the same time that Forbes urged escalation in attacks on the San Jose scale, that insect was showing surprising adroitness at defending itself. Although Forbes charged that Americans allowed the scale to overrun their farms without a fight, farmers around Clarkston, Washington, built their own plant to make lime-sulfur (then the best insecticide against the scale). Unfortunately, the insecticide killed fewer scales each year. Popular explanations blamed poor offense: the lime-sulfur was adulterated (a reasonable guess in a fraud-plagued industry), or farmers applied it incorrectly. But in 1914, an entomologist named A. L. Melander proposed the opposite explanation: good defense. Melander's tests showed that the most resistant scales lived in the most heavily sprayed region near Clarkston. Perhaps some scales were genetically resistant to sprays, he suggested, and passed their resistance along as a recessive Mendelian trait.[27] Melander's theory was controversial (among other things, it contradicted the idea that species were fixed) and did not catch on widely at the time.[28]

Unexpectedly strong defense was only one challenge. Another was what would, on human battlefields, be called "friendly fire." The idea that nature balanced itself was one of the most venerable in Western history among the public and scientists alike.[29] In the effort to control insects, entomologists believed that insect enemies were de facto human allies. As the title of an article in a popular magazine put it in 1916, the sides were "Men, Birds, and Fishes versus Arthropods."[30] Even insecticide makers recognized that their products could harm these allies. In early 1917, the insecticide maker Sterlingworth explained that "violent poisons" used as insecticides killed birds: "Man has upset one of the most important balances established by nature to control the insect growth and is paying for his folly by the increased numbers of these pests."[31]

Journalists made the same argument in popular publications. As *Living Age* put it, "Man himself – especially and before all, Man of the highest developed, Nordic type – has wantonly destroyed his beautiful and faithful allies the birds, has stupidly put out of existence many and many a harmless and useful reptile that only lived to devour insects and ticks." But there was hope. To be master of "an earthly paradise," "Man" could work toward "his vaguely adumbrated scheme of a balanced creation" involving himself and allies such as birds, lizards, fish, beneficial insects, and other "enemies of our enemies."[32]

While these writers blamed pest problems on the destruction of human allies in nature, another writer blamed some of history's worst problems with pests – and pestilence – on war. In 1916, Friedrich Prinzing published *Epidemics Resulting from Wars*. He pointed out that wars created troop concentrations, food shortages, exhaustion, poor sanitation, and refuse. As these ideal conditions for diseases worsened, commanders focused not on preventing disease, but on waging battles. Small wonder, Prinzing said, that epidemics ravaged troops and civilians in wartime.[33]

These epidemics were not just public health problems; they were military problems of the first order. Soldiers had a long history of seeing victory in war as resulting from what they did – recruiting and training troops, planning brilliant strategy, executing brave tactical maneuvers, and so on. When soldiers returned home after war, covered in the laurels of victory or the mud of defeat, who would question the idea that their glory or their disgrace resulted from clashes on the battlefield?

Perception and reality were two different things. Strategy, tactics, logistics, materiel, training, and all the other accoutrements of war taught in military academies certainly influenced the outcomes of battles. But, human pride notwithstanding, these human factors often took a back seat to nature in an objective calculus of military power. Throughout history, battles depleted military strength much less than did disease, weather, and accidents. As Hans Zinsser, an American medical officer, put it, "War is visualized – even by the military expert – as a sort of serious way of playing soldiers. In point of fact, the tricks of marching and of shooting and the game called strategy constitute only a part – the minor, although picturesquely appealing part – of the tragedy of war. They are only the terminal operations engaged in by those remnants of the armies which have survived the camp epidemics. These have often determined victory or defeat before the generals know where they are going to place the headquarters' mess."[34]

One of the worst war plagues was typhus fever. Typhus victims suffered chills, nausea, vomiting, violent headache, depression, fever, and rashes. Death claimed a fourth of the victims. When Prinzing wrote, no one knew how typhus fever was transmitted. But researchers were closing in on a theory: it seemed to be associated with body lice, which thrived in wartime.[35] The European War bore out Prinzing's thesis. Fighting wrecked villages, crowded refugees into small places, concentrated sick and wounded prisoners, swamped hospitals and their supplies, and left the miserable thousands without decent sanitary facilities. Typhus broke out in Serbia in November 1914 and spread with troops and refugees. The epidemic killed over 150,000 people in less than six months. Russia suffered an estimated 25 million typhus cases, leading to 2.5 to 3 million deaths, between 1917 and 1921. Hans Zinsser later remarked, "Typhus may not have won the war – but it certainly helped."[36] The typhus plague had little immediate impact on the United States, but it set in motion forces that would shape the way Americans thought about and fought human and natural enemies for decades to come.

So did gas warfare. In 1915, Allied troops huddled in trenches near Ypres, France, found themselves enveloped in a greenish-yellow cloud of chlorine gas released by German troops. Allied soldiers futilely tried to outrun the cloud, which reportedly killed 5,000 soldiers and injured 10,000 more. German military leaders lost the advantage when they failed to follow the cloud with a large-scale attack by soldiers, but they succeeded in demonstrating the military power that flowed from knowledge and control of chemicals.[37]

To observers on both sides of the front, gas warfare looked a lot like pest control. A German general at Ypres said, "I must confess that the commission for poisoning the enemy just as one poisons rats struck me as it must any straightforward soldier; it was repulsive to me."[38] A Dutch newspaper cartoon showed "Germania" sprinkling a can of chlorine on a horde of tiny soldiers, much as a homemaker would sprinkle insecticide powder on a horde of ants.[39]

Allied leaders assailed gas as illegal and inhumane. In the Hague Conventions and Declarations of 1899, Germany had agreed not to use projectiles emitting asphyxiating gases or weapons "calculated to cause unnecessary suffering."[40] British

Field Marshal John French charged that Germany "recognized gas's illegality" and caused victims to "die a painful and lingering death. Those who survive are in little better case, as the injury to their lungs appears to be of a permanent character, and reduces them to a condition which points to their being invalids for life."[41]

Allied propagandists seized on gas as a symbol of Germany's nefariousness. Dutch cartoonist Louis Raemaekers published a series of drawings portraying Germany as a criminal, an anarchist, and a snake for resorting to this form of warfare (Figure 2.1). Raemaekers's strategy worked. Journalist H. S. Villard judged that Raemaekers's cartoons "did as much as anything else, perhaps, to stir up the most intense kind of feeling" about the horror of gas warfare.[42]

Germany hoped gas would break the stalemate of trench warfare, but instead it touched off an arms race. Over the next three years, both sides launched gases of ever-increasing power and developed masks to counter them. Early gases, such as chlorine, harmed the respiratory system and could be protected against with just a mask. Later gases, such as mustard, harmed the whole body by burning and blistering the skin as well as the respiratory system, forcing soldiers to don protective clothing as well as masks. Chemical warriors also launched gases that made eyes water, shut down the central nervous system, and caused sneezing.[43] By the end of the conflict, gas would kill about 90,000 people and cause 1.3 million casualties.[44]

Poison gas helped catalyze a sea change in war by marrying science, technology, and war in the minds of European war planners. The parties had dated (and produced offspring) before: poisonous fumes had a long history in warfare, and the Union's victory in the American Civil War had owed a great deal to superior technology. But on the eve of the world war, European military strategists looked to Europe for inspiration more than to "provincial" Americans and their internecine conflict. One of the great students

2.1 "The Gas Fiend." One of the Allies' most effective propagandists, Louis Raemaekers portrayed Germany as a viper for using poison gas on unsuspecting Allied soldiers. From Louis Raemaekers, *The Great War, a Neutral's Indictment: One Hundred Cartoons* (London: Fine Art Society, Ltd., 1916), plate 68, Special Collections Department, University of Virginia Library.

of Napoleonic strategy, Karl von Clausewitz, had dismissed technology as an unimportant variable in war because both sides had access to roughly the same arms. "Superiority in numbers [of soldiers] is the most important factor in the result of an engagement," he believed.[45] Clausewitz's heirs looked at Napoleon and the Franco-Prussian War of 1871 and concluded that the keys to victory were big armies, quick movements, decisive battles, and civilian morale.[46]

The problem with the resulting "cult of the offensive" (besides its blindness to new technology) was its failure to take into account the ways in which enemy armies could defend themselves. Soldiers under attack in the European War dug holes in the ground to hide from enemy fire, introducing the term "foxhole" to the modern military lexicon. Small holes grew into elaborate, hard-to-storm trenches. Dreams of quick victory died in the mud of trench warfare.[47]

One response to the stalemate of trench warfare was to pump more men to the front, which belligerents did with lethal efficiency. Another was to dig a new well. That was where gas and other technology came in. Industrialization had already remade other labor-intensive industries by substituting machines for laborers and increasing productivity. Now belligerents did the same with war. "We have discovered that the modern economic organisation is in itself a fighting machine," observed British writer H. G. Wells. "It is so much so that it is capable of taking on and defeating quite easily any merely warrior people that is so rash as to pit itself against it."[48]

By 1916, the lesson had become clear. British Munitions Board Chief Hedlam declared, "The Du Pont Company is entitled to the credit of saving the British Army."[49] Chemists on the American side of "the pond" saw that technology's contribution to military power had soared. As a 1916 article in *Science* put it, "the present war is a struggle between the industrial chemical and chemical engineering genius of the Central Powers and that of the rest of the world. Quite irrespective of the war's origin, aims, ideals or political circumstances, these are the cohorts from which each side derives its power."[50] As the sinking of American ships increased tensions, the American Chemical Society helped plan mobilization of industrial facilities. Charles Herty urged the military to use, as a matter of policy, chemists for research rather than combat. He noted that chemical research "would prove much more vital to the power of the army than the presence of the individuals bearing arms."[51]

Other civilian scientists joined chemists in preparing for war. In 1916, a month after a German U-boat torpedoed a French ship carrying American passengers, the National Academy of Sciences placed the academy's services at the disposal of the president should the United States break diplomatic relations with any country. Two months later, the academy set up the National Research Council to promote the "national security and welfare" by organizing scientific research in government, industry, and educational institutions for the federal government.[52]

While the importance of technology in the European War was obvious to chemists in the United States, the obliviousness of the American army to the importance of technology was obvious in England. H. G. Wells complained, "In none of these [American army plans] is there evident any very clear realisation of the fundamental revolution that has occurred in military methods during the last two years." Instead, military leaders thought in terms of "rather imperfectly trained young men with rifles and horses and old-fashioned things like that."[53]

Nowhere did this lack of attentiveness glare more brightly than in gas warfare. American army leaders did nothing to prepare for gas warfare except write a few documents asking which part of the army had responsibility for supplying gas masks. In November 1916, almost two years after gas warfare started, a U.S. senator asked Colonel Charles G. Treat of the general staff, "Are they still using the poisonous gas over there, Colonel?" "The papers say so," Treat replied, "but we have not had any actual reports from our observers that they are using them."[54]

Wells's interest was more than analytical. It was easy to see that American resources could determine the outcome of the war even if the United States remained officially neutral. (Thus Germany's and England's efforts to blockade American merchant ships from enemy ports, an effort in which England held a decided edge.) From 1914 to 1916, "neutral" American banks lent $27 million to Germany versus over $2 billion to the Allies, and American exports to Germany fell 90 percent while quadrupling to the Allies.[55]

Wells, along with other British propagandists, sought to keep the United States neutral or, if possible, convince it to enter the war on England's side. A pro-German propagandist later called Wells "the biggest of the big propaganda guns.... Every detonation of his pen thundered throughout the world and reverberated with special force in the United States." Louis Raemaekers, the Dutch cartoonist whose drawings helped shape views of gas and the war in general, was said to be "worth an army corps to the Allies."[56]

In their broadly targeted campaigns, Wells, Raemaekers, and other propagandists turned to long-standing ideas about nature to influence popular views of Germany. Allied propagandists described Germany as a barbarian, ape, wolf, and bird. At the lowest level, Germany became a pathogen. Wells called the war "nothing more than a gigantic and heroic effort in sanitary engineering; an effort to remove German militarism from the life and regions it has invaded."[57] This reclassification implied that war was not just morally permissible, but morally necessary.[58]

In their efforts to convince the United States to enter the war (and boost morale at home by hinting at such an event), Wells and Raemaekers also relied on nature. Both recognized that Americans liked to view themselves as hardy individualists more interested in taming (or in a few cases contemplating) their own wilderness than in embroiling themselves in European squabbles. Raemaekers addressed this issue by portraying Uncle Sam as a pistol-packing, chaps-wearing, log-chopping frontiersman forced by an aggressive Germany to defend himself (Figure 2.2). Wells decided to hit just below the belt by implying that Americans would not become men until they tussled with other countries. "No longer a political Thoreau in the woods, a sort of vegetarian recluse among nations, a being of negative virtues and unpremeditated superiorities," Wells wrote, "she [the United States] girds herself for a manly part in the toilsome world of men."[59]

Americans had decidedly mixed opinions on the virtues of such girding, with ethnic and geographic factors playing important roles. Here we are interested in another factor, the perceived impact of the industrialization of war on democracy. Tocqueville had warned that war posed the single greatest threat to democracy because it increased the power of the state. Private commerce, he believed, abetted democracy. By the turn of the century, however, some "private interests" had grown so large that Progressives believed they too threatened to (or did) hold disproportionate economic and political power.

More threatening than government or business alone, some Progressives concluded, was an alliance between the two. In March 1915, a writer argued in *Harper's Weekly* that "private interests, with millions of dollars invested in plants, now have to urge constantly increasing military and naval expenditures so that their profits may continue." He charged that a "war ring" linked the army, navy, and industrial interests, leading to inflated costs for the taxpayer.[60] The First International Congress of the Women's International League for Peace and Freedom, held in The Hague in April 1915, saw "in the private profits accruing from the great arms factories a powerful hindrance to the abolition of war."[61] An editorial writer suggested in the *New York Evening*

2.2   "Two Giants." In this cartoon, Raemaekers suggested that barbaric
Germany forced the pacific United States to fight back. Like the pioneers
in Walt Whitman's poem (see epigraph), Uncle Sam carried his twin
weapons, the axe and the pistol, for conquering people and nature in the
wilderness. The caption read, "Germany: 'I destroy!' America: 'I
create!'" From Louis Raemaekers, *Raemaekers' Cartoon History of the
War*, vol. 3: *The Third Twelve Months of the War* (New York: Century,
1919), 84–85.

Post in 1916 that a "power elite" directly linked the military, industry, and the rich.[62]

Despite fears that private interests would push the United States into war, the country remained an official bystander for more than two years. Woodrow Wilson won reelection as president in 1916 with the slogan "He Kept Us Out of War."[63] True enough, but far from the whole story. The U.S. government stayed officially neutral, and American troops stayed on American soil. But outside of government, America was very much in the war, and the war's effects were very much in the United States. Our interest is mainly in the latter. Tocqueville had argued that nature was the most important factor encouraging American democracy because it fended off war. Oceans and wilderness defended the country from external enemies, and bountiful natural resources created a large middle class that quelled internal threats.

What Tocqueville did not consider was that American nature could go to war even if American people did not. Parts of nature did protect the United States from war, but other parts drew the country closer to it. American entrepreneurs transformed America's natural resources into technology, which went to Europe to help industrialize warfare. Money and ideas flowed back across the Atlantic, changing the way Americans interacted with each other and nature.

The impact was easiest to see in technology. The war transformed the American chemical industry from a middling competitor relying on bulk chemicals to a huge industry skilled at organic chemistry as well as its traditional products. This transformation in turn changed pest control by introducing a synthetic organic insecticide (paradichlorobenzene) and inspiring the search for others. The mushrooming explosives industry (along with other sources of demand) increased the value of cotton, which intensified the search for a boll weevil killer, which culminated in the introduction of the first effective insecticide (calcium arsenate) for this devastating pest. The industrialization of war in Europe hastened the industrialization of pest control in the United States.

The importance of chemistry for national defense prompted changes not only in the size of chemical companies but in the relationship between science and government. Chemists enlisted the aid of the federal government in protecting the nascent American organic chemical industry from German competition. They planned ways to mobilize their expertise for war by surveying manufacturing sites, suggesting draft exemptions for chemists, and supporting the creation of the National Research Council.

Most difficult to measure, but still important, was the impact of the war on ideology. Chemists welcomed the stature that "the chemists' war" conferred on them, and they promoted the idea that military power now derived more from chemistry than from muscle. Pest controllers and writers used the war in Europe to increase public awareness of the insect menace, promote stronger attacks on insects, and elevate the stature of entomology. European propagandists attacked the notion that nature would enable the United States to take a pass on entering the war, while at the same time they drew on traditional ideas about the control of nature to describe why Germany needed to be defeated and why gas warfare was inhuman.

The technology, organizations, and ideas developed during the European War worked together to increase the power of the United States *before* it entered the war. At the same time, these variables showed that few things in the world stayed the same, including enemies. On the battlefields of Europe, human enemies countered increased force with increased defense (and more force of their own). On the fruit farmers' fields of Washington State, insects too countered increased force with increased defense. The American way of war and the American way of pest control would have to evolve in response to their human and natural foes. To do so, they would evolve in response to each other as well.

3

Joining the chemists' war (1917–1918)

Once a democracy declared war, Tocqueville believed, its citizens would redirect their fervor for profit to fervor for victory, and nothing less than a clear victory would satisfy.[1] He was right. Once the United States declared war, it sent troops to Europe with flags flying, bands playing, and crowds cheering. Americans followed the fortunes of the American Expeditionary Force as it took on the Central Powers in battle. And many Americans called for destruction of Germany's ability to wage war ever again.

What Tocqueville did not foresee were the many other fronts on which a nation could go to war. The European War had, by the time the United States declared war, shaped American institutions, technology, and ideas. Declaration of war accelerated this process. By the end of the war, the country would evolve into something quite different from the nation in 1914. It emerged with a stronger federal government, a larger and more skilled chemical industry, closer links among the armed forces, science, military, and civilian advocates of chemical warfare, allied programs in chemical warfare and pest control, greater appreciation of the ability of institutions to shape public opinion, and increased confidence in the nation's ability to conquer human and natural enemies.

One of the clearest qualitative changes was incorporation of chemical warfare into the nation's arsenal. The U.S. Army's insouciance about gas continued until American troops suffered significant losses from gas on the battlefield. A month after his arrival in Europe, General John J. Pershing (commander of the American Expeditionary Force) scrapped the chaotic, divided system then in place and organized a Gas Service charged with equipping the army for offensive and defensive gas warfare.[2]

This decision converted an army engineer into probably the single most influential individual in the history of American gas warfare. Born in Oregon, Amos A. Fries had entered the Corps of Engineers on graduation from West Point in 1898. In the Philippine-American War, he saw action in a short campaign led by then-Captain Pershing. After returning to the United States, he had designed a harbor for Los Angeles and directed the army's military engineering education program. From 1914 to 1917, while war raged in Europe, he oversaw road and bridge construction in Yellowstone National Park.[3] Fries arrived in Europe with the American Expeditionary Force, expecting to do civil engineering. But, five days after Fries stepped ashore, Pershing named him chief of the Gas Service in Europe, and chief of a mess. Fries recalled, "There were no trained officers, no trained men, no gas masks, no gases, no policy." Fries had to train "the entire Army from the commanding general to the last private," protect American troops from gas, supply gas, and teach the army how to use it. For materiel, Fries had to rely on the Allies. The army bought 100,000 British and French masks to equip American troops. For troops, Fries drew on the Corps of Engineers. He organized six gas companies with some 1,600 troops.[4]

As Fries and his officers leaped into the gas fray, something unexpected happened: they grew to *like* gas. For one thing, gas was powerful. Although a new weapon, gas created a high percentage of casualties. Among American troops hospitalized, 27 percent landed there because of gas.[5] (Fries did not want to see Americans fall to gas, of course; he drew on those data because they were available and probably typical of what happened to other armies.) Gas was also humane (if humanity was defined as creating casualties without killing). Of the American soldiers "struck" by gas, only about 2 percent died.[6] Bullets and bombs, on the other hand, killed a much higher percentage of their victims. As Fries put it, gas was "at one and the same time the most powerful and the most humane method of warfare ever invented."[7]

This view flew in the teeth of public opinion. A lieutenant colonel won over to gas complained in 1918 that "widespread feeling has existed in this country to the effect that gas is more barbarous and inhumane than other weapons of warfare. This is really not the case."[8]

To explain the contradiction between their views and those of the public, chemical warfare advocates blamed propaganda. The anti-gas cartoons and pronouncements produced by the Allies in response to the original German gas attack blinded the public to the truth, they reasoned. The wartime experience of painter John Singer Sargent would only make things worse. An American who spent much of his life in Europe, Sargent was persuaded by the British War Memorials Committee to paint "British and American troops working together" on a huge canvas intended as the centerpiece of a proposed Hall of Remembrance. When Sargent got to the front in July 1918, however, he found that, although British and American troops worked together "in the abstract," they did not do so "in any particular space."[9]

Then Sargent came across a dressing station treating gas victims. He took "a lot of notes," started painting in October 1918, and finished in February 1919. The canvas, titled *Gassed*, was enormous – twenty feet by seven feet six inches. It was exactly the sort of art chemical warfare advocates despised. As one, a general, said after the war, "The judgment of future generations on the use of gas may well be influenced by the pathetic appeal of Sargent's picture of the first 'Mustard Gas' casualties at Ypres, but it must not be forgotten in looking at that picture that 75 percent of the blinded men he drew were fit for duty within three months, and that had their limbs and nerves been shattered by the effects of high explosive, their fate would have been infinitely worse."[10]

Images and words may have molded public hatred of gas, but firsthand experience created antipathy among nongas soldiers as well. Their reasons were practical: gas forced soldiers to wear cumbersome equipment, was hard to aim, blew back on the troops who launched it, and invited retaliation in kind. The assistant chief of staff commanding a corps in France refused to use gas unless "the gas officer would state in writing that if the gas was so used it could not possibly result in the casualty of a single American soldier."[11]

Some soldiers hated gas for ethical reasons as well. Imbued with the idea that warriors should spare civilians, they were appalled at the inability to control a weapon that literally shifted directions with every breeze.[12] When visiting France, Army Chief of Staff Peyton C. March "saw 195 small children brought in from about 10 miles from the rear of the trenches who were suffering from gas in their lungs, innocent little children who had nothing to do with this game at all." He reasoned, "War is cruel at best, but the use of an instrument of death which, once launched, cannot be controlled, and which may decimate non-combatants – women and children – reduces civilization to savagery."[13]

Chemical warfare advocates made it their mission to win the army over to gas. Among some staff officers and commanders, Fries noted, the hostility to gas was "outspoken and almost violent." So, along with becoming chemical officers, Fries and his officers became salesmen. Their "watchword," Fries said, was "'Chemical Warfare Service officers have got to go out and sell gas to the Army.' In other words we had to adopt much the same

means of making gas known that the manufacturer of a new article adopts to make a thing manufactured by him known to the
public."[14]

If Fries and company were the sales force for the "new article"
that was gas, Major General William Sibert was the chief executive
officer. Like Fries, Sibert was an army engineer who went to
Europe with the American Expeditionary Force expecting to do
civil engineering. (According to Sibert's biographer, "The military
engineers, of whom Sibert is one, changing their labors, as occasion and duty come, between the fields of war and of peace, front
today the enemy man, and tomorrow the enemy nature.") And,
like Fries, Sibert found himself ordered to become a chemical warfare officer. While Fries would oversee the Gas Service in Europe,
Sibert would manage research, development, and manufacturing
in the United States. He caught one of the next ships home to start
work.[15] Sibert brought impressive management experience to the
job. He had overseen construction of the Gatun Locks and Dam of
the Panama Canal, which accustomed Sibert to organizing
endeavors on a large scale. Sibert brought what others called his
"big business" approach to chemical warfare.[16]

And big it was. More than anything else, the "stupendous
scale" on which Sibert organized American preparations for chemical warfare astounded observers from around the world.[17]
Everything was big: in manufacturing, the United States achieved
quantities in three months that had taken the British and French
thirty months.[18] By January 1919, the United States could have sent
200 tons of gas – including 100 tons of mustard gas – per *day* into
battle. Germany, the United States believed, at armistice was able
to produce a maximum of only thirty tons of gas – including eight
tons of mustard gas – per day.[19] In personnel, the Chemical
Warfare Service (as it would come to be called) boasted more than
4,000 officers and 44,000 men (most draftees) by the end of the
war.[20] In research, 1,700 people – the largest research group ever

put together by the U.S. government (and probably the largest research group in the world) – held more doctorates and turned out more reports than researchers in any other country.[21]

Creation of this prodigious research effort owed more to civilian chemists than to Sibert or other military officers. In April 1917, the month the United States declared war, the National Research Council created a Subcommittee on Noxious Gases. The subcommittee set up a laboratory at American University in Washington, D.C., and arranged for help from such institutions as the Johns Hopkins University and the Mellon Institute. The Bureau of Mines, the federal agency with the most experience with poison gases until then, managed the effort. By the end of May, 118 chemists from government, industry, and academia worked in the laboratory. Many of the chemists involved were "dollar a year men" who stayed on their own universities' payrolls while doing research on chemical warfare.[22]

In their search for war gases, these chemists relied on chemicals (or relatives of chemicals) already known to be toxic. Because many of these killed insects as well as people, some had been used as insecticides before they became war gases. The first report from American University recommended that 45 percent of American gas be hydrogen cyanide. Since the nineteenth century, farmers and entomologists had used this compound to fumigate insects in orchards and buildings.[23] Other gases contained arsenic, an ingredient in the most heavily used insecticides at the time. The chemical warfare program eventually consumed a third of the country's arsenic supply, causing shortages of arsenic insecticides for agriculture.[24]

If profit motivated American chemists during the European War, patriotism became a powerful force once the United States declared war. James B. Conant, the war profiteer who had left the company he founded for a university position, was thinking about enlisting as a noncommissioned officer to work on defense against

gas when he saw James F. Norris of MIT. Norris, who was organizing one of the research teams at American University, offered
Conant the chance to lead one of the groups. Conant agreed. In
secret, Conant's group figured out how to make mustard gas and
lewisite (a highly toxic gas of American invention).[25]

Although Conant and his companions disliked researching
ways to wound or kill people, they rejected the view that gas
deserved special opprobrium. "To me," Conant recalled, "the
development of new and more effective gases seemed no more
immoral than the manufacture of explosives and guns.... I did not
see ... why tearing a man's guts out by a high-explosive shell is to
be preferred to maiming him by attacking his lungs or skin."[26]
Charles Herty of the American Chemical Society reached a similar
conclusion: "The first time I was out at the American University
here I saw a dog gassed, and I went away from there feeling, as a
chemist, almost degradation and a horror of the thing." But then
"someone said to me, 'Suppose you had been looking at a man
with his jaw shot off and his chest blown out; how would you feel
about that?' When you come to working it down to cold facts, the
thing comes down simply to this: It is simply another phase of
chemistry entering this field of war."[27]

Chemistry's entering a new field of war may have been simple
conceptually, but practically it was not. Military officers and civilian researchers valued different things, which made cooperation
rocky. Civilian researchers valued originality and freedom; military officers valued practicality and control. A frustrated Fries
complained that he "had constantly to impress upon research men
the fact that we wanted gases and other chemical warfare materials for use 'in this war' and not for some future war."[28]

This conflict in approach led to a fight over organizational
structure. Army officers wanted to bring civilian researchers into
the army, where they would be subject to tighter control. This
hope was part of a larger ambition to create a single organization

– a new part of the army – responsible for all aspects of gas warfare. Fries lobbied hard for this change in 1918, when, coincidentally, Germany reminded everyone of the importance of gas
warfare by launching major gas offensives.[29] The scientists wanted
to stay under the civilian Bureau of Mines, which in turn was overseen by the civilian National Research Council.[30]

The army won. In June 1918, Woodrow Wilson combined the
still-dispersed aspects of chemical warfare together in a single
organization. Civilian researchers were commissioned as officers
in what would soon be called the Chemical Warfare Service. The
National Research Council's Subcommittee on Noxious Gases dis-
solved in August 1918.[31]

Fries and Sibert may have wanted gases for this war, but they
needed an organization for the future. Wilson's order called for the
Chemical Warfare Service to disappear after the end of the war.
Chemical warfare officers thought such a plan foolish. In January
1918, almost a year before the armistice, a lieutenant colonel out-
lined a postwar plan for General Sibert. It stated what had become
articles of faith for chemical warfare officers: gas had proved its
usefulness and power on the battlefield; belligerents would use gas
in future wars (whether or not they signed treaties to the contrary); the best way to defend the United States was to prepare to
retaliate in kind and equip American soldiers with protective gear;
chemical warfare was, unlike any other part of the army, grounded
in "highly developed science"; to keep up to date, the army would
have to cultivate a "research reserve" in universities; and only a
separate, permanent branch of the army would master the science
and coordinate the institutional relationships necessary for gas
warfare.[32]

The war ended before chemical warfare advocates had the
chance to demonstrate what they saw as the full power of gas. The
armistice came shortly before the Chemical Warfare Service's huge
new factory at Edgewood Arsenal, Maryland, began producing in

quantity. The service thought a gas it developed during the war, lewisite, had great potential. Like mustard gas, it was highly toxic, quick acting, and highly vesicant (causing skin blisters). Unlike mustard gas, however, it was not persistent.[33] The United States started manufacturing lewisite, but the war ended before the new gas could be deployed.[34]

In addition to heading off use of lewisite, the armistice may have staved off large-scale aerial chemical warfare. Like gas, airplanes underwent rapid development during the war. For the most part, belligerents used airplanes against military targets (most dramatically in "dogfights" against other airplanes). But Germany and England bombed each other's cities from the air, and the United States developed the technology for many kinds of aerial attack: demolition bombs for buildings, fragmentation bombs for troops, and incendiaries for light structures and grain fields.[35]

Air power and chemical warfare advocates both promoted their technology as means to end the war more quickly. Aviators believed that attacking enemy cities, especially chemical factories, would bring Germany to its knees.[36] Demolition bombs would suit "precision" attacks on factories. But some leading chemical warfare advocates argued that the United States should aim to annihilate the enemy, military and civilian alike, with gas. William Walker, commander of the Chemical Warfare Service's Edgewood Arsenal, said the United States's one-ton mustard gas bombs would "account for perhaps an acre or more of territory, and not one living thing, not even a rat, would live through it.... We could have wiped out any German city we pleased to single out, and probably several of them, within a few hours of giving the release signal."[37]

Some combination of concerns, practical and ethical, among world leaders appears to have forestalled such plans. When Fries urged Pershing to use aerial gas attacks in the spring of 1918, Pershing declined, saying that Germany was not then attacking civilians with gas.[38] Walker, the Edgewood Arsenal commander, blamed the Allies. At first England opposed "wholesale attacks by air," then France complained that reprisals, and gas blowing back, would endanger France. So, France demanded that the Allies wait until they had pushed Germany far from French territory and controlled the air. That did not happen before the armistice. Walker believed that the Germans knew of these plans, and that "a big factor in that capitulation was the knowledge they certainly possess of our gas preparations." Walker regretted that "we had been cheated of our prey, but we were content. We felt sure the gas had done its work even though most of it still lay idle in our dooryard."[39]

If the United States had gone to aerial gas warfare, the evidence from aerial bombing suggests that the distance between airmen and their targets would have made such attacks more palatable (to those launching the attacks at least) than ground attacks. Will Irwin, an American journalist who visited the front, noted, "If you bayonet a child, you see the spurt of blood, the curling up of the little body, the look in the eyes.... But if you loose a bomb on a town, you see only that you have made a fair hit. Time and again I have dined with French boy-aviators, British boy-aviators, American boy-aviators, home from raids. They were gallant, generous, kindly youths. And they were thinking and talking not of the effects of their bombs but only of 'the hit.'"[40]

"The hit" joined a number of metaphors in helping Americans frame their understanding of the war. Like their European counterparts, American propagandists relied on ideas about nature (among others) to transform killing from a moral issue into a natural response to a natural threat. In a U.S. military recruiting poster, an ape, wearing a helmet labeled "militarism" and armed with a club marked "kultur," stepped ashore in America. The ape carried a partially disrobed woman shielding her eyes (a common symbol at the time for civilization). The poster called on Americans to "Destroy this Mad Brute: Enlist."[41] The ability of this and other propaganda to stir up popular frenzy astounded even the propagandists. It convinced George Creel, who headed the U.S. government's propaganda program, that advertising was a "real profession." Creel even titled his history of the wartime propaganda program *How We Advertised America.*[42]

Conversely, journalists and pest controllers continued to draw on war metaphors to shape the public's understanding of insects and entomology. The *St. Louis Post-Dispatch* described St. Louis's campaign to exterminate flies as "vigorous warfare" to "make the world safe for habitation" (a play on the war's goal to "make the world safe for democracy") (Figure 3.1). Stephen Forbes became more specific than he had been in his 1915 article. In June 1917, he charged that "fifty billion German allies" had already invaded American fields in the form of insects: the "chinch bug is pro-German in our present war, the Hessian fly is still Hessian, and the army worm is an ally of the German army."[43] L. O. Howard, chief of the U. S. Bureau of Entomology, described his bureau as waging "warfare against insect life," published an article titled "Entomology as a National Defense," and promised that threatening pests would be met with "a vigorous campaign."[44]

Such metaphors joined war itself in accenting insect threats, elevating the importance of entomology, and generating funding. As L. O. Howard put it, the war "intensified the work of the entomologists and enabled them to make the importance of their researches felt almost as never before." Increased appreciation could be measured in dollars: Howard's bureau received $441,000 in 1917 and $811,300 in 1918 on top of its regular appropriations. The Bureau of Entomology (with the Extension Service) used these funds to reach more farmers than before by fielding employees to demonstrate ways to control pests of crops, especially those considered important to the war effort.[45]

The Bureau of Entomology also worked with the army to solve insect problems of military importance. The most obvious prob-

"The Fly Must be Exterminated to Make the World Safe for Habitation"

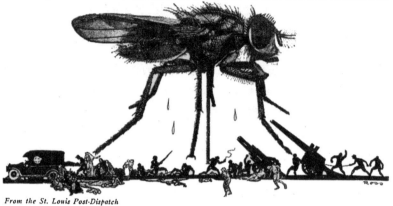

From the St. Louis Post-Dispatch
THE CITY OF ST. LOUIS IS CONDUCTING A VIGOROUS WARFARE AGAINST FLIES

3.1 "The Fly Must be Exterminated to Make the World Safe for Habitation." This newspaper cartoon showed soldiers launching artillery and grenades against a giant fly in much the same way as they did against human enemies in Europe. The outcome seemed uncertain and the costs high: the fly stood bloodied but unbowed, casualties littered the ground and filled an ambulance, and refugees fled the scene. From the *St. Louis Post-Dispatch,* reprinted in *American City* 19 (July 1918), 12; reprinted with permission of the *St. Louis Post-Dispatch,* copyright 1918.

lem was louse-borne typhus, which the army tried to control by heating clothing and bedding in large chambers to kill lice. This method could not prevent soldiers from being infested again, which often happened as soon as troops entered crowded, vermin-ridden trenches. Some 90 percent of American troops were lousy. Fortunately, few lice on the Western Front carried the typhus germ, probably because the Central Powers took pains to disinfest soldiers before transferring them from the typhus-ridden Eastern Front.[46]

This unintended help from the enemy was hardly something to count on. In hopes of finding a better method of louse control, federal entomologists worked with the Chemical Warfare Service to test war gases as insecticides. They hoped to find "a gas which can be placed in a chamber and be experienced safely for a short period of time by men wearing gas masks and which in this time will kill all cooties and their nits."[47]

These experiments stimulated more tests of chemical weapons as insecticides. The Chemical Warfare Service, Bureau of Entomology, and other government agencies researched a variety of war gases against dozens of species of insects. Most of the gases fell short, but chloropicrin, a compound that chemical warfare had lifted from obscurity, killed insects effectively. A laboratory curiosity before the war, chloropicrin was the most heavily used gas in World War I. Although sometimes lethal in its own right, chloropicrin found wide use primarily because it penetrated gas masks. The compound caused soldiers to tear and vomit, which led them to rip off their masks, which exposed them to less penetrating, but more lethal, gases mixed with chloropicrin.[48]

On a broader level, observations seemed to bolster the claims of some chemical warriors that they could wipe out life over broader areas altogether. *American Miller* magazine later reported that the "scarcity of insect pests around Rheims is attributed to the use of poisonous gases in that region during the World War."[49]

One product most companies avoided making in its final form, however, was poison gas. William Sibert and others in charge of mobilizing chemistry hoped at the outset that private companies would produce gas for the army. But most companies saw the work as dangerous, predicted little postwar demand for gas, and declined to make the product. Instead, the federal government had to build its own plants, most notably at Edgewood Arsenal. Supplying precursors to gas, on the other hand, was a different matter, and private companies sold the Chemical Warfare Service those chemicals in quantity.[50]

By the end of the war, chemists stood tall as the scientists of national defense. In 1919, Secretary of War Newton D. Baker said, "The Government of the United States, and particularly the War Department, owes a debt of gratitude and appreciation to the chemists of the United States.... I do not believe it will be discovered that any profession contributed a larger per cent of its members directly to the military service, or the results of the activities of any profession were more essential to our national success than that of the chemists."[51]

And the United States felt itself standing tall. To celebrate victory, the federal government published a poster showing a single American soldier in front of a devastated landscape. "And they thought we couldn't fight!" the poster read (Figure 3.2). The sentiment could have been a direct retort to Wells and others who had challenged America to prove its manhood by going to war.

The United States had done so in a thoroughly modern way: marrying science and technology to war; mobilizing civilians through industry and propaganda; and linking a variety of institutions – military and civilian, government and private – and nature into networks that produced what none could have done individually. It thus changed American ideas, science, technology, institutions, and nature in subtle and profound ways. The United States would not be the same country exiting the war it had been going in.

Yet Americans could still think of themselves in traditional ways. In 1893, Frederick Jackson Turner had formalized some of Americans' most cherished ideas about national development. In his "frontier thesis," Turner argued that the need to conquer wild people (Indians) and nature on successive frontiers had made Americans temporarily savage but ultimately individualistic, democratic, and antiauthoritarian.[52] The soldier in the victory poster was pure Turner: he stood alone; he had conquered the Germanic beast with the same dispatch he would use in hunting

3.2 "And They Thought We Couldn't Fight!" The United States celebrated victory and increased international stature in this poster. From MSS 5023, Collection of World War I Posters, Cartoons and Photographs, Special Collections Department, University of Virginia Library.

animals (see the game-like helmet on his belt); he was brave (bloodied and bandaged, but unbowed); he had become a savage for a short while so that he could create a better world; he had proven through action that European ideas about American inferiority were wrong; and he had done whatever was necessary to conquer nature (see the devastated landscape in the background) and human enemies. The European battlefield had been the latest of many frontiers renewing the American spirit. The young American had taken on the forces arrayed against him, and had won.

The next question was how this transformed American – image and reality alike – would fare in peace.

4

Chemical warfare in peace (1918–1937)

Turner's vision of history was ironic: the frontiersman's success was also his undoing. In conquering the hostile frontier, he made the land more suitable for civilization and less suitable for himself. So the moment of victory shown in the "couldn't fight" poster was also a moment of defeat. Like Turner's frontiersman, the soldier could not stay as he was, where he was. He would have to "re-civilize" himself to rejoin peaceful society, or he would have to move on to another frontier, another war, where his "savage" ways would be better suited.

So too for Amos Fries and his fellow chemical warfare advocates. In their minds, they had advanced civilization by developing a powerful, humane method of warfare. They had used it to defeat the savage "Bosch" and make the world safe for democracy. In the eyes of other soldiers and the public, though, chemical warfare was inhuman. Americans may have been forced into savagery by an uncivilized foe, but conquest of the foe enabled them to return to a more civilized state by banishing chemical warfare.

And so chemical warfare advocates spent the decades between the world wars struggling to survive in an inhospitable world they had helped create. They did so by making three main arguments.

First, civilization was fooling itself if it thought it had banished savagery from the world. If the United States wanted to protect its civilization, it would have to be prepared to unleash the dogs of war. Second, if the country did go to war, chemical weapons offered the most civilized way to wage it. Finally, gas belonged in a settled peaceful society because it offered a superior way to fend off natural enemies. Control of nature was a civilian affair, and because civilian affairs were peaceful, gas enabled Americans to wage "peaceful war."

The army and the president planned all along to banish the Chemical Warfare Service. The executive order establishing the service in 1918 also ordered its termination six months after the end of hostilities. Army Chief of Staff Peyton C. March and Secretary of War Newton D. Baker followed this order when, in December 1918, they transferred responsibility for gas to the Corps of Engineers. The latter would research poison gases for defense and retaliation but not for first use.[1]

Fries was astonished to learn that March agreed with the order. He found it inconceivable that "a military man will advocate abolishing a service that is at one and the same time the most powerful and the most humane method of warfare ever invented." The only explanation he could hazard was that March and his military allies were afraid that gas "will become too important and take from the infantry, the cavalry and the artillery some of the renown that they hold as the backbone of the Army."[2] In fact, March opposed chemical warfare on the grounds that it endangered entire communities (he had been distraught to see civilians harmed by drifting gases in Europe) and was a cruel and inhumane method of war.[3]

Practically, finding the reason for March's position was less important than finding a way to counter it. The resourcefulness Fries had displayed in Europe, where he had created a working Gas Service from a hodgepodge of gear and personnel, again served him well. If going up the chain of command failed, then Fries would go around it. That path led Fries and his allies to Congress and, less immediately important, to the public. The job was to change enough minds in Congress to save the Chemical Warfare Service. As Fries wrote to a chemical warfare veteran, "What we need now is good, sound publicity along lines showing the importance of Chemical Warfare, its powerful and far-reaching effects in war, and its humanity when you compare the number of deaths per hundred gassed with the number of deaths from bullets and high explosives for each hundred injured by those means."[4]

Fries cast a wide publicity net, which he hoped would land several congressional fish. In his files, Fries kept a draft resolution in favor of a separate Chemical Warfare Service, complete except for a blank where the name of an organization could be filled in.[5] He published an anonymous article in *Engineering News-Record* to drum up support from engineers. He got several chemical warfare veterans to lobby Congress and praise chemical warfare in public.[6]

Two of Fries's most important allies were the American Chemical Society, which had helped found the Chemical Warfare Service, and the *Journal of Industrial and Engineering Chemistry*. In 1918–1919, the journal published a series of articles on "Contributions of the Chemical Warfare Service," which it called on its readers to publicize to the public and to Congress.[7] Astounded that Congress was still considering abolishing the service by mid-1919, the journal's editor changed his September issue to "appeal to the chemists of this country to awaken the people of this country to what this proposition means." Votes by the American Chemical Society put some institutional muscle into these sentiments. In February 1919, the society voted to ask the president and Congress to maintain a separate Chemical Warfare Service.[8] In June 1919, the society sent a resolution to Secretary of War Newton Baker arguing that a separate Chemical Warfare Service was essential for preparedness.[9]

These efforts paid off for the Chemical Warfare Service and for Fries himself. The National Defense Act made the Chemical Warfare Service a permanent part of the U.S. Army in 1920. (The service was not a large part, consisting of about 500 men between 1922 and 1934, but it was a survivor.) The same year, Amos Fries took over as chief from William Sibert.[10]

Fries barely had time to catch his breath before the next dragon reared its head, this time in the form of an arms conference. Horrified by the destruction of (what Americans now often called) the world war, antiwar groups organized efforts to stop war – or at least put the worst of its technology back in its box. They had the ear of the highest leaders in the United States, including President Warren Harding. With his blessing, an international conference met in Washington to discuss limits on arms, including gas and submarines.[11]

Sentiment in favor of the conference grew not just out of fear of technology, but also from worry about large, armed populations in Asia. By 1921, China and Japan seemed restless and growing in armed strength. Newspapers and political leaders in England, France, Australia, and the United States warned of a possible conflagration in the Pacific. *Literary Digest* reported, "That war looms ominously on the Asiatic horizon – a war so appalling in its scope and consequences that even the World War would be dwarfed by comparison – is a belief exprest [sic] in many quarters." In California, where fears of a "yellow peril" ran strong, the *San Francisco Argonaut* quoted British Admiral Sir Cyprian Bridge as saying that "there is only one problem, and it is the problem of the coming conflict between the two halves of the human race, the white and the colored; it will be in the Pacific." Asia could mobilize "about one thousand millions of colored people as against some five hundred millions of white people."[12]

Along with technology and population, expansion in the scale of war spurred the Washington conference. One of the clearest critiques of this expansion came from Will Irwin. A journalist and propagandist in the world war, Irwin had been disillusioned by a visit to the Front. The Senate's rejection of the League of Nations further distressed him. In hopes of saving the Washington conference from the same fate, he wrote a book titled *The Next War* "at white heat." The publisher rushed it into print, and the book became an instant best seller.[13]

The turning point in the expansion of war came, Irwin believed, when Germany first released gas at Ypres. Before that, the world's greatest minds focused on improving life. Now they focused on destroying it: "great and little scientific minds, engaged hitherto in searching for abstract truth or in multiplying the richness of life and the wealth of nations, could be turned toward the invention of means of destruction whether they wished or no. A new area of human consciousness was brought to fruition. A new power in men was unloosed and this one most sinister."[14]

The "sinister power" of scientific warfare, Irwin argued, would not have been tapped had war been left to soldiers. Military life tended "to destroy originality," and professional soldiers wanted "to render warfare as merciful as possible," so they had rejected gas when it was still an abstraction. Once the stopcock on civilian imagination had been opened at Ypres, though, all sorts of horrors gushed into war: liquid flame (for "burning men alive"), tanks, more gases, high explosives, huge bombs, guns for launching more powerful shells, and airplanes.[15]

These new sources of military power made the civilians who produced them fair game, Irwin said: "Now since munitions and food had grown as important as men, since to stop or hinder the enemy munitions manufacture or agricultural production was to make toward victory, the women in war were fair game.... The same stern logic of 'military necessity' lay behind the continual air raids on cities." And thus the world returned to barbarism. Before the world war, Irwin argued, a "merciful though artificial body of ethics, built up by Christianity and all other humanitarian forces," had limited the destruction of war. At least in theory, armies used the least force necessary, avoided weapons that caused needless suffering, and abhorred senseless acts of cruelty. Armies spared prisoners, the wounded, civilians, and cities. But the world war sent civilization "back to the ethics of the barbarian hordes. The barbarians of the twentieth century B.C. killed in any manner which their imaginations suggested; so now did civilized men of the twentieth century A.D. The barbarian of the twentieth century B.C. killed the women and children of the enemy as tribal self-interest seemed to dictate; as now did the civilized men of the twentieth century A.D." Only two parts of "the code" – protection of prisoners and hospitals – survived the war.[16]

The impact of these scientific, technological, and ethical changes was easy to foresee, Irwin believed: mass aerial attacks on cities with poison gas, which could eliminate all life in such a city as Paris – or New York. For evidence, Irwin quoted Brigadier General Billy Mitchell, who said that "a few planes could visit New York as the central point of a territory 100 miles square every eight days and drop enough gas to keep the entire area inundated.... 200 tons of phosgene gas could be laid every eight days and would be enough to kill every inhabitant."[17]

Chemical warfare advocates thought Irwin and his ilk were, if not ill intentioned, dangerously naïve. "It can be accepted as an axiom that the more powerful a weapon the more certain it is that any attempt to forbid its use will result in failure," Fries argued. "Worse still, it puts a nation that can be depended upon to keep its word at the mercy of a nation which may be willing to break it."[18] The Chemical Warfare Service's journal, *Chemical Warfare*, editorialized, "Unless there is unrestricted opportunity for progress [in the development of poison gases and gas masks], the loss of power by a nation confronted suddenly may be likened to a state of suicide."[19]

The route to security and peace, chemical warriors argued, was not to limit the scale of war but to expand it – and thereby make it so terrible that no one would wage it. One way was to threaten massive gas attacks against enemy armies. Fries believed that "all nations should be given to understand that if we are forced into a war we shall use every known chemical method of warfare against hostile forces wherever they are located. That would be our permanent guarantee against attack." Another was openly to target enemy civilian leaders: "So long as the leaders of nations could carry on wars for years without harm to themselves, war was a sport," Fries wrote. "But today, with the development of chemical bombs and airplanes, no statesman or ruler is any more immune from attack than a private soldier.... Every development of science that makes warfare more universal and more scientific makes for permanent peace by making war intolerable."[20]

Against the publicity of Irwin and his allies, Fries and his allies launched a counteroffensive. In 1921, Fries and Clarence J. West (a major in the Chemical Warfare Service Reserves) published a book titled *Chemical Warfare* as part of an "enlarged program of publicity on the part of the Chief of the Service."[21] The mission of every chemical warfare officer, the journal *Chemical Warfare* stated, was "to carry the news of Chemical Warfare, to talk it at every opportunity, and to clear away many of the false ideas about it that exist in the minds of civilians, as well as the military."[22]

The publicity campaign reached a wide audience. Some journalists agreed that the best way to prevent war was to make it more terrible. One reflected that "the final consummate weapon of mass murder may itself bring the millennium, for war will no longer be an heroic contest of mind, courage, and prowess, but a mad mingling in mutual annihilation. Indeed, the chemical-warfare soldiers consider that they are conducting a war against war.... Nations wage war in the hope of victorious survival, but would eschew it if general slaughter were likely. The perfection of warfare, the advo-

cates of chemical warfare contend, prophesies the end of war; to
abolish warfare, make it increasingly terrible."[23] Others thought
singling out gas was irrational. The *New York Globe* wrote,
"There is no more to be said in favor of tearing men to pieces with
shells or bombs, macerating their flesh with high-power rifle bullets, or stabbing them in the face or intestines with bayonets than
there is for suffocating or burning them with gas. War is slaughter,
and can never be anything else, and victory will always go to the
contestant who is best at killing."[24]

But most journalists disagreed. "The theory that by making war
more and more horrible you diminish the chance of a war is an
amazingly faulty theory," said the *Baltimore American*. The
Louisville Courier-Journal argued, "There never will be a method
of warfare so terrible that men will refuse to engage in it....
General Fries overlooks the fact that as soon as an 'intolerable'
instrument of death appears, the immediate sequel is the invention
of protection against it. Armor counteracted swords and the bat-
tle-ax, just as the gas-mask was almost coevil [sic] with gas."[25]

Chemical warfare advocates' argument that gas was humane,
another aspect of the 1921 publicity campaign, also had a hard go.
"That poison gas warfare is 'humane' in character may come as a
surprize [sic] to the thousands of 'doughboys' who have not yet
recovered from the effects of gas during the World War," noted the
Seattle Times. "What is this 'humane' method of warfare of which
the chemists speak?" asked the *New York Evening Mail*. "Is it the
spreading of gas that will torture and poison honorable and gallant
men not only through their lungs but through their skins, that will
reach far behind the fighting lines and send women and children to
horrible death, that will kill all vegetation and secure the starvation
of peoples for years after war ceases? If this be a chemist's idea of
humane warfare, God deliver the world from its chemists!"[26]

One of the most influential opponents of chemical warfare was
Amos Fries's former mentor. War hero and Chief of Staff John J.

Pershing chaired an American advisory subcommittee to the Washington Conference; it recommended abolishing chemical warfare "as abhorrent to civilization. It is a cruel, unfair, and improper use of science. It is fraught with the gravest danger to noncombatants and demoralizes the better instincts of humanity."[27] In this face-off, Fries had little chance. "The stand of such a distinguished professional soldier as Pershing should have a tremendous effect upon public opinion everywhere," argued the *New York Evening Mail*. In contrast to Pershing's, Fries's "view is narrowed by his occupation" as chief of the Chemical Warfare Service, believed the *Louisville Courier-Journal;* "as a man lives, so does he think." In remarks that must have infuriated the battle-tested Fries, the *Philadelphia Evening Bulletin* said, "Here is practical military knowledge against civilian chemical theory." The *New York Evening Mail* said that chemical warfare "is not a soldier's idea of warfare, or General Pershing would have endorsed it. And, be it remembered, the soldier fights on the field, not in the laboratory."[28]

Chemical warfare advocates lost resoundingly. The American delegation accepted the Pershing subcommittee's recommendation, the conference as a whole adopted the American delegation's position, and Congress ratified the treaty in 1922. The vote in Congress was 72–0 (twenty-four senators did not vote). But that battle turned out not to have ended the war. The treaty would go into effect only if ratified by all the signatories. France decided it objected to the treaty's limits on submarines, rejected the treaty, and thus nullified it.[29]

It was a narrow escape, and an instructive one. Chemical warfare advocates had failed to convince the public or other military officers that chemical warfare had a place in a "civilized" world – especially one then at peace. Over the next several years, they changed tack and took their cue from Isaiah: to show that they promoted peace and life (rather than war and death), they beat their swords into plowshares. As *Chemical Warfare* reported in 1922, "It is a small job for a blacksmith to the [sic] beat the sword into the plowshare, but a large task for a scientist to use a war weapon in peaceful pursuits. This task has been accomplished in the application of various war gases of the Chemical Warfare Service to industrial and agricultural lines."[30]

The Chemical Warfare Service undertook a variety of "peace works," in collaboration with civilian agencies. (Some had started before 1922, but they became more prominent in the service's publicity.) With the Department of Commerce, the Chemical Warfare Service investigated ways to protect marine pilings from deterioration. It worked with the Bureau of Mines on gas masks. It trained and supplied municipal police forces with tear gas to quell civilian riots. It joined with the Public Health Service to kill rats. It developed a gas to kill earthworms that "damage the greens on golf courses." It killed gophers by releasing chlorine gas in burrows. It publicized its efforts in speeches, articles, interviews, and demonstrations to the public.[31]

The new theme brought a bonanza of free publicity, most of it favorable. On page one, the *New York Times* reported, "General Fries declared that the Chemical Warfare Service might well be named 'Chemical Peace Service,' since its present activities are mostly of a constructive nature."[32] The *Pittsburgh Gazette Times* cited Amos Fries as saying his service was doing "peace work principally."[33] In 1923, Secretary of War Weeks suggested that "it would be more logical and more in accordance with the facts to picture the results [of chemical warfare research] as being the destruction of agricultural pests, the limiting of the effect of germ diseases, and the reduction of the risks in industry," rather than "means of destroying life."[34]

One of the most popular projects "cured" disease with chlorine. Medical officers in the World War noticed that soldiers on the front lines fell prey to influenza less often than those in the rear. They theorized that gas immunized against the disease.[35] Beginning in 1922, the Chemical Warfare Service treated victims of colds, bronchitis, and whooping cough with inhalations of chlorine gas. Eighty-seven percent of the subjects said they felt better after treatment.[36]

The good news sent ripples of excitement among Fries's superiors, doctors, and journalists. The secretary of war relayed the findings to the president and to the press.[37] The *Journal of the American Medical Association* published the results. "Few announcements in recent years have occasioned more hope in the minds of the medical profession and the laity than did the report on chlorin [sic] as a therapeutic agent," noted a physician.[38] Journalists highlighted the significance of turning the first poison gas used at Ypres into a cure: "Fumes that Broke the British Front, Leaving Hundreds Dying, Now Cure Influenza, Bronchitis and Other Ailments," announced a *New York World* headline.[39]

The political value of the treatment was enormous. In a room near the Senate Appropriations Committee, the Chemical Warfare Service gassed more than 750 people, including 23 senators and 146 representatives. Even President Calvin Coolidge took the treatment. Those treated reported "nearly unanimous approval." The value of such approval became clear when Fries appeared before an appropriations committee. When someone mentioned that the New York Health Department condemned chlorine, a member of the committee retorted, "Oh well, you don't need to tell me about chlorine; I know, I was cured."[40]

The chlorine treatment was brilliant politics but, unfortunately for public health, bad science. The Chemical Warfare Service used no controls. When a physician at the University of Minnesota conducted a controlled experiment, he found that subjects recovered from colds no faster with chlorine than with other treatments. The "large percentage of recoveries within ... seven days under such a variety of medical treatments is evidence only of the self limited character and short duration of most colds," he concluded.[41]

Enthusiasm also exceeded results in some of the most heavily publicized "swords into plowshares" projects: attempts to use war gases as insecticides. "It is very possible that our investigations will demonstrate that the quickest and surest method in attacking crop destroying pests, whether ground squirrels, gopher, blackbird, crows, buzzard, rats, or grasshopper, is by clouds of gas," noted *Chemical Warfare*.[42] And unlike other measures then in use, poison gases offered the hope of eliminating certain pest problems forever. Gas, the service said, could produce the "complete extermination of certain types of animal life."[43] This potential lifted the hopes of pest control officials enormously. A member of the Mosquito Extermination Commission of Atlantic City, New Jersey, explained that draining marshes where mosquitoes bred solved the problem only temporarily. But "we hope by means of poison gases to destroy these danger centres [sic] permanently."[44]

The Chemical Warfare Service conducted its tests of gases as insecticides in collaboration with several civilian agencies, including the Bureau of Entomology of the U.S. Department of Agriculture. At the request of the service, the bureau detailed an entomologist to the service in 1924. He tested several organic compounds on tent caterpillars and concluded that one deserved future research. (Unfortunately, most of the chemicals effective against caterpillars also killed plants.)[45]

The most heavily promoted insecticide project aimed to find a better chemical to kill the boll weevil.[46] The Chemical Warfare Service tested nine chemicals against the weevil, none of which worked. But Fries was undeterred. In 1924, he announced, "It is known that there are poisons from one thousand to five thousand times as poisonous as calcium arsenate now considerably used to control the boll weevil."[47] The project expanded in 1924 when Senator Harris of Georgia inserted funds for boll weevil extermination into War Department appropriations.[48]

In the end, the Chemical Warfare Service had little to show. In 1926, its researchers reported that toxic gases were "ineffective against the weevil due to its apparent ability to suspend breathing more or less at will." However, they said they had found twenty chemicals that were superior to calcium arsenate. When they published their final report a year later, though, they recommended only two chemicals. Comparative tests found both products inferior to commercial calcium arsenate.[49]

Although of little use to farmers, the boll weevil project accomplished one of its promoters' most important goals: it convinced (at least some) journalists that the Chemical Warfare Service belonged in a peaceful, civilized world.[50] The *Washington, D.C., Herald* said the insecticide research offset "the ravages of war."[51] The *Boston Transcript* editorialized that if the boll weevil project met with even partial success, it justified the Chemical Warfare Service's appropriations.[52]

Simple utility was one reason for the laudatory publicity, but more was at work. Another Chemical Warfare Service claim to civilian utility – improvement in chemical manufacturing methods – spawned far less publicity. Perhaps the difference arose because killing insects more neatly resolved one of the ethical problems associated with gas: inhumanity. The *New York Times* made this argument when it editorialized, "It will not be necessary to argue that poison gases are humane agencies of warfare when the enemy is the boll weevil.... The sooner the General unlimbers his chemical batteries the better."[53]

Similarly, killing insects helped resolve a tension between bellicosity and pacifism. Americans traditionally considered war and the armed forces to be separate in time and space from peace and civilian life. They prided themselves on their skill in both areas, but they saw themselves as engaged in one or the other, not both at the same time. The country was at peace *or* at war. One was a soldier *or* a civilian.

This framework left little room for military skills and institutions in peacetime (and created the anemic military reputation that the "couldn't fight" poster was intended to answer). The War Department existed in peacetime too, of course, but in such an attenuated form and at such a remove from civilian life that it illustrated rather than belied this discomfort.[54] Control of nature offered a bridge between these seemingly incompatible aspects of American life. About pest control, Fries could say that "the arts of peace and war are identical" without fear of reproach.[55] On the contrary, the ability to find a niche in civilian life for chemical warfare was a source of amusement and even delight. The *Boston Transcript* used an oxymoron to describe the surprising compatibility between these ostensibly incompatible endeavors: "'peaceful' war."[56]

Ideas traveled both ways on this bridge. If pest control was a civilized form of chemical warfare, then chemical warfare was a militarized form of pest control. A 1921 pamphlet supporting the Chemical Warfare Service implied this point about chemical warfare technology: "Armed with such [poisonous] liquids and solids the airman of the next war will not need a machine gun or even bombs to attack the enemy underneath.... All he need do is to attach a sprayer to the tail of his machine and rain down poison on the earth beneath as the farmer kills the bugs on his potato field."[57] And in 1922 Amos Fries made the same point about the targets of chemical warfare: "We have given a good deal of attention to [the extermination of insects and other pests], and expect to give a great deal more to it in the future. The nearly four years that have elapsed since the close of the war have shown us that the human pest is the worst of all pests to handle."[58]

Along with carving out a niche for the ideology of chemical warfare in peacetime, pest control created a home for research in chemical warfare. In 1927, the Chemical Warfare Service said the boll weevil project created knowledge of chemical toxicity that would help solve "specific Chemical Warfare problems."[59] The flexibility of insecticide research posed a tremendous challenge to anyone who wanted to abolish research on chemical warfare. A scientist who worked on insecticides for the Chemical Warfare Service said that the development of insecticides made it "both certain and essential that research upon poisonous compounds will be continued."[60]

Small wonder that military funding of chemical research raised warning flags. In May 1922, *Current Opinion* said that "there is a well defined suspicion that recent expenditures by certain governments upon what is so euphemistically called 'science' are developments of chemical warfare for a future struggle that may exceed in barbarism all that has ever yet been recorded of poison gas.... There is already too much reason to suspect that chemistry is being transformed into a system of militarist privilege."[61]

If some groups (unnamed by *Current Opinion*) worried about the impact of peacetime research on battlefields of the future, hunters feared that using military technology in farm fields would endanger wildlife. When news of the Chemical Warfare Service's boll weevil project appeared, the American Game Protective Association complained to the Biological Survey of the U.S. Department of Agriculture. The survey apparently took the Chemical Warfare Service's publicity less seriously than many journalists did. The survey told the association that the "newspaper yarn about killing boll weevil with gas was without foundation in fact."[62]

Research and publicity about civilian applications of chemical weapons plummeted after 1927. Documents examined for this study are silent about the reasons, but the most likely explanation is the Senate's inaction on the 1925 Geneva Protocol. Once past that threat, the Chemical Warfare Service's need to change the views of journalists and the public dropped precipitously.

Under the belief that reducing arms traffic would reduce the risk of war, the League of Nations called a conference in Geneva in

May 1925. Despite Fries's efforts to the contrary, the American delegation introduced a gas resolution modeled on that of the Washington Conference. It banned "the use in war of asphyxiating, poisonous, or other gases, and of all analogous liquids, materials or devices" (as well as "the use of bacteriological methods of warfare"). The resolution passed, and the American delegation signed it.[63]

But signing the treaty was not the same as ratifying it, and the Washington Arms Treaty had taught chemical warfare advocates the importance of public opinion in influencing Congress. In the eighteen months between signing and the ratification vote, the Chemical Warfare Service and the American Chemical Society gave speeches and published articles. Fries emphasized reaching newspaper editors, a group he thought had pushed the Senate to ratify the Washington Arms Treaty by poisoning public opinion of gas. The campaign paid off when some editors switched their position. Some of the most important lobbying focused on veterans' groups. The American Legion, the Veterans of Foreign Wars, the Reserve Officers' Association, and the Military Order of the World War responded by passing resolutions against the gas protocol.[64]

These eighteen months of intense effort, along with publicity over the previous three years, bore fruit by placing a large amount of information in the public record. In the Senate, Military Affairs Committee Chair James Wadsworth led the floor fight against the protocol. Armed with data showing that gas killed victims at a lower rate than other weapons, Wadsworth believed that the United States' support for the Washington Arms Treaty had been based on misunderstanding, especially among the public, of gas. "Today we have much more information; in fact we have complete information, with the result that an entirely different picture is afforded in connection with the use of this weapon," Wadsworth argued.[65]

Wadsworth also emphasized preparedness, saying that other countries would be tempted to attack a United States that had chemically disarmed. This argument was a favorite red herring of chemical warfare advocates. The Washington and Geneva Treaties banned first use of gas, not stockpiling or retaliating, but treaty opponents implied that the treaties required complete chemical disarmament.[66]

Wadsworth mustered enough votes against the treaty to block ratification, but he did not have to use them. Rather than suffering outright defeat, treaty supporters asked that the protocol be returned to the Committee on Foreign Relations. No one objected, it was, and there it stayed until President Harry Truman withdrew it in 1947.[67] In 1932, when the Geneva World Disarmament Conference considered a ban on gas, President Herbert Hoover supported such a measure. But the conference adjourned without agreeing on the matter. As of 1934, the War Department's position was that the United States would be prepared to use chemical warfare "from the inception of hostilities."[68]

Such hostilities looked even more likely in the 1930s, especially as Japan and fascists in Europe armed themselves. The preeminent image of "the next war" was aerial gas warfare against civilians. *America* predicted in 1935 that "death will not march into Paris, London, Vienna, or Berlin in the next war. Death will come from the sky, with gases that sear and suffocate." In 1936, *Catholic World* suggested, "The next war (and short of a miracle there will be a next war) will be inconceivably horrible. We have grown used to prophecies that science may destroy the world, that civilization may be retarded a thousand years or blotted out forever … that death will drop upon us from the skies, that lethal gases will strangle us and explosive bombs blow our cities to dust, and that in fire we shall all perish in such agonies as not even the weird imagination of Dante could have pictured."[69]

In the early 1920s, inducing this sort of fear had struck Amos Fries as the ultimate in scientific rationality. The best way to prevent war was to make everyone fear annihilation. By the 1930s, however, Fries's successors had had enough. Public terror of their weapons struck them as hysterical, not rational. In 1936, one chemical warfare advocate condemned the trend toward "emotional, even hysterical" criticisms of gas by "horror-mongers and inflammatory journalists.... More than any other agent, chemical warfare has captured the popular imagination."[70]

In such publications as the *Saturday Evening Post, Current History, Scientific American,* and *Literary Digest,* Chemical Warfare Service officers and sympathetic journalists ridiculed the logic of those who predicted urban annihilation. Calling visions of chemical bombs or sprays that could "wipe out" cities "absurd," Chemical Warfare Service Captain Alden H. Waitt cited the physics of gas dispersion as a barrier to making such ideas a reality. "A plane might carry enough poison in one tank to kill every individual in a city if each molecule of the poison could reach its target – but that's the rub. Most of it will never reach a human being."[71]

Another Chemical Warfare Service officer said the military's commitment to efficiency would stay urban attacks. "If we also remember that war is an organized business and not just a mad riot of uncontrolled activities we will perceive that gassing large cities is a rather silly idea. New York would never be deluged with gas, even if there were no technical obstacles to overcome. Such an operation would not have the required military value."[72]

The ease with which civilians could protect themselves would also deter attack, chemical warfare advocates suggested. In a massive 1937 treatise on chemical warfare, the Chemical Warfare Service's Augustin M. Prentiss argued that "wars will not be won by aerial attack upon civil populations, using chemicals, if reasonable and relatively simple plans for the protection of the principal and most vulnerable centers of population are made."[73] Major General C. E. Brigham, former chief of the Chemical Warfare Service, said that preparations for gas attacks in other countries were designed mainly to ward off attacks from potential enemies by showing that such attacks would not be effective.[74]

Chemical Warfare Service officers repudiated another of Amos Fries's selling points. Fries had announced in the 1920s that the United States had developed a gas (presumably lewisite) more powerful than those used in the world war. It was so strong, Fries said, that the United States could "deal death from the air, three drops at a time" (referring to the tiny amount of the gas that, simply by contacting skin, would kill a human being). In 1935, Captain Waitt announced, "In spite of the innumerable reports about a super gas that have appeared in the newspapers of the world, there is no real evidence that such a compound has been discovered."[75]

Quite the opposite, the service's Augustin Prentiss explained in his chemical warfare tome. Chemical warfare researchers had surpassed any other form of warfare by making bloodless war realistic. "By means of molecular 'bullets,' man has finally learned the secret of waging war ... with something of the nicety of a skilled anesthetist," Prentiss wrote. It was "within the range of possibility to conduct a virtually deathless war with chemicals – a result entirely beyond the scope of explosive munitions or any other military agents heretofore devised."[76]

The same year Prentiss published this claim, the commander in chief repudiated the notion that chemical warfare had advanced civilization. Franklin Roosevelt had been appalled by a visit to the battlefields of the world war, where he saw "men coughing out their gassed lungs."[77] In 1937, a bill reached his desk that would have changed the Chemical Warfare Service to the Chemical Corps, signaling an elevation in status from subordinate (a "service") to equality with, say, the Corps of Engineers. Roosevelt vetoed the bill and issued a strongly worded policy statement. "It has been and is the policy of this Government to do everything in its power to outlaw the use of chemicals in warfare," Roosevelt

said. "Such use is inhuman and contrary to what modern civilization should stand for.... I hope the time will come when the
Chemical Warfare Service can be entirely abolished. To dignify this
Service by calling it the 'Chemical Corps' is, in my judgment, contrary to a sound public policy."[78]

The contrast between Prentiss and Roosevelt spoke volumes
about the ambiguous place of chemical warfare – and more
broadly warfare itself – in the United States. Americans liked to
think of themselves as minutemen, pacific workers of the soil who,
when forced, would abandon the plowshare and take up the
sword. Their fierceness in battle would vanquish the foe. Then the
minutemen would lay down their swords and return to their
plows. They, as Isaiah put it, "would learn war no more."

This bifurcated view made it hard to see the enduring impact of
even a relatively brief conflict such as the world war. The war created an institution (the Chemical Warfare Service) and interest
groups (chemical warfare veterans and other chemical warfare
advocates) that shaped American politics, intellectual life, international relations, and technology afterward. Chemical warfare
became (until 1945) the symbol of the expanding scale of war in
the twentieth century, and the touchstone for debates about the
wisdom of that expansion. Would it usher in the new millennium,
as advocates suggested, in which nations would abjure war – or at
least wage it without bloodshed? Or would it annihilate life, especially in cities? That was an empirical question, and one World
War II would help answer.

One of the currents in this debate was the role of the control of
nature. Long seen as a peaceful, civilian endeavor, it now pulled
the chariot of Mars. Were science and technology, the modern
ways of controlling nature, pulling that chariot into a better or
worse world? Was Mars driving this powerful team with the light-
est of hands, all but giving science and technology their heads? Or
was he yanking them where they would not otherwise go?

As in other parts of life, humor and metaphor offered some of the more appealing ways to deal with ambiguity. Oxymorons such as peaceful war went only so far because they highlighted rather than resolved the tension between categories. Reclassifying people as pests, and chemical warfare as pest control, did not leave people or technology perched on a conceptual divide.

Thus "dehumanizing," the usual term for using nature metaphors in war, tells us only half the story. It matters not just that propagandists moved people *out of* the category of human; it matters that they moved people *into specific categories* of the nonhuman. Saying people were pests was different from saying they were pets; the terms implied different ways of treating those people.

At the same time that chemical warfare advocates were drawing on entomological metaphors, institutions, and technology, pest controllers were doing the reverse. For them too, the borderland between war and peace offered an appealing territory to explore between the world wars.

5

Minutemen in peace (1918–1937)

H. G. Wells had tried to goad the United States into the world war by portraying war as a rite of passage. Only by joining the brawl would the reclusive, nature-loving, feminine youth of a country join the world of men, he had implied in his "Thoreau in the woods" broadside. Was entry to that world one of the reasons for the joy on the young, but no longer callow, face of the soldier in the "couldn't fight!" poster? If the soldier was not a career soldier–frontiersman specializing in (controlled) violence, but rather a mere youth–minuteman, his moment of triumph need not have marked passage from a world valuing his skills to one inhospitable to them. He had gone off a boy and returned a man, ready to take on the challenges of the next stage in life.

Such was the position of the chemical industry and, to a lesser extent, entomology at the end of the war. We have already seen how the world war increased the size, skills, tools, and prestige of industry and entomology during the war. In the interwar years, both would apply what they had learned to what they saw as their normal environment: peace.

So long as industry and entomologists focused their efforts on the control of nature, keeping alive the spirit of war served them well. Like chemical warfare advocates, they found reaching across the supposed divide between war and peace advantageous – but for the opposite reason. The perceived triviality of insects was one of their chief virtues for those trying to remove the moral stigma of poison gas. This same trait posed one of the chief challenges for pest controllers. Reclassifying pest control as war elevated its significance, associated it with patriotism and national priorities, and opened the door to humor that made otherwise unappealing topics attractive.

But, for the chemical industry, associations with war created hazards as well as opportunities. Suspicions of profiteering, largely muted during the world war, growled more loudly as the interwar years progressed. By the 1930s, chemical companies had become the iconographic "merchants of death" for those who believed that profit-seeking industrialists, in cahoots with professional soldiers, pushed nations into war at the expense of the common good.

The near-success of the Washington Arms Conference had prodded Amos Fries and his allies to redefine the Chemical Warfare Service as the Chemical Peace Service, partly by portraying chemical warfare as pest control. The same conference set the stage for the opposite strategy on the part of L. O. Howard and his allies. Morally unassailable as protectors of food supplies and human health, entomologists embraced the ideology and technology of the world war, including chemical warfare. They arrived in the same territory as chemical warfare advocates, although they started on the other side of the putative war/peace divide.

It was hard to escape the clamor created by the Washington Arms Conference. It reverberated not just in newspapers and speeches, but in the halls of the December 1921 meeting of the American Association for the Advancement of Science. L. O. Howard, chief of the United States Bureau of Entomology, chose in his address as retiring president of the association to promote a

new image for entomology. His speech framed "the war of humanity against the class *Insecta*" as "the next great world war." He
suggested, "It is too much, perhaps, to hope that the lesson which
the world has recently learned in the years 1914 to 1918 will be
strong enough to prevent the recurrence of international war; but,
at all events, there is a war, not among human beings, but between
all humanity and certain forces that are arrayed against it."[1]

Like propagandists in the world war, Howard urged his listeners
to think of enemy insect "forces" as inherently alien and antago-
nistic. Many would consider insects in that category already, of
course, but Howard accentuated the gap by portraying insects as
something   alien   to   earth   altogether.   Quoting   Maurice
Maeterlinck, Howard said that insects seemed to come "from
another planet, more monstrous, more energetic, more insensate,
more atrocious, more infernal than ours." And, like Forbes during
the world war, Howard portrayed entomologists as the career soldiers who led civilian armies into battle. Federal entomologists, "a
force of four hundred trained men," fought a "defensive and offensive campaign" against the insect hordes.[2]

Unlike the world war, however, this war saw no armistice.
Insects continued to attack "Man" from "every point" and
"threaten his life daily; they shorten his food supplies, both in his
crops while they are growing and in such supplies after they are
harvested and stored, in his meat animals, in his comfort, in his
clothing, in his habitations, and in countless other ways."[3]

With this speech, Howard moved military metaphors – which
had jostled with public health metaphors in entomological dis-
course – to the center of his agency's public rhetoric. Other entomologists repeated Howard's prediction that insects threatened
human survival. After quoting Howard's 1921 speech to a 1935
meeting of exterminators, another federal entomologist identified
the mix of motives – public service, professional advancement, and
profit – that made such rhetoric appealing: "People must be *taught*

that insects are enemies of man; and as the public becomes insect conscious the *opportunities for service* by the entomologist, the insecticide chemist, the chemical manufacturer and the exterminator *will increase.*"[4]

Howard's rhetoric struck a chord, and a flurry of newspaper and magazine articles on the insect menace followed. In May 1922, *Century Magazine* reported that the insect "menace" threatened human survival and "every effort at domination or mastery [of insects] has been futile." But there was hope if humanity modeled the insect war on the world war: "The Great War proved what can be accomplished in the field of science when concentrated and concerted energy is applied as the result of a powerful incentive.... Henceforth this warfare between man and the insects is to be one of relentlessness and determination. It will be a warfare which knows no armistice. Man's civilization, his future, his very life, are at stake."[5] In 1925, *Harper's Magazine* published a similar article: "The issue is vital: no less than the life or death of the human race. If man wins he will remain the dominant species on this earth. If he loses he will be wiped out by this, his most ambitious racial enemy." Against this "insect menace" stood L. O. Howard and the Bureau of Entomology. Those scientists were "the staff officers, the intelligence corps of the thousand-year war." Those "General Staffs of this war ... agree that the insects are gaining on man, that they threaten his very existence."[6]

For the rest of his career, Howard elaborated on these themes (and stated that he hoped they would increase public appreciation and funding for economic entomology). Following his retirement as chief of the Bureau of Entomology in 1927, Howard wrote three books in which he emphasized the insect danger. In 1930, he authored a classic history of applied entomology in the United States. In 1931, he published *The Insect Menace,* which combined a Darwinian belief in the struggle for survival, a Spencerian belief that struggle resulted in balance, and a Malthusian belief that human beings would soon overrun their food supply. In 1933, Howard published his autobiography, *Fighting the Insects: The Story of an Entomologist.*[7]

Howard's dire vision of the insect threat, and the implied response to them, struck critics as exaggerated. Soon after Howard launched his "war on insects" campaign, a scientist at the Vienna Natural History Museum wrote a newspaper article titled "Our Planet with No Insects – A Catastrophe which We Hope Will Never Occur." After listing benefits that insects brought to human beings, the scientist mused about what would happen if someone in the United States developed a method of controlling all insects. He decided the result would be catastrophic. Similarly, a 1935 article in *Scientific American* charged that economic entomologists had oversimplified and exaggerated the insect threat. It argued that insects helped as well as hurt people and had little chance of annihilating human beings.[8]

In his 1921 speech, Howard promoted the technology as well as the ideology of the world war. Three weapons seemed most promising for insect control: chemical weapons, airplanes, and flamethrowers. At the same meeting in which Howard delivered his speech, other entomologists reported on the first successful tests of aerial dispersal of insecticides. Howard cited these tests as opening new frontiers and, when *Chemical Age* reprinted his speech in 1922, a photograph of an airplane dropping insecticide dust graced the first page.[9]

Chemical warfare may have inspired this new method of insecticide dispersal. *McClure's Magazine* reported that a colonel returning from France to his job as an Ohio entomologist "knew that near the close of the war preparations were being made to sprinkle poison gas and liquid fire by airplane on soldiers in the trenches and he thought something like this could probably be used against caterpillars." The *New York Times* suggested a more mundane origin, saying that birds inspired aerial dispersal.[10]

Whatever the inspiration, the availability of military airplanes and the cooperation of the army made aerial dispersal feasible. In 1922, a newspaperman impressed by the Ohio entomologist's experiments told a congressional committee that the Army Air Service wanted to experiment with crop dusting to train pilots and develop a commercial auxiliary. The hearings led to a policy of cooperation between the Air Service and the Bureau of Entomology, which in turn led to the development of aerial dusting of cotton.[11]

This new method solved several problems facing cotton farmers. The most efficient dispersal technology then in use, ground sprayers, bogged down in muddy fields and spread insecticides inefficiently on windy days (forcing farmers to dust at night, after winds died). Airplanes soared over mud and, because their wings created downdrafts that pushed insecticide dusts forcefully to earth, allowed dusting on windy days. Plus, airplanes saved on insecticides (downdraft-directed dust adhered to cotton plants better than did dust from ground sprayers, cutting the amount of insecticide needed in half), time (one plane could dust 200–10,000 acres per day, versus 30 acres per day for carts), machinery (one plane did the work of 50–75 ground sprayers), and labor (one pilot replaced the workers needed on those dozens of ground sprayers).[12]

The army did not wait for civilian entrepreneurs to transfer this technology from experimental fields to the marketplace. In March 1923, the acting secretary of war declared that the army would help crop dusting "in a commercial way." Huff-Daland Corporation, which built experimental planes for the army, sent representatives to a Bureau of Entomology laboratory in 1923 to develop a dusting plane. The next year, Huff-Daland formed Huff-Daland Dusters, Inc. The chief of the flying section at the army's McCook Field became the company's chief of operations when the army temporarily released him. He in turn selected pilots and mechanics from army airfields to staff the new company. In 1925, Huff-Daland Dusters, Inc. began large-scale dusting in Louisiana. The following year, the company's chief of operations resigned from the military to work full-time for Huff-Daland. Before long, commercial crop dusters became prominent symbols of the war on insects, especially against the boll weevil.[13]

Although exciting to watch, crop-dusting airplanes frightened a number of people who, sometimes unexpectedly, found themselves in their path. Sharecroppers, whose houses were scattered among cotton fields, feared "that the poison dust would blow over the cabins and kill them all, along with the weevils." Researchers recognized that "the use of the plane might result in indiscriminate poisoning of every object on the property, including the cabins and everything in them." But they believed calcium arsenate harmless, for "this is equally true in the case of ground machines, and the latter have been used for several years without any apparent damage or danger."[14]

Development of aerial crop dusting came at the same time that the Chemical Warfare Service developed aerial dispersal of chemical weapons. In a well-publicized demonstration, airplanes bombarded ships with gas, partly to demonstrate gas's utility as a defense against invasion. When *McClure's Magazine* reported on the still-nascent technology of aerial dusting in 1924, a photograph of a gas attack on a ship accompanied the article. The magazine urged the Chemical Warfare Service and the Army Air Service to launch "a big wholesale sprinkling campaign against boll weevils, mosquitoes, flies and grasshoppers." But the magazine cautioned that chemical warfare against insects could go too far: "But if the gases used should be of the reputed superdeadly post-war developments – the kind that are guaranteed to end wars in one week – care would be necessary, otherwise the whole country might need to be thrown open for settlement again, as it was soon after the year 1492 when Columbus first discovered it."[15]

As we have seen, though, most chemical weapons did not work well against insects. Hope still lived in 1924, when Howard told a meeting of the Entomological Society of America that collaboration between the Chemical Warfare Service and the Bureau of Entomology had produced mountains of data of "undoubted value." But, Howard admitted, the Chemical Warfare Service was keeping almost all the results secret. In 1931, Howard laconically reported that the experiments were, in fact, "not promising, on account of the resultant damage to vegetation," which ended the Bureau of Entomology's public discussion of the war gas experiments. The exception was chloropicrin, the gas the world war had rescued from obscurity. It became a popular fumigant for clothing, households, and grain elevators.[16]

The failure of war gases was unfortunate, for Howard had looked to the branch of chemistry advanced in the world war, organic chemistry, to solve a persistent problem with pesticides: residues on food. Arsenic residues on apples and vegetables had been blamed for illness and death, and federal regulators stepped up their enforcement of laws limiting residues in the interwar years.[17] In one eight-month period in the early 1930s, the Food and Drug Administration seized 221 shipments of sprayed fruit and vegetables, versus 103 the previous year. By 1933, residue enforcement ate up a third of the Food and Drug Administration's budget.[18]

Chemical companies shared Howard's hope that organic chemistry would solve pest control problems, and they turned to research to find new insecticides. This effort was part of a larger commitment to research stimulated by the world war. Before the war, few companies invested in continual research. When they wanted new ideas, they turned to Germany, the acknowledged leader in chemical research, or consultants. "The chemists' war," which placed a premium on new ideas, convinced a generation of chemists to try a new approach. In 1919, one analyst of the chemical industry concluded, "The European War may be credited with having awakened what bids fair to become a real interest in scientific and industrial research.... Truly the war has taught us the value of sustained, continuing research."[19] In 1921, another analyst located the origin of the commitment to research more specifically in chemical warfare: the "mobilization of two thousand American chemists at the Government experiment station in Washington by the Chemical Warfare Service when America entered the war may be said to have marked the real beginning of our chemical industry," he said.[20]

Much of that research focused on America's war child, organic chemistry. At first, in-house research meant looking for new uses for surplus chemicals. Then companies began synthesizing new compounds tailor-made for customers. At Du Pont, four laboratories kept 1,189 people working on dyes, intermediates, explosives, paints, and other products. So many new products flooded the market that the "Age of Synthetic Chemistry" became a catchphrase for the era.[21]

The ability of companies to invest in research flowed largely from the capital and skill created during the war. Du Pont came out of the war with its assets quadrupled and a surplus of $68 million to invest in new fields. Two thousand experienced chemists surged onto the civilian market from the Chemical Warfare Service alone. "How long we should have had to wait for such independence [in organic chemistry] but for the war, no one knows," mused one observer in 1919.[22]

Even if companies had not been drawn to organic chemical research, the changing marketplace would have kicked them into it. The United States demobilized rapidly after the war, yanking the floor out from under the military market for chemicals. To survive, companies had no choice but to turn to the civilian market. To compete in that market, it soon became clear, a company needed research. As Monsanto's vice president in charge of manufacturing put it, "In the organic chemical industry, the fellow who moves fastest gets the profits. The man who is second gets a much lesser prize, and the third and fourth fellows get left out in the cold."[23]

Two by-products of the world war stoked the hope for finding insecticide uses for organic chemicals. Innis, Speiden & Company successfully marketed chloropicrin, the tear gas, as an insecticide (especially as a fumigant).[24] Paradichlorobenzene (PDB), the explosives by-product, found a larger market. By the early 1940s, farmers used 1.5 million pounds of PDB yearly against peach tree borers, and 12.5 million pounds went to control clothes moths.[25] Some companies also manufactured synthetic chemicals developed by the Department of Agriculture, such as ethylene oxide and carbon dioxide, as fumigants.[26]

Finding the right product, several organic chemical companies concluded, could unlock a much larger insecticide market. Hoping to produce a safer substitute for the arsenic compounds then creating residue problems, Rohm and Haas introduced one of the first organic insecticides developed in-house. Called Lethane, it was not very effective, was of questionable safety, and did not find a large market.[27]

Along with increasing their in-house research, chemical companies turned to universities to help them find new insecticides. In 1928, Hercules established a fellowship at the Georgia State College of Agriculture in Athens "to determine the value of Hercules naval stores products in insecticides and related products." Fellowships and research grants to several other universities followed. But finding a good insecticide was not easy. One Hercules fellow tested more than 6,000 compounds between 1938 and 1941. By the outbreak of World War II, Hercules had only one commercial insecticide.[28]

Difficulty finding new insecticides was not the only brake on sales, especially in the household insecticide market. The insecticide industry's reputation for producing fraudulent and dangerous products also slowed sales. In 1925, the president of the Insecticide and Disinfectant Manufacturers Association blamed dishonesty, inexperience, and bad publicity for limiting growth. He lamented that "a prominent newspaper publishes as a news item that the best insecticides are as dangerous to humanity as the insects they destroy." In 1926, a vice president of John Powell & Co. complained that "the housewife – if she knew there was such a thing as an insecticide – bought a package in fear and trembling lest its contents kill her and her family and oftentimes did not buy unless the need for relief was pressing indeed." Manufacturers believed the same factors hindered agricultural insecticide sales, especially by leading government entomologists and extension agents to regard the industry and its products warily.[29]

Industry executives believed the key to overcoming consumer ignorance and distrust was advertising. To separate consumers from their experience with dangerous "bug killers," the common term for their product, manufacturers promoted the term "insecticide." The (in fact synonymous) term caught on slowly. The Scientific Committee of the Insecticide and Disinfectant Manufacturers Association complained in 1925 that the word "'insecticide' has not been sufficiently popularized.... When the housewife was asked why she did not use a good insecticide to rid her home of an infestation of roaches, carpet beetles, ants, etc., or whatever the problem might be, the answer invariably was: 'What is an insecticide and where can I buy one?' The expressions, 'bug killer', 'fly killer', are better known to the housewife, but to some they imply poisonous or dangerous materials of one kind or another."[30] But overall, manufacturers did see progress. In 1926, a vice president of John Powell & Co. said, "The tremendous development of the insecticide industry of late years has been largely due to the aggressive educational advertising in the daily press and popular periodicals."[31]

Insecticide makers drew on public health campaigns and military metaphors to describe struggles with nature and insects. In

1926, Major M. A. Reasoner of the Army Medical Corps delivered a speech on insect-borne diseases to a convention of manufacturers. Insects, Reasoner said, had "overthrown dynasties" and "wiped out whole countries or civilizations or reduced them from a position of commanding superiority to one of helpless subordination." Against this threat, he concluded, people had to wield insecticides, the "symbols of our long deferred superiority and victory" over insects.[32]

The Publicity Committee of the Insecticide and Disinfectant Manufacturers Association distributed a summary of his speech (titled "Insects More Deadly Than Bullets") to local magazines and newspapers "to stimulate the sale of all disinfectants and insecticides." The summary contrasted the traditional view of insects as a source of discomfort with the army and health department view of insects as "menacing disease carrier[s]" and praised the spread of "the Army idea in insect extermination as a means of prevention of disease." The story called for "ruthless warfare" on insects using insecticides.[33]

Pleased with the reception to its first release, the Publicity Committee widened the scope of its campaign. It sent the text of Reasoner's address to 44 trade journals, 8 trade associations, 144 medical journals and state health departments, 450 metropolitan newspapers, and 4,000 small-town weekly newspapers. Outlets in each medium, including 800 small-town newspapers, reprinted the releases.[34] Although military metaphors were not new, the growth of advertising in the interwar period provided new opportunities to promote them. As Thomas Dunlap has suggested, it is difficult to resist the idea that the appeal of insecticides arose partly from their promise of victory over, rather than coexistence with, insect enemies.[35]

Along with military metaphors, manufacturers relied on humor in advertising their products. One of the leaders was Stanco, the Standard Oil division that made a household insecticide called Flit. In the mid-1920s, Stanco created an insect-plagued cartoon family of "Ma, Pa, Little Betty, Uncle Bob, and Lightnin', the maid." The company published cartoons featuring this family in a number of newspapers, advancing its publicity from south to north as the weather warmed and the insect season arrived.[36]

Flit sparked more smiles in the late 1920s, when it hired Dr. Seuss (Theodor Geisel), later famous as an author of children's books, to draw cartoons advertising Flit.[37] The strategy worked. As a publishing industry magazine put it, "Flit literally has smiled its way into the market." Radio joined with print to help make Flit a part of the national parlance. Flit sponsored the most popular comedy act on radio in the 1920s, Billie Jones and Ernie Hare, who were known as the Flit Soldiers.[38] This moniker perhaps seemed appropriate because the Flit can featured a drawing of a soldier. Flit (and military metaphors) captured so much of the market that the popular name for a pump-action sprayer (made by any of several companies) was Flitgun.

Not all companies entering the insecticide business had Stanco's eye for markets and marketing. In the late 1930s, a chemist named Paul Müller at the Swiss dye company Geigy (later Ciba-Geigy) found that an obscure chemical made from chlorine, hydrogen, and carbon (thus a member of the family called chlorinated hydrocarbons) seemed almost ideal as an insecticide: it killed insects at low doses for long periods with low (acute) toxicity to humans. In 1941, Geigy offered the chemical to its United States subsidiary, but the subsidiary declined to market it. The chemical's only known use was to kill the Colorado potato beetle, and the subsidiary did not think the new chemical would compete well with an arsenic insecticide already on the market.[39] World War II would give the chemical, then known as Gesarol and later as DDT (for *d*ichloro*d*iphenyl-*t*richloroethane) a second crack at American insects, but in the meantime it remained unknown in the United States.

So too did another new class of insecticides, the organophosphates, albeit for different reasons. In the mid-1930s, a chemist named Gerhard Schrader at the giant German chemical combine I. G. Farben was looking for new insecticides. He began with a compound (chloroethyl alcohol) known to be toxic to people and dogs, varied the atoms on the molecule, and screened the resulting compounds on insects. A series of substitutions led him to a little-studied family of compounds called organophosphates, which killed insects effectively. In 1936, Schrader found an especially effective insecticide by attaching cyanide to his basic organophosphate molecule. The resulting compound killed aphids at the tiny concentration of one part per 200,000. Further research led to a whole family of organophosphate insecticides, the most famous of which would be parathion and malathion. But the organophosphates had a big drawback. Unlike DDT, which seemed harmless to people, several of Schrader's compounds were lethal to humans as well as insects. Undesirable in an insecticide, this trait was valuable in a chemical weapon. Schrader's find seemed like a good candidate for a war gas, so I. G. Farben sent a sample to the chemical warfare section of the army in May 1937. Schrader traveled to Berlin to demonstrate its effects. Later named tabun, the compound was the first organophosphate nerve gas.[40]

So while creating a new class of insecticides, Schrader was also creating a new class of chemical weapons. In 1938, Schrader found a compound whose potential "as a toxic war substance" he judged to be "astonishingly high." On animals, the substance tested ten times as toxic as tabun. Schrader dubbed it sarin. Other nerve gases followed. Through his superiors at I. G. Farben, Schrader reported 100 to 200 highly toxic compounds to the government in the late 1930s and early 1940s. In 1939, Germany set up a pilot plant to make tabun for the army.[41]

The public knew nothing about Schrader's success. Some journalists suspected that Germany was up to something, but they could only surmise. In 1934, *Nineteenth Century* magazine published documents showing that a German (not Schrader) believed to be involved in making poison gases took out a patent for a "procedure for the attainment of a field of drops from great heights with especial reference to the combating of pests." The patent described ways to increase the height from which "a field of drops" could be dropped to above 500 meters. The article pointed out that the patent "does not explain why insects and other pests should be combated by poison gas 'from great heights' at all. But if the 'pests' upon whom this rain from heaven is to fall are assumed to be troops, or the inhabitants of cities, [the] technique becomes intelligible."[42]

During the interwar years, American chemical companies discovered nothing remotely so powerful against people as the organophosphates (nor, for that matter, did they discover anything remotely so powerful against insects as the organophosphates or DDT). But they suffered from a growing perception that their knowledge of science useful in war, along with desire for profits and ties with the armed forces, gave them disproportionate power over the world's military affairs. By the mid-1930s, chemists had fallen from grace. No longer were they heroes of the chemists' war; they were villains who profited from, and perhaps even started, wars.

Suspicion of a sinister military-industrial web antedated the world war, but wartime fervor had dampened its fire. The return of peace allowed this concern more air. Defeat of arms treaties, persistence of conflict after a war to end all wars, publicity of wartime profits, the symbolic importance of chemical warfare, and eventually economic distress helped fan suspicion's flames and blow them toward chemical companies. The contrasting fates in the Senate of the Washington Arms Treaty and the Geneva Protocol helped focus attention on chemical companies. Publicity campaigns of chemical warfare advocates notwithstanding, public disapproval of gas did not change radically between 1922 and 1927. But the Senate, which unanimously ratified the Washington Arms Treaty, buried the Geneva Protocol.

A number of journalists, especially on the left, blamed small, but politically powerful, interest groups for the shift. The "recent shelving, in the Senate, of the innocuous poison-gas treaty was an unmistakable demonstration of the rise, power, and growth of the new bosses of war – the chemists," thundered Robert S. Allen in the *Nation* in 1927. By "the chemists," Allen meant military and civilian chemists alike. With his forceful personality and high public profile, Amos Fries became a lightning rod for such criticism. Allen called Fries a "super-military agitator."[43]

Prominent liberals embraced the idea that a small but powerful alliance of military officers and industrialists needed to be reined in. In 1927, W.E.B Dubois, Felix Frankfurter, David Starr Jordan, Fiorello H. LaGuardia, and Arthur M. Schlesinger endorsed a book by Norman Hapgood titled *Professional Patriots.* Hapgood identified Fries and Elon Hooker, president of Hooker Electro-Chemical, as examples of "professional patriots" who issued "persistent propaganda" that degraded "the name of patriotism to the service of the dollar," partly by defaming liberal and left causes. Many of these interests gained power in the world war, Hapgood argued, with the ironic result that the United States had become more like Germany and now subjected "the individual to more constraint than before the conflict."[44]

Suspicion percolated throughout the late 1920s and early 1930s that the chemical industry had not only profited from war, but stimulated war. In 1928, the House of Representatives considered a resolution to prohibit the export of "arms, munitions, or implements of war to belligerent nations."[45] The biggest watershed came when these ideas migrated from liberal circles and "the people's house" to arenas that were more conservative. Collapse of the economy into the Great Depression undermined faith in business leaders and their solutions to problems. Then, for reasons that are unclear, *Fortune* magazine published an unsigned article in 1934 titled "Arms and the Men." The work of several members of the magazine staff, the article charged that arms makers supplied "everything you need for a war from cannons to the *casus belli*." The "axioms" of arms makers were to "(a) prolong war, (b) disturb peace" because "killing is their business."[46]

It was big business. In the world war, *Fortune* reported, belligerents spent about $25,000 to kill a soldier. Every "time a burst shell fragment finds its way into the brain, the heart, or the intestines of a man in the front line, a great part of the $25,000, much of it profit, finds its way into the pocket of the armament maker," the magazine said. Compared to European arms makers, Americans were "small fry" but "not quite so virginally innocent in this business as we might like to suppose," *Fortune* declared. The magazine listed Du Pont, Midvale, Colt's, Remington, and Bethlehem Steel as war profiteers.[47]

Suddenly Americans could not get enough of war profiteers. Senator Gerald P. Nye of North Dakota had "Arms and the Men" reprinted in the *Congressional Record*. *Reader's Digest* published a condensation.[48] Two popular books followed fast: *Merchants of Death*, by Helmuth C. Engelbrecht and Frank C. Hanighen, and *Iron, Blood and Profits*, by George Seldes. Like "Arms and the Men," both argued that arms makers fomented and profited from wars. As Seldes put it, "certain business interests, certain manufacturers and producers and their bankers, do want war, they intrigue for war, they have dragged nations into wars and are in favour of war because of the profits they gain from it." These interests, Seldes charged, led the campaign for American preparedness and intervention in the world war. *Merchants of Death* noted that the United States gained 21,000 new millionaires during the world war.[49] Both books used gas as a symbol of their thesis. The first page of Seldes's book showed a photograph of civilians, including a girl, putting on gas masks. Engelbrecht and Hanighen included three photos of people in gas masks.

The "merchants of death" thesis gained wide currency. *Merchants of Death* became a best seller and a Book of the Month Club selection in April 1934. President Franklin Roosevelt charged that "the private and uncontrolled manufacture of arms and munitions and the traffic therein has become a serious source of international discord and strife." Making similar statements were the premier of France, two former secretaries of state, the League of Nations, the *Christian Science Monitor,* members of Congress, pacifist organizations, religious leaders, the *Wall Street Journal,* and the *Chicago Journal of Commerce.*[50]

So widespread were the suspicions, and so accepted was poison gas as a symbol of modern war, that the *Minneapolis Tribune* ran this poem:

> Munitions men, bowed down with care,
> And worries here and everywhere,
> Each nite must breathe this little prayer –
>
> Now I lay me down to snore,
> I hope tomorrow there'll be war –
> Before another day shall pass
> I hope we sell some mustard gas;
> Bless the Germans, bless the Japs,
> Bless the Russians, too, perhaps –
> Bless the French! let their suspicions
> Show the need for more munitions!
> Now I lay me down to snooze;
> Let the morrow bring bad news![51]

With pressure from women's and pacifist groups, the U.S. Senate appointed a special committee in 1934 to investigate the munitions industry. Senator Gerald Nye, a Progressive Republican from North Dakota, served as chair.[52] When a member of the du Pont family charged that the Communist Third International fomented criticism of arms makers in the hopes of making capitalist countries vulnerable, Nye retorted, "During four years of peacetime the du Ponts made only $4,000,000. During the four years of war they made $24,000,000 in profits. Naturally, du Pont sees red when he sees these profits attacked by international peace."[53]

From the start, the committee saw investigation of the Du Pont company as of "paramount importance." The growth of chemical warfare, which in future wars looked (in the committee's words) to "be on a scale so vast as to make the casualties in the last war seem infinitesimal," was one reason for the interest. Others were Du Pont's large size, key role in the world war (when it supplied 40 percent of all propellant powders used by the Allies), and its extensive "world-wide connections."[54] In a 1935 speech, Nye predicted that the "next war" would be fought "to make the world safe for Du Pontcracy."[55]

When the committee issued its report, it used Du Pont as its first example of the importance of war for munitions makers. The company delayed building the Old Hickory powder plant for three months in the world war, the committee charged, because of its desire for "exorbitant" profits. These profits made the world war "the turning point" for the company. Business had been depressed in 1913–1914. The war brought profits of over $228 million and dividends of 458 percent of the par value of the original stock during the war years. After the war, the company used its profits to expand its product lines, including purchase of other companies. Du Pont also, according to the committee, succeeded in lobbying for a protective tariff and against poison gas control in the 1920s as a means for building up itself, especially vis-à-vis the German chemical industry.[56]

The committee also used links between the Chemical Warfare Service and Du Pont to exemplify nefarious alliances between the armed forces and private capital. In 1928, when Congressman Theodore Burton of Ohio introduced a resolution to ban export of weapons to belligerent nations, Amos Fries wrote Irenee du Pont to warn him of dangers the bill posed to the chemical industry. The Nye Committee quoted the letter in its report. Because so many chemicals served civilian as well as military purposes, Fries wrote, the bill was "exceedingly bad" for the chemical industry and would "encourage the radicals and communists to continually attack the United States in its commercial relations with other nations."[57]

One of the committee's most damning conclusions was that the arms business in the United States had come to resemble Germany's on the eve of the world war. An industry so closely tied to national defense "constitutes an unhealthy alliance in that it brings into being a self-interested political power which operates in the name of patriotism and satisfies interests which are, in large part, purely selfish, and … such associations are an inevitable part of militarism, and are to be avoided in peacetime at all costs."[58]

Although committee members agreed on the problem, they disagreed on the solution. The majority recommended that the United States rely on government arsenals to make munitions because "during the World War the munitions companies insisted throughout on their pound of flesh in the form of high profits for their production, and did not let their patriotism stand in the way of the 'duty as trustees' to the stockholders." The committee minority feared that government arsenals would be expensive, wasteful, and create their own "impulse to armament." It concluded "that the public welfare, from the standpoint of peace, defense, and economy can be better served by rigid and conclusive munitions control than by nationalization." On the other hand, the committee reached "remarkable agreement on the need for neutrality legislation" after examining evidence about events in the world war period, and its members helped pass new neutrality legislation in 1935 and 1936.[59]

The idea that chemical manufacturers were merchants of death continued to enjoy wide currency after the hearings. In 1936,

Catholic World reported, "The munitions-makers are no longer Public Enemy No. 1. Their place has been taken by the chemists.... Sooner or later the chemists and physicians will invent or discover something that can blow us all to atoms, or make us evaporate like steam."[60] Such views reflected not just sentiments growing out of the world war, but awareness of events in increasingly restive European and Asian countries. When conflicts in those regions boiled over into the second world war, powers of the magnitude described by *Catholic World* would look far more attractive.

6

Total war (1936–1943)

In October 1941, an insecticide importer published an advertisement promoting "Total War on Insects." It provided a benchmark of the state of warfare among people as well as against insects. The world war (now the *First* World War) had expanded so many features of war – science and technology, propaganda, and attacks on enemy cities, to mention a few – that no one had figured out a widely accepted name for this expansion until after the war. Before the United States entered World War II, though, "total war" had become so familiar a term that an insecticide maker could use it as a synonym for extermination.

Military theorist Giulio Douhet came close to coining the term "total war" in 1921. He wrote that "prevailing forms of social organization have given war a character of national totality – that is, the entire population and all the resources of a nation are sucked into the maw of war. And, since society is now definitely evolving along this line, it is within the power of human foresight to see now that future wars will be *total* in character and scope."[1]

The stress on a broad foundation of military power, resting on civilian science and technology as well as armed forces, gained force among military planners in the 1920s.[2] German General

Erich Ludendorff elaborated on these ideas and gave them the specific name "total war" in a 1935 book titled *Der Totale Krieg;* an English translation appeared the next year. The unfamiliarity of the term could be seen in the quotation marks added to the title of the translation, *The "Total" War.*[3]

The text of the translation of Ludendorff's book gave this military strategy a decided ideological bent by translating "total war" as "totalitarian war." Fascist countries certainly put the strategy into effect. In the 1930s, Italy bombed Barcelona and gassed Ethiopians armed with spears, Germany bombed Guernica (an event Picasso commemorated with a mural for the 1937 Paris World Exhibition that year), and Japan bombed Chinese civilians.[4] In 1938, *Commonweal* reported that Germany had adopted "an ultra-modern, 'streamlined' theory of military operations" called "totalitarian war." Its features included attack without warning; destruction of hostile armies, navies, and shipping from the air; and attacks on cities. In accomplishing the last objective, "the bombing squadrons must inexorably and without pity attack the enemy's cities and population centers as well as his railroads and industries," *Commonweal* noted.[5]

The strategy of total war, especially attacks on civilians, lost much of its opprobrium when Great Britain met Germany's aggression with some of the same methods, including by trading incendiary attacks on cities.[6] Whether the United States should enter the war remained a matter of debate until Japan decided the issue by attacking Pearl Harbor. The United States declared war on Japan, Germany and Italy declared war on the United States, the United States declared war on Germany and Italy, and the country plunged into what was by then commonly called total war.[7]

Wrapping one's mind around such a huge undertaking was both simple and complex. Simple, because self-defense was one of the most obvious and justifiable reasons to go to war. Complex, because one could choose from almost countless ways to think about the enemy, the means used to wage war, and the goals the war should achieve. Different people chose different ways to think about and carry out those tasks. Our interest here is not in all the ways, but in those that drew on nature (especially the part of nature with six legs). As it turned out, insects offered some very useful ways to think about total war.

Similarly, thinking about natural enemies (again, especially those with six legs, and more specifically those insects that threatened human health and food supplies) was both simple and complex: defending oneself against threats was an obviously sensible thing to do, but one had almost countless ways to think about and carry out the tasks involved. Again we are not interested in all the ways, but those that (to reverse the direction) drew on (or were shaped by) war. And, as it turned out, total war offered some especially useful ways to think about and alter pest control.

The usefulness of nature in thinking about human enemies and the goals of war could be seen in a letter to the *New York Times* published the day after the attack on Pearl Harbor. Albert Hirst of New York noted that Franklin Roosevelt had compared Nazis to rattlesnakes. Hirst thought the comparison apt, for "In America ... one retreats before a rattler only in order to pick up a stone or a stick and to kill it. Every little boy kills rattlers. This shows that they are little feared. In the well-settled parts of America the rattler, because of this incessant hunt, has become practically extinct."[8] In Roosevelt's metaphor, Hirst saw a way to think about Nazis (dangerous but not feared) and the appropriate American response (stand one's ground, attack right away, and perhaps exterminate the foe).

When using nature metaphors, Americans applied them differently to Germans and Japanese. In fixing blame for German aggression, Americans usually fingered a subset of the population – Hitler or Nazis. For Japanese aggression, Americans often spoke of all Japanese (or more commonly "Japs") as the culprits. As a British official put it, Americans in Europe saw themselves fighting "great individual monsters like Hitler, Goebbels, Goering, and Mussolini." Against Japan, Americans often saw themselves fighting a "nameless mass of vermin."[9] When Ernie Pyle visited the Pacific after seeing some of the worst fighting in Europe, he also noticed the contrast: "In Europe we felt our enemies, horrible and deadly as they were, were still people. But out here I gathered that the Japanese were looked upon as something subhuman and repulsive; the way some people feel about cockroaches or mice."[10]

Several factors contributed to seeing Germans and Japanese differently. A long-standing fear of a Yellow Peril played some role. A letter to the New York Times argued that the attack on Pearl Harbor resulted from Japan's "age-old dream of world mastery."[11] The attack on Pearl Harbor was one of the most important factors. It came without warning or clear provocation, killed Americans, took place in American territory, and occurred during talks between high Japanese and American officials. Germany did similar things, but to Europeans, not Americans. Brutal treatment of American prisoners of war made things worse. The Japanese killed captured American aviators and, in the Bataan Death March, oversaw the deaths of 8,000 of 12,000 American prisoners. Killing prisoners of war, Representative Robert L. F. Sikes of Florida told Congress in 1943, meant the Japanese "should be cast out from the world family of nations. There is no place for mad dogs."[12]

The experience of battle also played an important role in shaping perceptions. Only about one percent of Japanese fighters surrendered, and American soldiers found such tenacity inhuman. A Guadalcanal veteran wrote, "The Japanese seem to get a grotesque pleasure from self-destruction, from planned death, whether by their own hands or by the hands of others."[13]

Many similar experiences convinced American soldiers that they would have to exterminate (rather than capture) Japanese soldiers. General Henry H. Arnold said, "The Germans are smarter, but the Japs are tougher. When a German outfit is cut off, it is usually smart enough to give up – but not the Japanese. We have to bomb and burn and blast them out."[14] A June 1943 conference of naval commanders concluded, "The only way to beat the Japs is to kill them all. They will not surrender and our troops are taking no chances and are killing them anyway."[15]

Official and unofficial propaganda reinforced the tendency to view America's human enemies as pests. America's official propaganda agency, the Office of War Information, produced a cartoon of a caterpillar saying "What! Me sabotage that guy's victory garden? What do you take me for – a Jap?" (Figure 6.1). Private companies promoted much the same idea. In an insecticide advertisement, the Rohm and Haas Company paired a drawing of a soldier shooting a Japanese soldier (in the back) with a drawing of another person shooting a fly with a Flitgun. "Whether Japs or flies," the text read, "it's fast action that counts."[16]

Such propaganda cut both ways: along with portraying war as pest control, it portrayed pest control as war. And it worked on more than one level: along with framing views of human and natural enemies, it helped frame views of the technology used to control both kinds of enemies. A Flitgun maker (Hudson) used military technology to reinforce the notion that sprayers were weapons in a battle against insects. In an advertisement, the company suggested, "For every enemy up ahead, thousands lurk treacherously in and behind the actual battle lines. Mosquitoes, lice and other disease carriers are a constant, dangerous threat. That's why our fighters all over the globe are equipped with two kinds of guns – firearms to fight the human foe – sprayers to fight the insect foe."[17]

Conversely, a bomber crew and a photojournalist used Flitguns to help them think about military technology (and human ene-

6.1   "What! Me Sabotage that Guy's Victory Garden?" In this cartoon created for the Office of War Information, Bo Brown implied that a "Jap" was an even lower creature than an insect. From 208 COM 278, Still Pictures Branch, NARA.

mies) in a way that was both playful and serious. When Margaret Bourke-White arrived in England to photograph the first heavy bombers sent from the United States, one of the crews asked her to name their plane. She suggested "Flying Flitgun." The delighted crew "ran out to their bomber with pails of paint," Bourke-White recalled, "and on the nose of the B-17 they painted a bright yellow flit-gun, spraying down three exotic insects, with the faces of Hitler, Mussolini and Hirohito." The bomb group's commanding officer read a speech that concluded, "May the *Flying Flitgun* bring to the enemy the devastation its godmother has brought to the 97th" (Figure 6.2).[18]

Although the crew of the Flying Flitgun did not know it yet, chemical warfare would play a central, yet often unrecognized, role in devastating the enemy. Experts and laypeople alike used the term "chemical warfare" interchangeably with "gas warfare" (likewise "chemical weapons" with "poison gas"). Equating the two obscured the fact that chemical warfare included more than gas. In World War II, one of the most important chemical weapons was fire.

The Chemical Warfare Service had worked on incendiary weapons during World War I, but, faced with tight budgets in the interwar years, had all but dropped that line of research in favor of what it saw as its more powerful weapon and main concern, poison gas. Therefore, the Service had no incendiary bombs on hand in December 1941.[19] Within the Chemical Warfare Service, the main advocate for incendiaries was a reserve officer, Columbia University chemist J. Enrique Zanetti. Zanetti had worked on incendiaries for the Chemical Warfare Service in World War I. He thought fire, not the poison gases on which the debates about chemical warfare had focused in the interwar years, posed the biggest danger to cities in wartime. Gas dropped on cities from airplanes would dissipate; fire, the "forgotten enemy," would propagate.[20]

6.2 "The Flying Flitgun." Photojournalist Margaret Bourke-White, who suggested the "Flying Flitgun" name to the crew, appears here with unidentified men. Photographer unknown, from the Department of Special Collections, Syracuse University Library.

In the 1930s, Zanetti thought awakening the world to the destructive potential of fire would advance peace. In a 1936 article, he predicted that "little by little the realization of the enormous, irreparable damage that can be mutually inflicted will dawn upon the nations of the world and only collective insanity could drive them to settle their differences by resort to armed conflict."[21]

Zanetti was a better chemist than prognosticator. The ink of his article had scarcely dried before events proved him wrong. (Either that, or the nations of the world had descended into "collective insanity.") In April 1941, he published another article, this one not a prediction but a call to arms: "Whether one is prepared to accept the long-foreseen 'all-out' type of warfare, in which the destruction of civilian morale plays such an important part, or whether one condemns it as brutal, inhuman, and uncivilized matters little," he argued. "All out warfare is here and must be faced."[22]

William Porter, chief of the Chemical Warfare Service, agreed. He recalled Zanetti to active duty in July 1941; soon Zanetti headed a new Incendiaries Branch. By October 1941, Porter gained permission to obtain over 25 million incendiary bombs and began letting contracts.[23] Porter also arranged for the Chemical Warfare Service to gain sole custody of incendiaries. Ordnance, with which the Chemical Warfare Service shared responsibility, wanted to focus on explosives and agreed to the relinquishment. With full custody of incendiary bombs came an economic windfall. When the Chemical Warfare Service took over Ordnance's part of the program, $69 million of Ordnance's money came with it. Pushed mainly by demand for incendiaries, the Chemical Warfare Service returned to the level of big business. After scraping by on a few million dollars a year, the service spent about $1.7 billion on procurement during World War II. The incendiary program was the single most important item in that growth: the service spent more money on, devoted more personnel to, and obtained a larger number of incendiaries than any other item. The service that had no incendiary bombs on hand in December 1941 had, by December 1945, obtained almost 255 million.[24]

The incendiary program owed much of its rapid growth to civilian chemists. Vannevar Bush, president of the Carnegie Institution in Washington, D.C., took the lead in organizing civilian science for war. Bush believed that the armed forces did not yet appreciate the extent to which modern war was a matter of science and technology. With the blessing of Franklin Roosevelt, Bush organized the National Defense Research Committee to mobilize civilian scientists for war research. One of his first recruits, James Conant, had gone from researching poison gas in World War I to becoming president of Harvard. Conant assumed that Bush would follow the World War I American University model by gathering scientists from around the country in one place. The committee did so for a few projects, most famously in a project Conant supervised for the committee, the development of the atomic bomb. (Conant thus helped develop the emblematic weapon of World War I, poison gas, and of World War II, the atomic bomb.) But, in most cases, Bush would follow a new model: keeping scientists in their home institutions and supporting them with research contracts.[25]

Bush asked Conant to oversee chemical research. Conant recruited a fellow Harvard chemist, Louis Fieser. Fieser considered poison gases inhumane and unlikely to be used, but said he "swallowed my personal feelings" and recruited a new group of Harvard Ph.D.'s for the project. Before they started work, however, Fieser visited the Chemical Warfare Service's Edgewood Arsenal, learned that the service had done no research on incendiary gels, and got permission from the National Defense Research Committee to use his colleagues and funds to research incendiaries instead of gases. Fieser's group found that mixing two compounds (aluminum naphthenate and aluminum palmitate) with gasoline produced a tough, sticky, flammable gel. Fieser dubbed the mixture napalm, from the first letters of *na*phthenate and *palm*itate. By the spring of

1942, researchers had figured out a way to package and ship the thickener long distances, making much easier the wide use of flamethrowers and incendiary bombs (later known as napalm bombs).[26]

From the start, incendiary developers envisioned using fire on enemy houses. Tests of incendiaries at Huntsville Arsenal, Alabama, took place in June 1942 on "rickety old abandoned farmhouses, barns, and settlers' shacks." Another set of tests in July 1942 at Jefferson Proving Ground, Indiana, used "substantial houses in village and farm groups." These tests showed that napalm and other incendiaries produced "beautiful fires," in Fieser's view. One napalm bomb burned down a house in two to three minutes. Another landed on a barn and set a fire that jumped to two sheds. A third landed in front of a house, but splattering gel ignited the house and three sheds.[27]

But would incendiaries would work as well on German and Japanese homes? To answer this question, William N. Porter decided in 1943 to build model towns at military sites in Florida, Maryland, and Utah. He hired three German Jewish architects, who had fled the Nazis, to design the German buildings. Crews then built the buildings, taking care to install the types of wood, furniture, bedspreads, rugs, and drapes used in Germany. For the Japanese houses, crews ransacked Hawaii and the West Coast of the United States to find Japanese straw floor mats. At the Dugway, Utah, site, an air force observer noted that the buildings were "as truly authentic as humanly possible, down to the last detail. They were 'typical' even insofar as the curtains, children's toys, and clothing hanging in closets were concerned. Nothing was overlooked." The towns included factories, shops, and businesses as well as homes. Tests on these buildings enabled researchers to develop incendiary bombs suited to each nation's architecture.[28]

The tests in May–July 1943 produced convincing evidence that American bombers could burn up enemy cities. During the fall of

1943, National Defense Research Committee scientists helped the air force write plans for bombing Japanese cities with incendiaries. In 1944, Vannevar Bush sent General Henry Arnold a memo describing incendiary bombs as ideal for strategic bombing because of their efficiency and impact on morale. He suggested that incendiary bombing "may be the golden opportunity of strategic bombardment in this war – and possibly one of the outstanding opportunities in all history to do the greatest damage ... for a minimum of effort. Estimates of economic damage expected indicate that incendiary attack of Japanese cities may be at least five items as effective, ton for ton, as precision bombing of selected strategic targets as practiced in the European theater. However, the dry economic statistics, impressive as they may be, still do not take account of the further and unpredictable effect on the Japanese war effort of a national catastrophe of such magnitude – entirely unprecedented in history." Researchers developed a large bomb (the M-69) especially for Japanese cities. It weighed about 500 pounds, opened at an elevation of 5,000 feet, and released a cluster of six-pound bombs. Each of those exploded and spread flaming jellied gasoline for a radius of thirty yards.[29]

Fieser and his colleagues also developed a tiny incendiary that could be attached to bats (the mammalian kind). The idea was that an airplane would release armed bats over a Japanese city. The bats would seek shelter under eaves of buildings, and a timer would then set off the incendiaries. In December 1943, Fieser joined the Chemical Warfare Service for tests of bat bombs in the model Japanese village at Dugway Proving Ground, Utah. Fieser rated the results "good." He used the data from the test to estimate that bat bombs dropped over Tokyo by one B-25 bomber would start at least 3,725 destructive fires. This figure meant that bat bombs were 3.7 times more efficient than the M-69 cluster bomb, which was then the most efficient method available. Fieser thought this would be an ideal way to destroy Tokyo. "Imagine, then,"

Fieser later wrote, "a surprise attack on Tokyo in which a succession of bombers would operate at high altitude for about half an hour, say starting at midnight, each delivering a load of bat-bombs equivalent to some 3,700 fires. There would be no explosions or fire bursts to give warning, and the bombers would depart. With the activated mechanisms all set for a four-hour delay, bombs in strategic and not easily detectable locations would start popping all over the city at 4 A.M. An attractive picture? All those working on the project thought so."[30]

Civilian chemical warfare researchers faced two institutional hurdles in getting their ideas for weapons into the field. One was getting the Chemical Warfare Service to accept them. The service was not opposed to incendiaries, as Porter and Zanetti's efforts showed, but the service's ideas about how to proceed differed from those of civilians. Civilian scientists thought military officers lacked talent and vision; military officers thought civilian chemists were arrogant and impractical. By April 1942, cooperation in chemical warfare was "in a fair way to be nullified by hard feeling" between civilians and Chemical Warfare Service officers.[31] Then the new chief of the technical division of the Chemical Warfare Service reduced tensions by appointing a liaison officer from the service to the civilian committee. The National Defense Research Committee reciprocated by placing the chairmen of its three chemistry divisions on the officer's staff. By the end of the war, the two organizations were "working hand and glove on mutual problems."[32]

Bush also addressed this problem (and others like it with other parts of the armed forces) by reorganizing his committee and its mission. Again with Franklin Roosevelt's approval, Bush created a new entity called the Office of Scientific Research and Development; the last two words signified that civilians would do "applied" as well as "basic" steps in weapons development. At the same time, Bush incorporated medical research into his purview.

The old National Defense Research Committee (now the second tier in the Office of Scientific Research and Development) continued to oversee weapons development. A new Committee on Medical Research oversaw civilian work in military medicine.[33]

A second hurdle, faced by civilians and military officers alike, was getting the air force to use incendiaries. In Porter's view, the air force held a "prejudice" against incendiaries. The Chemical Warfare Service began shipping incendiary bombs (a 100-pound version called the M-47) to the air force in Europe in June 1942. But American air strategy stressed pinpoint destruction of industrial targets, for which high explosives were better suited, and the incendiary bombs went unused.[34]

This lack of interest meant the Chemical Warfare Service was, at the time, in danger of watching the war from the sidelines. Although the War Department's position was that field commanders could start gas warfare when they saw fit, civilian leaders soon reined in that authority.[35] Franklin Roosevelt, who had condemned chemical warfare in his 1937 veto of the bill making the service into a corps, maintained his position in World War II. According to Chemical Warfare Service records, the navy's Bureau of Aeronautics planned to add tear gas to shells and bombs around the time of the United States' entry to war, but Roosevelt stayed their hand by presidential order.[36] The secretary of the navy apparently agreed with Roosevelt, writing the secretary of state in January 1942, "the attitude of the Navy Department is against the use of such gasses in warfare."[37] In April 1942, Chief of Staff George Marshall elevated decisions about initiation of chemical warfare to the chief of staff of the army and commander-in-chief of the U.S. fleet.[38]

With options closing inside the armed forces, the Chemical Warfare Service launched a public relations offensive in civilian publications. The main spokesperson was Colonel Alden H. Waitt, who, in April 1942, told the readers of *The New Republic* that a gas offensive "will come very soon. When it does come, it will be initiated with greatest surprise and on a scale never before witnessed … Massed airplanes, carrying tons of gas, will drop their chemical from the sky in amounts that may prove overwhelming." Chemicals would "produce the decision."[39] Articles in *Time* and *Popular Science,* and a book authored by Waitt, elaborated on familiar reasons why chemical warfare was the "ideal weapon": it was powerful, efficient, humane, well suited to modern war (especially aerial warfare), and inevitable.[40]

Then Allied leaders all but shut the door on first use and on gas publicity. England and the United States agreed to make decisions about starting gas warfare jointly, and they never decided to do so. The reasons cited most often were that gas would divert resources (especially airplanes) from other missions, complicate the battlefield, be inhumane, raise public criticism, and invite retaliation in kind.[41] The War Department adopted a policy of minimizing news about gas in order "not to arouse opposition to use of various weapons of Chemical Warfare on the part of sentimentalists."[42] In June 1943, Roosevelt set a policy against first use when he announced that "use of such [chemical] weapons has been outlawed by the general opinion of civilized mankind. This country has not used them, and I hope that we never will be compelled to use them. I state categorically that we shall under no circumstances resort to the use of such weapons unless they are first used by our enemies." But should an enemy use chemical weapons, "We promise to any perpetrators of such crimes full and swift retaliation in kind."[43]

Such a policy did not bind the country's enemies, of course, and the Chemical Warfare Service helped make the threat of aerial chemical warfare visible through a traveling demonstration. Titled "Action Overhead," it was seen by about 1.5 million civilians in twenty-eight states and about eighty-five cities in the first nine months of the war. The demonstrations featured explosions of incendiaries and dispersal of gas simulants. In New York City, a "harmless white smoke" used as a demonstration "piled up as high as the tallest skyscrapers."[44]

As some Americans equipped themselves with gas masks, they struggled to make sense of this new part of their lives. At least one artist seemed to think that gas masks – perhaps because of the lack of individuality and menace they suggested – led people to resemble insects. *The New Yorker* published a cover illustration of a masked maid peering at herself in a mirror. One of the magazine's writers later interpreted the image: the maid "seems transformed from a docile butterfly into a predatory insect. As she gazes into the mirror, can she be dreaming, just this once, of overpowering her endlessly demanding charges and dragging them off to her den belowstairs, there to devour them at her leisure?"[45]

Aside from a few ineffectual incidents, Germany and Japan did not attack the forty-eight states. But their insect allies did. With food rationed and civilians planting victory gardens, every pest did the work of a saboteur. Insects accidentally imported from – and named after – Germany and Japan made especially good targets for journalists. *Science News Letter* singled out the Hessian fly and the Japanese beetle as "insect saboteurs" working in aid of the enemy.[46] Many publications (including the *New York Times*) and entomologists even changed their name for the latter to "the Jap beetle" after Pearl Harbor.[47]

As we saw briefly earlier, an insect did not have to originate overseas to become an enemy on the home front. Nor were war metaphors anything new. But the scale on which public and private organizations publicized war metaphors soared. A booklet prepared for dairy farmers, apparently by the Bureau of Entomology, was called "War on Insects." Commercial firms bought and distributed more than 3 million copies to milk, butter, and cream producers.[48] Department of Agriculture posters urged gardeners seeing insects to "shoot to kill!" Monsanto and van Ameringen-

Haebler compared insecticides (or at least their odor) to chemical weapons. An importer of pyrethrum (the active ingredient in many household insecticides) suggested that its customers could expect "the knockdown and total war on insects [to] surpass past experience." *House and Garden* advocated "an all-out attack on fifth columnists in the garden."[49]

The supply of words and images promoting a war on insects seemed to be limitless, but the supply of weapons for such an attack was not. As the war prodded crop prices higher and higher, farmers dusted insecticides on their crops to eke out every bushel. Cotton, for example, became more valuable as demand increased for clothing, bandages, oils, and fats.[50] A member of the U.S. Department of Agriculture complained, "There simply is not enough arsenic in the world to take care of the demand that can be made by cotton farmers when the price of cotton is 21 cents and when they have been permitted or encouraged to buy calcium arsenate indiscriminately."[51]

These demands led the Bureau of Entomology to change its arm's-length partnership with industry. In hopes of finding an effective substitute for pyrethrum and rotenone, the bureau revised its policy against testing proprietary products.[52] It furnished weekly reports of insect outbreaks to manufacturers to guide insecticide distribution.[53] R. C. Roark (one of the members of the bureau with closest ties to industry before the war) joined a committee of entomologists created to work with the Agricultural Insecticide and Fungicide Association. An entomologist who participated in, and wrote a history of, entomology in World War II believed this committee was "instrumental" in gaining recognition for the role of insecticides in the war effort.[54] P. H. Groggins of the Office for Agricultural War Relations (a Department of Agriculture office with close ties to industry) told L. S. Hitchner, secretary of the Agricultural Insecticide and Fungicide Association, that "our obtaining the cooperation of the Bureau of Entomology and Plant

Quarantine has been the outstanding accomplishment of our activities in the field of insecticides and fungicides."[55]

The domestic war on insects included threats to public health as well as agriculture. Before the war, a stagnant economy had joined with stagnant pools of water to send the malaria rate climbing. With public health mainly a state and local responsibility, and medicine a private profession, the federal government had played a limited role in trying to reverse the trend. War made malaria a federal – and more specifically a military – threat. Civilians with malaria, most of whom lived in the South, formed a "reservoir" of disease that mosquitoes could spread to soldiers. So, the federal government intervened on a vast new scale. General James Simmons, the army's chief of preventive medicine, called this effort "the most gigantic mosquito-control campaign carried out in the history of the world." The Army Surgeon General's Office funded improvements on bases, and the U.S. Public Health Service launched the Malaria Control in War Areas program around bases and war industries. The program cooperated with governments of twenty states, the District of Columbia, and Puerto Rico. It protected over 1,000 "war establishments" by 1944, including army installations, navy stations, "critical war industries," and recreational sites for war workers or military personnel.[56] The rate at which troops were admitted to the hospital for malaria dropped from a peacetime average of 2.3 per thousand men per year in 1931–1940 to less than 0.3 per thousand men per year in 1943.[57]

In the Pacific, meanwhile, ignoring malaria created a disaster. There, the Surgeon General's Office lacked the authority it held at permanent bases to order mosquito control measures. In the field, troop health was a command responsibility. Medical officers advised, but did not control, commanders. Unfortunately, the attitude of too many commanders was, as one officer put it: "We are here to kill Japs, and to hell with mosquitoes." After the Guadalcanal invasion, months passed before malaria control personnel set foot on the island, by which time malaria was epidemic.[58] Some units became so sick that they were evacuated before they did any fighting at all.[59]

Nature, as it turned out, posed a much bigger threat to American military power than Japanese soldiers. A Canadian military attaché concluded that the Japanese army did not even make the top three: "The Japs are not the main enemy in the South Pacific. We figure they are a bad fourth Public Enemy," behind climate, scrub typhus (a relative of the European disease), and malaria. All took bigger tolls on Allied soldiers than did Japanese soldiers.[60] Early in the Pacific war, malaria caused *eight to ten times* as many casualties as battle did. Averaged over the course of the war, malaria caused five times more casualties in the South Pacific than combat had.[61]

The problem started at the top, and so did the solution. General Douglas MacArthur realized that malaria had defeated him on Bataan and knew that his troops in Papua fell to malaria at a high rate in 1942. He did not want that to happen again. As he complained to a medical officer, "This will be a long war if for every division I have facing the enemy I must count on a second division in hospital with malaria and a third division convalescing from this debilitating disease."[62]

Field commanders were not simply ignorant or hardheaded (though some were both). Malaria control required supplies and labor, two items at a premium. To solve the logistical problems, Army Surgeon General James C. Magee proposed the creation of special units to plan and carry out malaria control. Each unit would include malariologists, entomologists, parasitologists, sanitary engineers, trained enlisted men, and laborers. After intensive lobbying, he got permission to deploy the first units in January 1943. The same year, MacArthur acted decisively to control malaria. He ordered commanders to use malaria control units, raise the shipping priority for anti-malaria supplies, order troops to take prophylactic drugs (quinine and atabrine), establish a standard mosquito repellent, survey bivouac sites to avoid malarious areas, and train troops in the importance of malaria.[63]

A publicity blitz formed an important part of this effort.[64] Chief of Staff George Marshall concluded that in "some tropical theaters of operation, malaria has hospitalized ten times more soldiers than have battle casualties. This loss in fighting manpower is due largely to failure of Army personnel of all ranks to appreciate the necessity for control measures of all types."[65] In 1943, the army prepared what it called "educational propaganda" about malaria. It flooded theaters with posters, films, radio broadcasts, pinup calendars, signs, manuals, matchbooks, ration containers, and maps, all warning soldiers to protect themselves from malaria (Figure 6.3). Cartoon movies bore such titles as *Silent Battle* and *Private Snafu vs. Malaria Mike.*[66]

The campaign drew on several aspects of GI culture. One was the fear of poison gas dating from World War I: "You can be made as chronic an invalid from malaria as from poison gas," noted one training circular. "Malaria can make you weak and puny, and good for nothing."[67] The campaign also capitalized on cheesecake. Nearly every tent and Quonset hut in the South Pacific featured cartoon pinups of *Anopheles* mosquitoes, the genus that carried malaria.[68] Theodor S. Geisel (Dr. Seuss), who had drawn cartoons for the insecticide Flit before the war, created a mosquito version of a femme fatale. ("This is Ann; she's dying to meet you," read the caption. "Her full name is Anopheles Mosquito and her trade is dishing out Malaria.") When an army detachment in New Guinea chose Rosemary La Planche as "Miss Mosquito Junction of 1943," she donned a mosquito net as a cape and carried a Flitgun as a scepter.[69]

Many materials linked the war against malaria to the war against Japan. One poster featured a creature with a mosquito's body, a head with stereotypical Japanese features, and wings with the rising sun of the Japanese flag. The poster credited "Japs" with just one casualty for every eight due to malaria.[70] Another poster pointed out that war made the malaria problem worse because ruts, abandoned roads, blocked ditches, foxholes, and shell holes

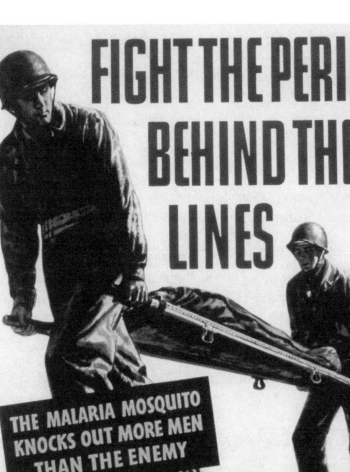

6.3 "Fight the Peril behind the Lines." This poster reminded soldiers that malaria endangered them more than the enemy did. Other posters specified the casualty ratio early in the Pacific war, which ran eight malaria casualties to one combat casualty. From 44PA 763, Still Pictures Branch, NARA.

were ideal for mosquito breeding. In fact, war more than doubled the number of malaria mosquitoes (Figure 6.4).

The new strategy worked. In 1943, malaria hospitalized more Americans in the Southwest Pacific than all other causes. By June

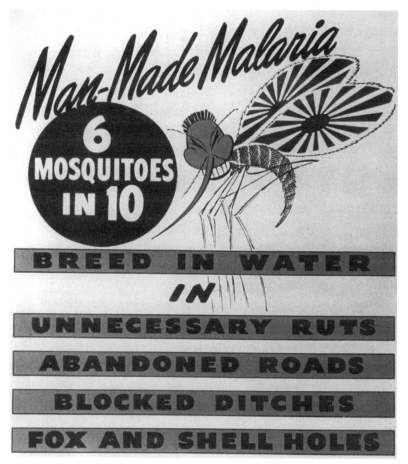

6.4 "Man-Made Malaria." As part of its "educational propaganda" efforts in the Pacific, the armed forces often merged portrayals of Japanese and insect enemies. The mosquito body in this 1944 poster bore a stereotypical Japanese head (slanted eyes, short hair, buckteeth), and the wings resembled the Japanese flag. Human activity in war areas, according to the poster, created breeding places for 60 percent of malaria mosquitoes. From USGPO, 44 PA 1327, Still Pictures Branch, NARA.

1944, the malaria rate had dropped 95 percent. Serving in the Southwest Pacific had become little more dangerous than serving at home: in 1944, the "non-effectiveness" rate from all causes, including battle, was about the same (only 0.003 percent higher) as in the United States. In June 1944, MacArthur's headquarters announced that MacArthur had won "one of the greatest victories ... in the Southwest Pacific Areas – a victory by Science and discipline over the anopheles mosquito."[71]

Now the United States had the chance to turn an enemy into an ally. Malaria had plagued Japanese as well as American troops; if it continued to attack the Japanese while "sparing" Americans, it would debilitate the Japanese army. So, the U.S. Army publicized the results, but not the means, of the victory over malaria.[72]

Giulio Douhet had proved prescient. The "next war" had indeed sucked "the entire population and all the resources of a nation ... into the maw of war." War was no longer a matter of armies fighting armies; total war pitted nations against nations. The incorporation of civilians as home front allies was one of the easiest changes to see. Civilian scientists organized themselves to research weapons and medicines. Civilian companies and workers manufactured war materiel. Civilians also entered "the maw of war" as targets of attack. Scientists developed tools for destroying enemy homes and, though some acknowledged this more openly than others, the people who lived in them.

Less obviously, total war sucked nature into the maw of war. Nature was an important ally on the home front, supplying food and raw materials for industry. Ideas about nature also served the war effort. They helped frame and express views of the enemy, oneself, and the proper interaction between the two. In the era of mass production and mass attack, thinking of human enemies as masses of insects was useful – especially if one believed war should aim for extermination.

Total war also sucked nature into its maw as an enemy. Insects that ate crops or carried disease to soldiers and war workers threatened military power as concretely as, and sometimes more effectively than, enemy soldiers or saboteurs. Military need drove the federal government and cooperating institutions to control insects on a scale never before seen. This effort in turn changed the way people interacted with each other, including by drawing institutions closer. War even offered the army the chance to tame a natural enemy (malaria) and employ it as an ally in the fight against enemy soldiers. It was not biological warfare in the sense of releasing diseases, but it was a reliance on disease as a weapon in warfare.

These changes in American life, which seemed simultaneously radical and inevitable, obliterated the traditional distinctions between military and civilian life, and between people and nature. Small wonder that humor, one of the common ways to deal with incongruity, so often merged ideas about human and natural enemies.

7

Annihilation (1943–1945)

In 1944 and 1945, two periodicals published similar images. Both showed half-human, half-insect creatures, talked of the "annihilation" of these vermin, and touted modern technology as the means to accomplish that end. One piece, a cartoon in the U.S. Marine magazine *Leatherneck,* showed a creature called "Louseous Japanicas" and said its "breeding grounds around the Tokyo area … must be completely annihilated" (Figure 7.1). A month after the cartoon appeared, the United States began mass incendiary bombings of Japanese cities, followed by atomic blasts that leveled Hiroshima and Nagasaki. Although *Leatherneck's* cartoonist surely intended his cartoon to be humorous and hyperbolic, annihilation of human enemies had, by the end of the war, become realistic.

So too with insect enemies. The second cartoon, an advertisement in a chemical industry journal, promoted perfumes to eliminate insecticide odors (Figure 7.2). The text began, "Speaking of annihilation." The accompanying image showed three creatures, each with a stereotypical head of a national enemy on an insect body. The Italian creature lay on its back, an allusion to Allied victory over the Italian army and over typhus-carrying lice. German

119

Louseous Japanicas

The first serious outbreak of this lice epidemic was officially noted on December 7, 1941, at Honolulu, T. H. To the Marine Corps, especially trained in combating this type of pestilence, was assigned the gigantic task of extermination. Extensive experiments on Guadalcanal, Tarawa, and Saipan have shown that this louse inhabits coral atolls in the South Pacific, particularly pill boxes, palm trees, caves, swamps and jungles.

Flame throwers, mortars, grenades and bayonets have proven to be an effective remedy. But before a complete cure may be effected the origin of the plague, the breeding grounds around the Tokyo area, must be completely annihilated.

7.1 "Louseous Japanicas." In 1945, U.S. Marine Sgt. Fred Lasswell praised efforts to annihilate "Louseous Japanicas." From Sgt. Fred Lasswell, USMC, "Bugs Every Marine Should Know," *Leatherneck* 28 (Mar. 1945): 35–37, see 37; reprinted by permission of *Leatherneck*.

and Japanese creatures remained standing as guns blasted all three with chemical clouds. The image fit the times. As the ability to control pests rose, some entomologists called for the extermination of entire species.

In many ways, these developments followed their own paths: the United States did not use the same compounds against cities and against insects, for example. But their paths also crossed. Extermination of lice supplied a metaphor for extermination of human enemies and vice versa. The United States could quickly spray insecticides in the Pacific because the Chemical Warfare Service had already developed equipment that could be adapted to this purpose. Spectacular success against insects inspired military and civilian researchers formally to link institutions working on chemical warfare and pest control.

Two to go!

Speaking of annihilation — the odors created by our adept perfume-chemists for your insecticides, slay the killing agent, *pronto* and quietly depart the battle scene. No trace remains—perfumed or otherwise.

Send us a gallon of your unperfumed spray We want to show you what we consider a perfect perfuming job

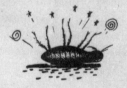

VAN **AMERINGEN-HAEBLER** INC. · 315 FOURTH AVENUE · NEW YORK 10, N. Y.

7.2 "Two to Go!" This 1944 advertisement, which appeared in a journal that served the National Association of Insecticide and Disinfectant Manufacturers, took it for granted that national and insect enemies required annihilation. From *SSC* 20 (Apr. 1944): 92.

Against human and insect enemies, the scale of annihilation in the last two years of the war depended on moving new technology from civilian laboratories (organized by the Office of Scientific Research and Development) to field tests to deployment. In the insect war, the key laboratory was the U.S. Bureau of Entomology's facility in Orlando, Florida. The Army Surgeon General's Office asked the federal entomologists to find ways to control a number of insects that carried disease. The two most important were lice and mosquitoes.

For both pests, entomologists set out to find new technology suited to military, not necessarily civilian, needs. The standard method of controlling mosquitoes in settled areas (which the Malaria Control in War Areas project used with great success) was to kill mosquito larvae by draining, oiling, or poisoning breeding areas. But the Orlando scientists believed that this method poorly suited the "highly mobile type of warfare such as is used in the present war." Even if the Army started "larviciding" areas as soon as they were invaded, troops "may be exposed for several weeks to infected vectors already present.... By the time antilarval measures are able to reduce the mosquito populations troops may move into new infected areas." So, the researchers focused most of their effort on finding "an effective and rapid means" to kill *adult,* rather than larval, mosquitoes.[1]

One breakthrough came from research federal entomologists had started shortly before the war. Flitguns, the standard way to kill adult insects, sprayed insecticide in coarse drops that settled quickly (and often left behind an unattractive residue on household items). In 1941, federal entomologists discovered that insecticides dispersed in an aerosol (a mist so fine it resembled smoke) spread widely and killed insects effectively. Compressing insecticide and gas into a metal cylinder, then releasing the contents through a fine nozzle, offered a workable way to disperse an insecticide aerosol almost anywhere a soldier happened to be. In the summer of 1942, manufacturers developed a small metal container with freon-12 as the propellant and pyrethrum as the insecticide. Weighing about one pound, each container treated 150,000 cubic feet of space. Small, round, and born in war, these containers soon became known as aerosol "bombs." By March 1943, manufacturers turned out about 600,000 aerosol bombs for the armed forces.[2]

Louse-control technology, largely unchanged since World War I, also suited mobile warfare poorly. The large chambers used to heat clothing and bedding were cumbersome to move, did not prevent reinfestation, and sent out smoke that enemy gunners found ideal for targeting. A member of the Army Surgeon General's Office suggested that an insecticide powder, which soldiers could carry and apply to themselves any time, might work better. So, the Orlando entomologists set out to find a louse powder.[3]

They soon succeeded by combining pyrethrum (the active ingredient in many household insecticides) with other chemicals that improved pyrethrum's performance. Packed in small cans, the powder could be shipped and distributed relatively easily. The Rockefeller Foundation handled many of the field tests. It successfully tested the powder against artificial infestations of lice on conscientious objectors in 1942. The foundation then tested the powder, again successfully, against "natural" louse infestations in Mexico and North Africa. To treat large numbers of people quickly, Rockefeller and military researchers experimented with power dusters (some made for agriculture), which sped up the dusting process by eliminating the need for disrobing.[4]

Aerosol bombs and louse powders suited war needs in many ways, but they shared an Achilles' heel. Both relied on pyrethrum, which came from chrysanthemum flowers grown overseas. Naval warfare had slashed imports so drastically that, in July 1943, Army Chief of Preventive Medicine James S. Simmons told civilian researchers the most important thing they could do for military medicine as a whole – not just for preventing insect-borne diseases – was "finding a substitute for pyrethrum."[5]

Enter the hero, DDT. A lot had changed since 1941, when Geigy's American subsidiary had seen little market for the chemical in the United States. War opened a market for killing lice that had not existed before, made synthetics attractive because imports of botanical and arsenic insecticides were slashed, and led to free research and development by the U.S. government (which, before the shortage of botanicals, had restricted its testing of proprietary products). In October 1942, Geigy gave the Bureau of Entomology, which had never heard of DDT, some Swiss reports showing that DDT killed insects and was "relatively non-toxic to man and animals." It sent a sample to the bureau in November.[6]

Tests in Orlando made DDT look "magical": it killed lice and mosquitoes at low doses for a long time. According to one story, ducks flying from treated to untreated ponds carried enough DDT on their bodies to kill the mosquito larvae in the untreated ponds. DDT powder killed lice for four times longer than pyrethrum powders did. Sprayed on walls of buildings, DDT killed adult mosquitoes for months. And, as a synthetic, DDT could be manufactured in the United States. Although DDT surely would have found a market without World War II, Simmons noted that "recognition of [DDT's] full possibilities might have been delayed indefinitely, had it not been for the problems posed by global war."[7]

Early tests raised doubts about DDT's safety for people, but the army gambled and won. Researchers at the Food and Drug Administration and the National Institutes of Health fed animals DDT to see its effects. Simmons recalled, "The preliminary safety tests, made with full strength DDT, had been somewhat alarming. When eaten in relatively large amounts by guinea pigs, rabbits and other laboratory animals, it caused nervousness, convulsions or death, depending on the size of the dose." But the army was desperate for an insecticide, so, Simmons said, "in spite of the earlier rather startling toxicity reports we had asked our people to start a limited manufacturing program" of DDT.[8]

Further tests quelled safety concerns about DDT louse powders, which soldiers (unlike the test animals) presumably would not eat. After three months of working with DDT, subjects and researchers in Orlando showed no toxic symptoms. Tests on animals by the Food and Drug Administration convinced researchers that DDT dusts were safe.[9] In May 1943, federal entomologists recommended, and the army adopted, DDT as a louse powder.[10]

Researchers had not concluded that DDT was harmless. Rather, they believed, as the Food and Drug Administration's lead scientist, H. O. Calvery, put it in July 1943, "the hazards must be weighed against the great advantages of the materials." Research at the National Institutes of Health showed that DDT in solutions behaved differently from DDT in dusts. When painted on bellies of rabbits, DDT solutions led to tremors, paralysis, and sometimes death. These findings led Calvery to warn the army that DDT solutions should not be allowed to contact skin. In August 1943, Calvery reported that rubbing rabbits with DDT ointments daily for twelve weeks led, even at low doses, to necrosis of muscles and organs, kidney damage, atrophy of testes, dermatitis, dehydration, emaciation, and death. In feeding experiments, almost all test animals showed "slight to moderate liver damage." Some showed "slight terminal gastric bleeding," "slight to moderate testicular atrophy," or "degenerative cellular changes" in the thyroid. The effects varied among species. Calvery concluded that more studies would be needed before one could judge DDT's safety for long-term use, but he thought using DDT against insect-borne diseases that threatened soldiers was a good idea.[11]

Further tests on people – rather than lab animals – set to rest the concern that inhaling DDT might be dangerous for soldiers. Research by Paul A. Neal of the National Institutes of Health's Division of Industrial Hygiene showed that human beings displayed no "evidence of subjective or objective signs of poisoning" when exposed to DDT aerosol. In September 1943, Neal reported that DDT was safe when used as an aerosol, dust, or mist.[12] Neal's findings gave the army "final assurance that the material is not dangerous for use under the conditions which we had selected," and the army requested "a great expansion" in DDT production.[13]

Although the army wanted to cloak DDT in "complete secrecy," and although research on the chemical was classified, word soon got out to the entire insecticide industry.[14] In June 1943, P. H. Groggins of the Department of Agriculture told a meeting of the National Association of Insecticide and Disinfectant Manufacturers that a new synthetic insecticide was being produced in the United States. Had enemy spies been in the audience, they would have had an easy time identifying the substance, for Groggins cited the British patents for DDT by number, if not by name.[15] In July 1943, the cat jumped entirely out of the bag. A trade journal printed a diagram of the structure of DDT and a recipe for its manufacture.[16]

As it turned out, Germany had no need of American trade publications to learn about DDT's wonders. Based in neutral Switzerland, Geigy had the opportunity to work both sides of the conflict. The company had applied for a patent on DDT in France in March 1941, nine months after France had surrendered to Germany, and apparently patented DDT in the Third Reich in May 1943. After Germany's fall, Allied intelligence agents learned that I. G. Farben had obtained samples of DDT from Geigy, made 100 tons per month following the Geigy process, and supplied the Wehrmacht with DDT louse powders.[17]

But the German commitment to research on DDT paled in comparison to the American one. Researchers in Orlando soon found that DDT's remarkable powers extended to mosquitoes as well as lice. In February 1943, they learned that DDT killed *Anopheles* "at the extremely low concentration of 1 part of DDT

to 100 million parts of water.... There was reason for real optimism: here was a material exactly 100 times as toxic to mosquito
larvae as was phenothiazine, the most effective synthetic organic
larvicide previously known." Further tests showed DDT was
twenty-five times as effective as Paris green, the standard anophe-
line larvicide. Just two quarts of 5-percent DDT solution were
effective for controlling larvae over an acre of wetland. Twenty-
five gallons of crude oil would have been required for the same
area, with less certain results. Such a dramatic reduction in volume offered the promise of slashing costs for material, equipment, and labor. The Bureau of Entomology concluded that "the
advantages of DDT are readily apparent" when one noted that
"one operator with DDT preparations can accomplish as much as
was possible to do with perhaps six men using oil and at a frac-
tion of the cost."[18]

The United States ramped up production just in time for DDT
to make one of the more dazzling debuts in public health history.
In December 1943, General Dwight Eisenhower cabled the United
States that twenty cases of typhus had broken out in Naples. Other
personnel infected with typhus were traveling from the Balkans to
Italy and would spread the disease to civilians. The month when
typhus traditionally soared, January, was fast approaching. All
these factors made typhus an "actual threat to Military Personnel
in occupied Italy"[19] (Figure 7.3).

Allied health organizations responded by dusting over a million
civilians in Naples with louse powder. Older pyrethrum powder
(and rotenone powder, another plant-derived insecticide favored
by the British) "broke the back" of the epidemic, and DDT swept
in to finish the job. Medical officers credited success to several
aspects of the campaign, including finding and isolating typhus
cases, but DDT got the lion's share of publicity. This event, the first
instance a typhus epidemic was halted in wintertime, was cause for
celebration. *Saturday Evening Post* reported that in Naples, "Army

7.3. "Typhus Is Spread by Lice." Typhus historically had killed many more soldiers in European wars than had battle. Louse powders developed for World War II enabled individual soldiers for the first time to protect themselves. The can shown here contained two ounces of powder, an amount easily carried in each soldier's backpack. Posters such as this one (issued in 1944) reminded soldiers to use the powder regularly. From 44 PA 2182, Still Pictures Branch, NARA.

doctors are winning their battle against a foe that has killed more men than all the weapons of war."[20]

The widely publicized success against lice in Naples lifted hopes for "total victory" against other insects. *Reader's Digest* promised "total victory on the insect front." Simmons, the army's chief of preventive medicine, told the Associated Press, "The wartime development of effective repellents and insecticides will probably constitute the biggest contribution of military medicine to the civilian population after the war."[21]

DDT played such a heroic role in wartime publicity that it became a cultural icon and inspired poetry (or at least doggerel). On learning that DDT killed "lice, termites, moths, roaches, bedbugs, fleas, Japanese beetles, corn borers, and other insect pests," David McCord published "Dusty Answer" in a 1944 issue of *The New Yorker*:

> Little insect, roach, or flea,
> Have you met with DDT?
> In the foxhole, up the line,
> DDT gets eight in nine.
> In the tank, beside the gun,
> DDT means battles won.
> Bunk and barrack, tent and cot:
> Now we know the answer, what?
> Termite, moth, lamented louse:
> DDT is on the house.
> Should you enter with the cat,
> DDT takes care of that.
> Dusting DDT about
> Cures the cat but cuts you out.
> Do you fly, or do you crawl?
> DDT will fix you all.
> Beetle, borer, bedbug – these
> Horrors worse than DDT's –
> On the leaf, in corn, in bed
> DDT has knocked 'em dead.

This our weal and this their woe
In the kit of G.I. Joe,
East and west, a world away:
Letters tough as O. P. A.

Letters cripple us civilians
But they kill bugs by the millions.[22]

The Naples dusting and subsequent use of DDT in Europe prevented disease and killed "bugs by the millions," a scale of extermination that set the stage for the "Speaking of annihilation"
advertisement a few months later. But the advertisement alluded
not just to annihilating lice. Its title, "Two to go!" referred to annihilating the two remaining human foes whose heads adorned the
louse bodies, Hitler and Hirohito. In that effort, incendiaries
would play an important role once the air force revised its thinking. Although lethal to anyone who happened to get in the way, the
American air force's philosophy of "precision" strategic bombing
did not make civilians the target of attacks. Nor did it make incendiaries the first choice among weapons; explosives served better for
precise targeting. General William Porter, chief of the Chemical
Warfare Service, identified two turning points in getting the air
force to use incendiaries. Both came in the summer of 1943.

The first came when the air force experimented with incendiaries on industrial targets in France. Porter credited a Chemical
Warfare Service colonel, who represented the service in Europe,
with persuading Colonel Curtis E. LeMay of the air force to do the
experiments. The second turning point occurred with the
Hamburg bombing. In July 1943, British and American bombers
attacked Hamburg for seven days and nights. British flyers
dropped most of the incendiaries while American flyers relied on
explosives. In combination, the methods were astonishing. *Life*
magazine noted, "This was a new kind of warfare. It was not
merely RAF area bombing or United States pinpoint bombing. It

was rather a combination of both, having for its objective the complete obliteration of Germany's largest city." "Dante's Inferno," said an eyewitness, "was incomparable with Hamburg. Entire city districts were wiped out." An estimated 42,000 people died.[23]

The Hamburg bombing swayed the rest of the Eighth Air Force. After the Hamburg raid, it "began to scream for incendiaries ... and CWS was hard put to meet the demand."[24] In July 1943, the Eighth Air Force dropped 250 tons of incendiaries. In 1944, it dropped more than 5,000 tons per month. By December 1944, incendiaries made up 40 percent of American bomb loads.[25]

One of the most spectacular uses of incendiaries came in February 1945, when British and American bombers dropped demolition and incendiary bombs over two days on Dresden. The resulting firestorm could be seen 200 miles away. Germany announced that Dresden was "an ocean of fire," and that the attacks had killed 70,000 people. *Newsweek* reported that "Allied air chiefs had decided to adopt deliberate terror bombing of German population centers as a military means of hastening the Reich's surrender by snarling up communications and sapping morale."[26]

As J. Enrique Zanetti had predicted, fire turned out to be an efficient way to annihilate cities – better than explosives and probably better than gas. The Strategic Bombing Survey concluded that, in Europe, fires destroyed more residential areas than did other weapons and that most of those fires were set intentionally with incendiary bombs.[27]

Outside some religious circles, Americans generally approved of bombing German cities. In 1944, twenty-eight clergymen and "national leaders" called on the United States to halt the "'obliteration' bombings of German cities – this 'carnival of death.'" Representative Samuel A. Weiss of Pennsylvania excoriated the twenty-eight and quoted to Congress an editorial from the *McKeesport (Pa.) Daily News*. "It is total war, waged not alone by uniformed men in battle phalanx but by every man, woman, and child able to lift a hand to fashion an instrument for the death of someone else," argued the editorial writer. "Criminal and un-Christian now is the continued determination of the German people to resist – a flagellant decision by a people who have sown the wind to reap the whirlwind. They deserve no mercy. They shall have none."[28]

If anything, such sentiments were even stronger when directed toward the Japanese. The cartoonist who drew "Louseous Japanicas" was not alone in merging images of human and insect foes and calling for their annihilation. We have already seen "educational propaganda" posters merging malaria mosquitoes and Japanese soldiers. As American GIs fought their way across the Pacific, they continually encountered posters calling on them to annihilate both malaria mosquitoes and the Japanese enemy (Figure 7.4). Soldiers and journalists regularly used terms similar to those in the posters. Pilot Robert Scott, Jr., named his airplane "Old Exterminator," and said every time he killed a "Jap" he felt he "had stepped on another black-widow spider or scorpion." After three weeks of bloody battle on Iwo Jima resulted in an American victory, *Time* reported that "the Pacific's nastiest exterminating job was done."[29]

It is impossible to quantify the impact that ideas about insects (and other parts of nature) had on the conduct of war. But at least some participants thought them key. Novelist Herman Wouk, who served aboard a destroyer in the South Pacific, included this passage in a novel: "This cold-bloodedness, worthy of a horseman of Genghis Khan, was quite strange in a pleasant little fellow like Ensign Keith. Militarily, of course, it was an asset beyond price. Like most of the naval executioners at Kwajalein, *he seemed to regard the enemy as a species of animal pest.* From the grim and desperate taciturnity with which the Japanese died, they seemed on their side to believe they were contending with an *invasion of large armed ants. This obliviousness on both sides to the fact that the opponents were*

7.4 "Enemies Both." This 1944 U.S. government poster, drawn by "Frank Mack 23rd Bomb.," showed a pistol-packing Uncle Sam calling on American soldiers to "eliminate" both human and insect enemies. From USGPO, 44PA 720, Still Pictures Branch, NARA.

human beings may perhaps be cited as the key to the many massacres of the Pacific war."[30] For an officer who served in the Philippines, reclassifying human enemies as vermin transformed fighting from a moral quandary – he espoused pacifism – into a practical responsibility and perhaps a moral good. He explained, "I'm more of a pacifist than I ever was, but as long as there are vermin like Japs and Nazis, they have to be exterminated."[31]

As soldiers fought their way across the Pacific, they saw ever more powerful ways of exterminating insects as DDT arrived and worked wonders against mosquitoes. Effective in tiny concentrations, DDT made spraying realistic on a scale never before seen. By 1945, the armed services could blanket "thousands of acres" with DDT using a variety of airplanes, from small combat planes to large transports. Aerial DDT spraying was economical. At a fort in Trinidad, aircraft sprayed DDT over 5,000 acres about every three weeks at a cost of $35,000 for oil and DDT. The previous method, installing permanent ditches, would have cost an estimated $2.5 million.[32]

The army was able to start spraying DDT around the world as soon as the chemical arrived in combat theaters because it had already deployed chemical warfare equipment. Theater surgeons worked with the Chemical Warfare Service and the air force to experiment with spraying DDT. They soon found that the Chemical Warfare Service's M-10 smoke tank, which was already standard equipment in all theaters for smokes and poison gas, needed only a nozzle change to spray DDT.[33]

Chemical Warfare Service field officers welcomed responsibility for insecticide spraying. As a report from the Pacific theater put it in November 1944, a chemical officer oversaw spraying DDT using "C. W. spray tanks, air operations companies, and C. W. techniques." Although the work in the Pacific was an ad hoc arrangement, the report suggested that it would be a good idea for the service to continue this work after the war.[34]

Although advantageous in many ways, similarities between chemical warfare and insecticide spraying had a major drawback: the enemy might believe the United States had started chemical or biological warfare (and perhaps retaliate in kind). Early in the development of aerial spraying, entomologists and medical officers foresaw spraying beachheads with fast combat planes *before* invasions, thereby protecting soldiers during a time they were especially vulnerable to mosquito bites. But the similarities between gas and germ warfare and DDT spraying derailed this vision. A malariologist for the air force in the Pacific noted the conflict between the desire to spray "soon after the landing" of invading forces and the need "to prevent the misinterpretation of our procedure by the enemy as gas or bacteriological warfare." In July 1944, MacArthur ordered commanding generals alone to determine when to start spraying DDT, and to do so cautiously, "because of the possibility that the enemy may interpret such spraying operations as bacteriological warfare."[35]

Misinterpretation by the enemy was only part of the danger; so was misinterpretation by Americans. In August 1944, a malariologist arranged to spray Cape Sansapor with DDT from B-25s shortly after the invasion. To make sure "the Ack-Ack at Sansapor" did not "mistake our spray with Gas and give us a few shots," four P-38s escorted the DDT-spraying bombers "just to show the ground troops that we are friendly."[36]

A mistake at Iwo Jima showed that fears of misinterpretation were realistic. DDT spray planes were supposed to fly only over areas held by American troops, but, the naval medical officer reported, "irregularly drawn battle lines resulted in some spraying of enemy-held territory. Later interrogation of prisoners revealed that the Japanese first thought the cloud of spray was gas. Presumably their observation that most of the spraying was done over American lines allayed this fear."[37]

Another drawback, less worrisome in the short run but more so in the long run, was that DDT spraying devastated some islands. (In many cases, the solvent, rather than the DDT itself, may have been the culprit.) A naval medical officer reported that the first use of DDT in the Pacific had led to "complete destruction of plant and animal life." On Saipan, one of the islands seen as a great success for DDT because it slashed hospital admissions for dengue fever (another debilitating mosquito-borne disease), DDT reportedly caused something "approaching a condition of devastation.... There was scarcely a living thing on it. No birds, no mammals, no insects, except a few flies, and the plant life was decreasing."[38]

At home, DDT spraying inspired military and civilian researchers to link chemical warfare and pest control in new ways. Within the Office of Scientific Research and Development, the National Defense Research Committee oversaw most chemical warfare research, while the Committee on Medical Research oversaw pest control research. Then DDT spraying, in the words of one researcher, revealed "the parallelism of approach in the field of insect and rodent control and in the search for chemical warfare agents." Both involved finding toxic compounds, learning ranges of toxicity for various kinds of life, and discovering mechanisms of poisoning and therapy. Of the two fields, chemical warfare researchers thought their own was "far advanced" over pest control and "promised great assistance" for the latter.[39]

This conviction led the Office of Scientific Research and Development to link both halves of its organization – weapons and medicine – with a new Insect Control Committee. Milton C. Winternitz, a physician overseeing research on medical aspects of chemical warfare, chaired the new committee and added supervision of some research on insecticides to his responsibilities.[40]

Chemical Warfare Service Chief William N. Porter welcomed the merger of research on chemical warfare and pest control, for the two endeavors struck him as two faces of the same problem. "The problem of insect control is fundamentally one in applied toxicology," Porter reasoned. "We wish, at the moment, to poison insects because they threaten the health of our troops. Coincidentally the Chemical Warfare Service.... is actively at work in an attempt to improve our methods for poisoning Germans and

Japanese.... The fundamental biological principles of poisoning Japanese, insects, rats, bacteria, and cancer are essentially the same. Basic information developed concerning any one of these topics is certain to apply to the others."[41]

Along with supporting the merger of civilian research (in the Office of Scientific Research and Development), Porter incorporated research on insects into the Chemical Warfare Service's in-house program. In 1944, the service started researching the toxicity, physiological effects, and dispersal of insecticides. Much of this research took place in the service's Medical Research Laboratory at Edgewood Arsenal, Maryland. The service also looked for new insecticides, especially by testing derivatives of chemical warfare agents.[42]

Along with starting its in-house program, the Chemical Warfare Service directed some of its civilian collaborators to add pest control to their research. Collaborators included scientists at Harvard, Chicago, MIT, Virginia, and Rohm and Haas.[43] By December 1944, chemical warfare laboratories were sending about 300 chemicals a month to the Bureau of Entomology lab in Orlando for testing.[44]

In developing insecticides, these laboratories used the same approaches and methods they employed with chemical weapons. In its research contracts, the Chemical Warfare Service spelled out objectives for chemical weapons and insecticides in identical language.[45] The University of Chicago Toxicity Lab, which tested poison gases by putting compounds on the skin of human volunteers, used the same protocol to test DDT and insect repellents for irritancy.[46]

Along with researching insecticides, the Chemical Warfare Service and its collaborators developed new methods of dispersal. Some methods worked well. Decontamination sprayers (which spread neutralizing chemicals over areas contaminated with gas) dispersed DDT solutions effectively. So did smoke generators, which military and civilian researchers developed during the war to screen invasions and other military activities from enemy sight.[47]

Another line of research, explosive charges, did not work well. Entomologists and chemical warfare researchers investigated DDT grenades, shotgun cartridges, bombs, and mortars.[48] They thought grenades would be "useful for troops attacking a village," for one could "throw in the grenade and thus clear the area of insects before the troops entered."[49] Mortars offered the possibility of clearing "whole areas."[50] Aerosol bombs, to be dropped from 20,000 feet, would keep airplanes out of reach of enemy anti-aircraft fire.[51] None was adopted by the end of the war.[52]

To enhance the flow of information, the army transferred an entomologist who had been working on malaria control for the Army Surgeon General's Office, Vincent Dethier, to the Office of the Chief of the Chemical Warfare Service to act as liaison officer.[53] Publications also helped spread news. The Chemical Warfare Service issued monthly progress reports covering the chemistry, engineering, entomology, and medicine of insecticides.[54]

As the war in Europe wound down and the United States focused its effort on the Pacific, the chances of using poison gas increased. Despite Roosevelt's 1943 pronouncement, high military leaders seriously considered using gas against Japanese troops and civilians. The Allies no longer feared retaliation from Germany (whose gas capability the Allies considered much stronger than Japan's), thought gas would work well against dug-in Japanese troops, and predicted gas would terrorize civilians who would then be faced with a choice between urging their government to surrender and "extermination." With a 1945 article titled "Should We Gas the Japs?" the War Department appears to have begun testing (or trying to channel) the waters of American public opinion.[55]

The United States never did start gas warfare in World War II. Nor did other belligerents, with the exceptions of Japan (which reportedly used gas in China) and Germany (which used hydrogen cyanide in the Holocaust).[56] The search for a single explanation seems doomed to failure, for different people made different decisions at different times for different reasons. Instead, the best explanation seems to be that a variety of factors combined to create restraint in a way that no one factor could have. At one point, Winston Churchill called for "a cold-blooded calculation made as to how it would pay us to use poison gas.... I want the matter studied in cold blood by sensible people and not by that particular set of psalm-singing defeatists which one runs across now here now there." Churchill's military leaders argued against gas for tactical and strategic reasons: it would divert aircraft from other missions, invite retaliation, and likely fail to produce a decision. Churchill seemed to think he could have overcome military *or* cultural objections, but the two in concert proved stronger than he was: "Clearly I cannot make head against the parsons and the warriors at the same time," Churchill lamented.[57]

The same barriers did not exist against incendiaries. The reason, then and later, was unclear. Perhaps, as J. Enrique Zanetti suggested, people feared fire less than gas because it was more familiar. Perhaps it was because poison gas had a reputation as a laboratory creation, while fire seemed "natural." Perhaps it was because fire resembled traditional, direct-blow sorts of fighting more than gas, which seemed insidious and unsporting. Whatever the reason, the American air force relied mainly on incendiaries in its spectacular campaign of urban annihilation against Japan in 1945.

The air force described the difference between its strategies in Europe and Japan as arising from differences between German and Japanese cities. At the same time that American flyers began precision bombing in Europe, American industrial analysts estimated that 90 percent of the buildings in Japan's cities would burn easily, versus only 10 percent in Germany. Japanese cities often suffered "conflagrations" in peacetime, while German cities almost never did. In many cases, workers lived and manufactured goods in the same flammable buildings. As a result, the air force said, it was logical to use a "new kind of strategic blitzkrieg." Mass attacks on cities would destroy factories, disrupt utilities and transportation, "dehouse" workers, and cause "loss of life," air force analysts said. This approach made sense in Japan because "speed is perhaps the most important measure of the worth of a strategic bombing campaign," and such an approach would work fast in Japan. The United States "could do the job far quicker, more thoroughly and at infinitely less cost in lives and materiel than ever dreamed of by the British in the case of Germany."[58]

And "the Japs" had attacked the United States. The desire for retaliation went deep, and the tendency to hold the Japanese in general (rather than individual leaders or a political party) responsible for Pearl Harbor encouraged support for attacks on civilians. So it was generally welcome news when, in April 1942, Lt. Col. James H. Doolittle led his bombers in incendiary attacks on Tokyo, Kobe, Yokohama, and Nagoya.[59] Representative Randolph of West Virginia spoke for many when he praised "the splendid work which our Army flyers did in connection with the bombing of Tokyo and other cities of the Nipponese Empire."[60] *The New Republic* identified more specifically the emotions that made the attacks look "splendid." It called the bombings "Things to Cheer About" because they "relieved some of the burden of frustration and impotent anger the Americans have felt ever since Pearl Harbor."[61]

Between 1942 and 1945, as we have seen, the war in Europe boosted the air force's appreciation for incendiary attacks. At the same time, civilian researchers developed, and industry manufactured, incendiary bombs designed just for Japanese cities. In

March 1945, the air force began a "campaign to obliterate all important industrial areas in Japan by fire bombing."[62] In one of the biggest raids, planes dropped more than 1,000 tons of incendiary bombs over fifteen square miles in the Tokyo city center, where industrial, commercial, and residential districts adjoined. The resulting fires could be seen eighty-five miles away.[63] The Chemical Warfare Service later reported that "70% of Tokyo was destroyed by incendiaries."[64]

Annihilating Japanese cities gave some leaders pause. When Secretary of War Henry Stimson heard about the fire raids, he felt betrayed. He had had the impression that bombing in Japan would be restricted to "the precision bombing which it (the AAF) has done so well in Europe." Stimson believed that the "reputation of the United States for fair play and humanitarianism is the world's biggest asset for peace in the coming decades," and he "did not want to have the United States get the reputation of outdoing Hitler in atrocities."[65]

But many shared the opinion of the air force's Curtis LeMay, who announced that the incendiary attacks on Tokyo "shortened this war. To what extent they have shortened it no one can tell, but I believe that if there has been cut from its duration only one day or one hour my officers and men have served a high purpose. They will pursue that purpose stubbornly."[66] Elliott Roosevelt, the president's son, called for bombing Japan "until we have destroyed about half the Japanese civilian population." Paul V. McNutt, chairman of the War Manpower Commission, said in April 1945 that the United States should pursue "the extermination of the Japanese in toto."[67]

The United States did not achieve McNutt's desire, but it did annihilate people along with buildings. In nine months, American air attacks on Japanese cities caused about 806,000 casualties, including about 330,000 fatalities, most from fire.[68] The Tokyo fire raid killed 79,000 to 130,000 people and left about one million more homeless.[69]

To get a handle on the scale of this destruction, at least three comparisons are useful. One is temporal scale. In Europe, it took years for Allied bombers to kill 300,000 people, injure about 780,000 more, and render 7.5 million homeless. In Japan, American bombers wounded and killed roughly the same number of people in months. Another is military versus civilian casualties. Overall, Allied air forces dropped twice as many tons in "area attacks" on cities as they launched against all manufacturing targets combined. When measured in absolute casualties, this urban strategy meant that soldiers and civilians (at least in Japan) bore the burden of World War II roughly evenly (806,000 civilian versus 780,000 military casualties, with 330,000 civilian versus 460,000 military deaths.)[70]

The third comparison involves the type of bomb. The spectacular nature and post-World War II importance of the atomic bomb have sometimes obscured our vision of World War II behind a mushroom cloud. Physics may have been the pinup science of World War II, but chemistry was the workhorse science of urban destruction. Of the areas of Japanese cities destroyed by American bombers, atomic bombs accounted for only about 3 percent. Atomic bombs were important when it came to casualties, but still took a back seat to incendiaries; atomic bombs caused about a fourth of the casualties suffered by Japanese civilians. General Carl A. Spaatz, commander of the strategic air force in the Pacific, pointed out that the atomic bomb was (in the words of the *New York Times*) "only a comparatively insignificant weapon in his arsenal. The great incendiary and demolition assaults by huge fleets of Superfortresses still have the main burden of destroying the Japanese capacity to fight, and the B-29's are accomplishing their task with an efficiency and skill hitherto unheard of in warfare."[71]

There was no denying, though, that the atomic bomb made annihilation more efficient. After the Hiroshima blast, President

Harry Truman threatened to "obliterate more rapidly and completely every productive enterprise the Japanese have above ground in any city" unless the country surrendered. The *Washington Post* reported on August 8, 1945, "The Japanese themselves now realize that their country faces total destruction." Japan did not surrender after the Hiroshima attack, so the United States dropped a second atomic bomb on Nagasaki. The *New York Times* reported, "Literally tens of thousands of persons had been blasted and burned to death," and "big and little buildings within the immediate target areas had crumbled and disintegrated under the devastating effect of the atomic bomb." Truman announced that the United States would use atomic bombs "until we completely destroy Japan's power to make war, and only a Japanese surrender will stop us." The *Washington Post* surmised that this threat "made it clear to the Japanese people as well as to the Tokyo regime that Japan literally faced extinction."[72]

Ending the war was undoubtedly a good thing, and the reaction of many Americans was, in the words of Paul Fussell, "thank God for the atom bomb!" The *Washington Post* said that Americans should be "unreservedly glad that science put this new weapon at our disposal," for it would shorten the war, perhaps make an invasion unnecessary, and save American lives.[73]

Japanese surrender did end the war, but some Americans thought the war had not achieved its aim. In a letter to the editor of the *Milwaukee Journal*, a woman wrote, "Japan is a terrible evil in the world, as were the brutal Nazis. Then why isn't the evil wiped away, completely, once and for all? When one sets out to destroy vermin, does one try to leave a few alive in the nest? Most certainly not!" The newspaper titled her letter "Extermination for the Japanese."[74]

Others wondered whether the United States had won a pyrrhic victory. The morning after the Hiroshima blast, the *St. Louis Post-Dispatch* asked whether science had "signed the mammalian world's death warrant" and "deeded an earth in ruins to the ants."[75] Such apocalyptic – and entomological – quotations would become increasingly common after the war, especially once the Cold War heated up. But such a fate was not the legacy scientists (or the armed forces) intended to leave. On the contrary, they hoped to head off postwar problems by planning ahead.

8

Planning for peace and war (1944–1945)

Some nine months before the end of World War II, President Franklin Roosevelt asked his chief science lieutenant to plan for peace. He requested that Vannevar Bush, director of the Office of Scientific Research and Development, recommend ways to use science "in the days of peace ahead for the improvement of the national health, the creation of new enterprises bringing new jobs, and the betterment of the national standard of living." Bush's response, a report calling for federal support of science, became one of the seminal documents in shaping postwar relations between science and the federal government. Like the federal government at the end of World War I, Bush turned to Turnerian themes to make the case for ways the United States could capitalize on the violent world of war to advance the world of peace. He titled his report *Science: The Endless Frontier.*[1]

Roosevelt and Bush were not alone. In military, scientific, medical, agricultural, and industrial circles, leaders looked for ways to build on wartime success in peacetime. That World War II had wrought big changes in ideas, science, technology, and institutions was easy to see. How best to meld wartime developments with a world at peace was, however, a matter of debate.

At root, the debate turned on power. Who should have power? Why? How much? Subject to what controls? World War II demonstrated that enormous power – personal, professional, institutional, economic, political, military, and geopolitical – flowed from the control of nature (usually under the term "science"). And it demonstrated the power of war to accelerate the control of nature, especially by the federal government and the armed forces.

Here we focus on three case studies grounded in chemical technology. Each illustrates a different way in which World War II changed ideas about the distribution of power among institutions. Through them war changed the distribution of power among people and nature during and (as we will see in the next chapter) after World War II. The cases focus on intellectual property, professional domains, and "environmental" values.

World War II undermined corporate control over intellectual property, which accelerated the manufacturing and the use of insecticides. One way was by enabling the United States to claim intellectual property for free. In 1944, Allied governments organized teams of civilian and military investigators to follow in the wake of conquering armies. They were charged with finding not only military secrets, especially those of use in the war against Japan, but also industrial intelligence. Vannevar Bush sent members of his office to join the teams; the War Production Board also sent representatives. Requests for information came from the armed forces, government agencies, and private companies. The intelligence teams combed through "industrial firms, factories, laboratories, military bases, storage depots, testing grounds, experiment stations, research establishments, universities and technical institutes, and the people who owned, managed, and staffed them."[2] Gerhard Schrader's laboratory was a gold mine. It revealed the secrets of organophosphate nerve gases and insecticides, neither of which the Allies had known about. Schrader himself wrote the most thorough report on his work for the investigators. That report came out in two forms: a classified complete version and an unclassified revision omitting discussion of nerve gases. Any American company wishing to make organophosphate insecticides could do so free of patent or licensing restrictions.[3]

The war also undermined the control of an individual corporation over DDT. The commitment to DDT placed tremendous pressure on the army and the War Production Board. Geigy expected to make 1,000 pounds of DDT per week in May 1943 and 10,000 pounds a week in July, which roughly equaled the world production of pyrethrum. Even that level of production fell short, however, as the army demanded "a great expansion in [DDT] production" in 1943.[4] So the army and the War Production Board began approaching other companies about making DDT. Some companies slowed the expansion program, and their own profits, by asking for excessive remuneration, and the government returned their applications for revision downward. Du Pont, on the other hand, took a longer view. The company had been searching unsuccessfully for a good synthetic insecticide since the 1930s and had predicted that the market would grow severalfold should someone find the right chemical. The army's desperation equipped Du Pont with a powerful lever for separating Geigy from its hammerlock on the DDT patent. According to the army surgeon general, Du Pont created a crisis by refusing to begin manufacturing until guaranteed a license to sell DDT after the war.[5] Eventually, Geigy granted Du Pont the license.[6]

Compared to the army's need, however, even bringing Du Pont on board left the ship several rowers short as demand continually accelerated. In November 1943, the army wanted 350,000 pounds per month. Geigy produced only a tenth of that, 35,000 pounds per month, and its factory would top out at 50,000 pounds. Du Pont – which had not begun manufacturing by the end of November – expected to make 100,000 pounds more per month, leaving the army with less than half the amount it wanted.[7] The War Production Board quickly raised the priority ratings for Geigy's (Cincinnati Chemical Works) and Du Pont's factories, which enabled them to obtain scarce materials to expand.[8] Soon, Geigy and Du Pont together were scheduled to produce 350,000 pounds per month, the estimated military need. Then the army, navy, and relief organizations doubled their estimated need to 700,000 pounds per month.[9]

The army surgeon general threw his weight behind greater expansion, saying that unless DDT production increased, the "Army in the field may be compelled to alter major plans due to lack of facilities for combatting insect-borne diseases, particularly typhus and malaria."[10] The Chemicals Division of the War Production Board concurred, calling insect control "the most important problem facing the armed forces of the United States and the United Nations in the field."[11] The War Production Board approached Merck, Hercules, Monsanto, Pennsylvania Salt, and General Chemical about making DDT, and the army got Geigy to agree to allow companies to produce DDT without licenses.[12] In January 1944, the War Production Board approved another expansion by Geigy and Du Pont and brought Merck and Hercules into the fold of DDT producers.[13] In June 1944, the estimated need for DDT doubled again, to 1.7 million pounds per month, and fourteen factories belonging to eleven companies joined the DDT program.[14]

As it did for Du Pont, the chance to make DDT fulfilled Hercules's dreams dating from the 1930s. Hercules had spent large sums of money on fellowships and research, out of which had come a synthetic insecticide called Thanite. The war-induced shortage of botanicals had been good for Thanite, boosting sales from 397 gallons in 1942 to 365,643 in 1944. But Thanite irritated human skin and had a bad odor, and these problems became more apparent as its use increased. In 1943, Hercules had hired entomologists to look for new insecticides.[15] Now it was handed the right to make the best insecticide anyone had ever seen.

The finances of making DDT could not be beat. The Chemicals Bureau of the War Production Board recommended that all DDT manufacturers receive Certificates of Necessity, which enabled companies to write off on their taxes, over a five-year period, the cost of constructing or modifying facilities. In theory, if products had postwar value, the write-off was 35 percent, while products with "a strictly war value" could be written off at 100 percent.[16] Although Du Pont had indicated its interest in civilian markets when it demanded a license to sell DDT after the war, the War Production Board granted Du Pont 100 percent tax amortization (perhaps later reduced) for $1.39 million of facilities.[17] Other DDT manufacturers apparently amortized at 35 percent.[18] In addition, the government built some DDT plants – Hercules operated such a plant at Parlin, New Jersey.[19]

Companies entering the DDT business in World War II had little worry about price competition. Production lagged so far behind demand that the government bought all the DDT produced at prices ranging from about $.85 to $1.60 per pound.[20] And production did lag. Du Pont's program ran a month behind schedule, and Hercules waited to expand until it got financing from the government's Defense Plant Corporation. Production met a measly 8 percent of demand by the end of January 1944, but that was enough to supply the Naples dusting. And production soon soared.[21]

Nor did companies have much doubt about the postwar market. At the July 1944 meeting of the National Association of Insecticide and Disinfectant Manufacturers, which set records for attendance, "DDT and aerosol insecticides were on every tongue."[22] A trade journal noted that "the war brought tremendous demands" for insecticides while cutting off supplies of raw materials. This had enabled synthetics, which had been struggling for markets, to gain sudden acceptance, and DDT was the premier synthetic insecticide. Manufacturers predicted "greatly expanded markets after the war."[23] The postwar market looked large for political as well as agricultural and public health reasons. General Stanhope Bayne-Jones of the Army Surgeon General's Office thought DDT's ability to help in "regenerating" governments by preventing diseases vested DDT with "political, as well as health, implications that may change the history of the world."[24]

World War II also influenced science by encouraging some fields to challenge others' turf. A dispute over the postwar fate of the Insect Control Committee illustrated this dynamic. With the benefit of hindsight, we now know that this committee would have little impact on entomology in the long run. But that was not clear at the time. The committee's founders aimed to revolutionize pest control, and entomologists saw the committee as a major affront to their authority.

The spectacular success of insect control during World War II, and the institutional structure that helped make it possible, set the stage for other fields to storm entomology's gates. As we have seen, Vannevar Bush created the Insect Control Committee to link work in the two bodies of his organization, the National Defense Research Committee and the Committee on Medical Research. Seeing advances in pest control as one of the most valuable contributions to the Office of Scientific Research and Development, Bush wanted the Insect Control Committee to continue after the war, so he suggested that a similar committee be set up in the National Academy of Sciences. Unlike Bush's organization, which would go out of business at the end of the war, the National Academy of Sciences functioned in peacetime.[25] Bush convinced the secretaries of the army, navy, and interior, as well as the administrator of the Federal Security Agency (where the Public Health Service was located) to support the idea of an Insect Control Committee in the National Academy of Sciences.[26]

Bush failed, however, to gain the support of the Department of Agriculture. Assistant Secretary of Agriculture Charles Brannan questioned the notion that a new committee in the National Academy of Sciences was needed to handle civilian pest control (which had been the purview of the Department of Agriculture since the nineteenth century). He suggested that committees organized by the departments involved (a thinly veiled criticism of Bush's role in organizing the National Academy of Sciences Committee) had worked fine in the past. Brannan refused to join other departments in requesting the committee, although he did agree to appoint a representative should the committee be formed.[27] A testy exchange of letters between Bush and Brannan followed, with Bush arguing that the new committee would supplement rather than encroach on the "responsibilities and privileges of the Department of Agriculture."[28]

The National Academy of Sciences Insect Control Committee got under way despite these conflicts, but its organization continued to rankle the Department of Agriculture. The National Academy of Sciences Insect Control Committee had almost identical membership as the Office of Scientific Research and Development Insect Control Committee, which meant that it was dominated by medical doctors and chemists who had specialized in chemical weapons.[29] No entomologist sat on the committee, even after the committee had operated for months.[30] In March 1945, Brannan wrote to Frank Jewett, head of the National Academy of Sciences, to express his "concern" that no entomologist "nor anyone with extensive background in that field" had yet been appointed to the committee.[31] In a reply drafted for Jewett, Insect Control Committee Chairman M. C. Winternitz wrote, "Your point about the absence of an entomologist on the main committee is well taken, but was not an oversight." Winternitz saw no reason to add an entomologist, saying that the Department of Agriculture's appointment of two entomologists as liaisons was sufficient for the time being.[32]

Entomologists were outraged. The executive committee of the Entomological Society of America unanimously protested "the erection of committees of national scope dealing with entomological problems being made up without entomological members appointed thereon."[33] E. O. Essig, president of the American Association of Economic Entomologists, lodged a protest.[34] After these complaints, the National Academy of Sciences appointed the state entomologist of Connecticut to the Insect Control Committee in July 1945, about ten months after its founding.[35]

Winternitz had another rationale for making chemical warfare researchers so important on a committee devoted to insect control. As news of Schrader's organophosphates flowed out of captured Germany, members of the Insect Control Committee concluded that the United States needed to centralize information about chemicals in much the same way as Germany. Walter Kirner, who had headed efforts to synthesize and test chemical weapons for the Office of Scientific Research and Development, would succeed Winternitz as chair of the Insect Control Committee. He believed that Germany would not have discovered the usefulness of bug-killing organophosphates as nerve gases had it not nationalized chemical knowledge.[36] The Insect Control Committee offered a way to do the same thing in the United States.[37]

The Insect Control Committee's chair was unusual in explicitly aiming to demote entomology. The changes wrought by World War II did, however, lead other institutions to enter entomology's domain, usually more by exploring institutional or technological boundaries than by laying claim to territory entomologists thought was theirs. One such expansion was the institutionalization of the Malaria Control in War Areas project. James S. Simmons, who was president of the National Malaria Society as well as chief of preventive medicine for the army, titled his malaria society presidential address "American Mobilization for the Conquest of Malaria in the United States." After praising wartime mobilization, he said he feared that triumph over the Axis would lead to defeat in the domestic war on malaria. "We must not demobilize until we have defeated our enemies," he stressed.[38]

Simmons got his wish. In July 1944, Congress authorized the Public Health Service to expand its operations from the areas around war establishments (about 2,000 by then) to the vast area considered "the traditional malaria belt in the southeastern United States." This expansion resulted partly from concern about malaria in returning service members.[39] In 1945, this "extended program" of the Malaria Control in War Areas project became the Communicable Disease Center, which later became the Centers for Disease Control in Atlanta.[40]

Another new – or, more accurately, revived – presence in federally funded entomology was the Chemical Warfare Service. The service planned to promote specific pieces of technology, already in use by the armed forces, for civilian insect control. Most promising, it thought, were decontaminating apparatuses, mortars, and smoke generators for spraying DDT and other insecticides. Technologies it thought useful in other endeavors included flamethrowers (for removing water, vegetation, ice, and snow), incendiary mixtures (for removing crabgrass from lawns), smoke generators (for protecting fruit trees from frost), war gases (for riot control, apprehending "desperadoes," and fumigation), and gas masks (for industry).[41]

The Chemical Warfare Service's civilian collaborators joined with public servants and private companies to demonstrate some of these new technologies to the public before the end of the war. In April 1945, Seymour Hochberg (who investigated dispersal of chemical weapons and insecticides for the Office of Scientific Research and Development) joined entomologists and manufacturers to demonstrate mortar-launched insecticide explosives in a New York state park. The demonstrators thought this method of dispersal was "one of the most promising methods for dispersing DDT sprays or powders" in wooded areas.[42]

In March 1945, Dr. R. D. Glasgoe of the State Geological and Natural History Surveys Commission of the New York State Museum said that high explosives and army mortars loaded with insecticides would be useful for eliminating mosquitoes in the United States. The method would be "quick, economical and [give] surprising coverage."[43]

An alliance between another civilian scientist working for the armed forces and a private party showed that military smoke generators could disperse DDT in agricultural fields. An engineer working with the navy wondered, "Suppose this fog was impregnated with that wonder insecticide [DDT], and ground covered as fast and as completely as in battle – wouldn't that kill bugs quicker and cheaper than all this spraying and dusting of crops?" To get civilian tests approved, the engineer's father (an Arizona rancher) told the navy that farmers in war-torn Europe "might need this quick modern weapon against insects. It might make the difference between feast and famine." The navy sent two "highly secret fog generators" to Arizona, where the manufacturer and entomologists marveled that the poison fog killed "everything in the shape of an insect." They were also "fascinated" with "the absence of highly-paid workers."[44]

Domestic tests also reinforced hopes for aerial dispersal of DDT by civilians. After spraying 127 square miles of woodlands infested with gypsy moths in 1944–1945, a federal entomologist found "no persisting infestation." DDT not only killed gypsy moths better than earlier insecticides did, but it cost far less. Aerial spraying of DDT cost $1.45 per acre, compared to $15 to $25 per acre for ground spraying of older insecticides.[45]

Dispersal technologies were supporting characters for the star of this drama, DDT. The most enthusiastic promises for DDT's civilian applications came from the army. Journalists eagerly relayed these promises to the public. Typical was an article General James Simmons published in *Saturday Evening Post* titled "How Magic Is DDT?" The final sentence answered the title's question:

"In my opinion it is the War's greatest contribution to the future health of the world."[46]

The army, journalists, and manufacturers predicted that DDT would conquer agricultural and household pests as well as it had conquered public health pests. Looking ahead to the postwar world, *Reader's Digest* promised "total victory on the insect front."[47] In an article titled "Our Next World War – Against Insects," *Popular Mechanics* reported that "Uncle Sam, fighting one World War, is preparing for the next – and this one will be a long and bitter battle to crush the creeping, wriggling, flying, burrowing billions whose numbers and depredations baffle human comprehension."[48]

Recognizing that they never could have funded publicity on the same scale themselves, chemical companies gratefully basked in the glow of free praise for their products. As the National Association of Insecticide and Disinfectant Manufacturers noted, "BUGS! Bugs! Bugs! All through the war, bugs and how to kill them received a billion dollars worth of publicity – every dollar of it a mighty valuable sales asset to the insecticide industry."[49] A Hercules manager said, "It is only within the past war years that the American people have become insecticide conscious and this has been largely due to insistence by the Army and Navy that our troops should not fall prey to typhus, malaria, and other insect-borne diseases."[50]

Hundreds of similar articles cemented, in the eyes of the public, DDT's reputation as a miracle worker. Federal entomologists noted in 1944 that massive publicity of the army's adoption of DDT, especially of its use in delousing programs in Naples and North Africa, had created civilian expectations that DDT would solve all pest problems "in houses, gardens, and orchards."[51] As a speaker at a meeting of DDT producers put it, "The general public has been led to believe that DDT will perform miracles under all circumstances."[52]

Statements by some entomologists increased these hopes by describing species eradication as within reach. In his December 1944 presidential address to the American Association of Economic Entomologists, E. O. Essig called for "An All Out Entomological Program." Noting that the world had never been so conscious of insect control as during World War II, Essig urged entomologists to seize "the great opportunities" and create "a new day" for entomology. He thought one of the "most promising prospects" was "the strong emphasis being placed on the *complete extermination* of not only newly introduced pests but also those of long standing in the country."[53] *Science News Letter* summarized Essig's talk as calling for "total war against man's insect enemies, with the avowed object of total extermination instead of mere 'control.'" Although Essig had not mentioned DDT, *Science News Letter* emphasized that DDT would be a "powerful agent in these *postwar wars* to make crops less costly and personal life safer, more comfortable."[54]

Other entomologists regarded these expectations and predictions with delight and trepidation. Although gratified that DDT boosted public appreciation of the significance of insects and entomologists in human affairs, they feared that hopes reached beyond what DDT could deliver. In December 1944, federal entomologist Sievert Rohwer reported to the American Association of Economic Entomologists on behalf of a Special Committee on DDT. The committee concluded, "Never in the history of entomology had a chemical been discovered that offers such promise to mankind for relief from his insect problems as DDT." DDT's promise extended to public health, households, and agriculture. The committee warned, however, that more tests were needed to resolve concerns about DDT's effects on humans and other species, especially when used in agriculture.[55]

Entomologists wondered about DDT's effect on crops, beneficial insects (e.g., honeybees), and animals. Initial tests showed that

DDT could damage all three.[56] The impact on beneficial insects was ironic: trying to kill pests, entomologists believed, could worsen pest problems. One study found a six-fold increase in aphid infestations in sugar cane plots dusted with DDT. Predators commonly attacked aphids in untreated plots, but they were absent from treated plots. Similarly, fruit trees sprayed with DDT became infested with mites and spiders after predatory lady beetles were killed. So, the Bureau of Entomology's Sievert Rohwer concluded, "Irrespective of the residue problem the Bureau does not feel justified in recommending the use of DDT insecticides for codling moth control." This was an important statement, for codling moths and boll weevils created the two largest markets in the United States for insecticides.[57]

Pharmacologists joined entomologists in calling for more testing. In a chemical industry journal, H. O. Calvery and his colleagues at the Food and Drug Administration warned in 1944 that feeding experiments showed "small amounts of DDT in the diet will produce toxicity in experimental animals," and that "the safe chronic levels would be very low indeed." They said that studies of longer duration would be needed to assess DDT's chronic toxicity. The next year, other Food and Drug Administration scientists reported on the effects of DDT fed to dogs. They found that DDT accumulated in body fat and was excreted in milk.[58] In a technical journal published in July 1944, M. I. Smith and two colleagues from the National Institutes of Health described DDT's effects on nerve cells, spinal cords, brains, muscles, kidneys, and livers.[59]

In an article that reached a more general audience, *Science News Letter* repeated Smith's and his colleagues' conclusions in a piece titled "Insect War May Backfire": "The toxicity of DDT combined with its cumulative action and absorbability from the skin places a definite health hazard on its use." In laboratory animals, "small single doses given repeatedly lead to chronic poisoning." Before seeing DDT used in agriculture, "scientists would like to know whether the liver or other organs may be seriously damaged by eating it on vegetables and fruits. The amount on each apple or tomato would be small, but in the course of a few years, quite a lot might accumulate in the body from such sources."[60]

One of the reasons for the contrast between military and civilian views was the difference between military and civilian criteria for evaluating DDT. At a press conference on May 31, 1944, F. C. Bishopp warned that two traits that made DDT ideal for the armed forces – persistence and a broad spectrum of activity – were the same traits that gave the Bureau of Entomology pause. In agriculture, a persistent chemical could leave poisonous residues on food, and broad lethality could create pest problems by killing predators and parasites that kept pests in check.[61]

The failure, intentional or not, of knowledge to travel from expert to popular spheres contributed to the public's lack of information about expert's concerns. Secrecy was one factor. When Army Surgeon General Norman Kirk asked the National Cancer Institute to study DDT's potential carcinogenicity, he told the institute to keep the research classified to "avoid disturbing rumors."[62]

The way scientists published their findings created a second obstacle. When scientists shared their results in professional journals and meetings, they reached their peers but often not the public. Popular publications, especially those geared to readers with interests in science or conservation, sometimes picked up the DDT story and spread it to a larger audience. But glowing articles and newsreels about DDT far outnumbered those voicing concerns, and the public came away with the view that DDT was entirely safe. As one user recalled, "I am a member of a generation that watched newsreels of South Pacific natives being sprayed with DDT and was told that the substance was safe enough to spray right in the room. So we did that at my house."[63]

Another obstacle was the tendency to simplify. Experts saw DDT as a chemical of many faces. It could be used in two major forms (dusts and solutions). It could be dispersed in several ways (dusting cans, aerosol bombs, spray guns, fog machines, and air-planes). It could be used for several purposes (public health, agri-culture, and nuisance control). It could be used for varying periods of time (short in wartime, long in civilian agriculture). It could have unintended negative effects on any number of species (peo-ple, beneficial insects, fish, birds). Experts argued that different combinations of form, method of dispersal, purpose, and time frame merited separate calculations of dangers and benefits. But complicated views often got simplified, even in professional jour-nals. This 1944 headline from the *American Journal of Public Health* was typical: "DDT Considered Safe for Insecticidal Use."[64]

This brings us to the surprising regulation of DDT for "environ-mental" reasons, concerns that some historians have argued did not arise until after World War II.[65] Entomologists wondered whether DDT might wipe out all life when broadcast over large areas. These concerns were based not on idle worry, but on field tests. After experiments in Panama, two members of the Bureau of Entomology wrote, "Biological deserts may be produced by heavy treatments of DDT and these would be, of course, highly undesir-able. In fact, any upset in the balance of nature is very apt to pro-duce conditions unfavorable to the general welfare of the plants and animals present. If, for example, insects are eliminated from a large area, young birds may subsequently starve as the result." Another federal entomologist voiced a similar sentiment: "In con-nection with DDT over large areas, serious consideration must now be given beneficial insects, as well as other animal and plant life because areas devoid of life might be created by too generous and indiscriminate applications of DDT."[66]

Fish and wildlife biologists shared the concern about DDT, especially when broadcast over large areas. In May 1945, Clarence Cottam of the Fish and Wildlife Service asked that DDT not be released for civilian use until the service could assess its effects on wildlife.[67] The Fish and Wildlife Service conducted tests at Patuxent River Refuge in Maryland during the summer of 1945. These tests found that even small doses of DDT (one-half pound per acre) killed fish, and larger doses (five pounds per acre) "drastically reduced" bird populations as well. These experiments seemed important enough that Robert F. Griggs, chair of the National Research Council's Division of Biology and Agriculture, journeyed to Patuxent to look at them firsthand. He concluded that the Patuxent project leaders showed "thoroughness and vision."[68]

Colonel J. W. Scharff, a British malariologist who praised the role of DDT in protecting troops from malaria, found wide damage to nontarget species acceptable in war but not in peace. "As an entomologist and lover of nature," he said, "I believe that the use of aerial spraying with DDT should be reserved for serious military emergencies. DDT is such a crude and powerful weapon that I cannot help regarding the routine use of this material from the air with anything but horror and aversion."[69] Nature writer Edwin Way Teale shared his distress: "Given sufficient insecticide, airplanes and lackwit officials after the war, and we will be off with yelps of joy on a crusade against all the insects." Teale was sure of the result of this "bug-blitz binge": a "conservation headache of historic magnitude."[70]

In April 1945, the army and the U.S. Public Health Service acted on these concerns when they announced restrictions on domestic aerial spraying of DDT. At the time, the War Production Board's priority system gave these two agencies virtual hammerlocks on nonexperimental use of DDT in the United States. (The Public Health Service's activities fell into the military category because it ran the Malaria Control in War Areas project, which protected soldiers on bases and workers in defense factories from malaria.) These two agencies decided to protect what would later be called "the environment" from potential harm by banning aerial spraying except in exceptional cases. (They allowed use on smaller scales, such as by dusting individuals or spraying rooms.) "Much still must be learned about the effect of DDT on the balance of nature important to agriculture and wild life before general outdoor application of DDT can be safely employed in this country," the press release stated.[71] A special army committee (with advisors from the Public Health Service, Bureau of Entomology, and Fish and Wildlife Service) reviewed all requests for aerial spraying of DDT inside the United States. As of August 8, 1945, the committee approved only seven projects, all on military bases.[72]

These two agencies also argued that, in their eyes, different criteria should govern military and civilian evaluations of the costs and benefits of technology. Soldiers overseas faced a high risk of serious disease and short exposure to DDT, while civilians encountered a lower risk of disease and long exposure to DDT. On battlefronts, where destruction reigned, killing birds or fish seemed trivial. At home, where livelihoods and recreation depended on "the balance of nature," killing beneficial insects, fish, and birds carried a higher price. As the April 1945 press release announcing restrictions put it, "It may be necessary to ignore these considerations [of the balance of nature and impact on wildlife] in war areas where the health of our fighting men is at stake, but in the United States such considerations cannot be neglected."[73]

The federal government had the power to regulate DDT in this way because of the war. In the short run, army and U.S. Public Health Service policies amounted to de facto federal policy because these agencies controlled most DDT used in the United States. Over the next several months, the amount they used (mostly overseas) soared. In June 1945, manufacturers churned out an astounding 3 million pounds of DDT per month, up from none in 1942 and 193,000 pounds in all of 1943.[74]

This tidal wave of production eroded the authority of the Army and Public Health Service and gave more control over DDT's fate to the War Production Board, which oversaw production of DDT and other materials of military value. So long as military demand outstripped supply, the board required producers to sell all their DDT to the federal government, which in turn decided how to use the chemical. But by July 1945, the War Production Board thought a small surplus of DDT over military needs would appear in the fourth quarter of 1945.[75]

This surplus gave the War Production Board the freedom to allow sales of DDT to civilians to control insects in homes and on farms. Freedom for the War Production Board amounted to freedom for DDT manufacturers. The board (made up of industry representatives temporarily working for the government) usually followed the advice of its chemicals division (made up of chemical company managers temporarily working for the government), which usually accepted the advice of its DDT Producers Industry Advisory Committee (made up of representatives of companies that made DDT and its precursors).[76] Companies wanted to sell new chemicals. Chemical companies had doubled their production in World War II. After the war, they aimed at least to equal their wartime production level. To do that, they focused their energies mainly on newer chemicals, which offered higher profit margins than older compounds.[77]

Under the pre-World War II regulatory system, no government agency had the authority to keep pesticides off the market. The Department of Agriculture had the power to enforce labeling requirements, and the Food and Drug Administration had the authority to seize foods with pesticide residues above specified levels. But neither agency had the power to stop a company from selling an accurately labeled chemical.[78] Moreover, the War Production Board had announced that it wanted to avoid surpluses and would make conversion to civilian use a priority. (After World War I, the United States had cut back sharply on military production with little provision for switching to civilian production, and the country had tumbled into depression.) The DDT producers' decision followed that policy.[79]

Some DDT makers wanted to keep DDT off the market until they knew how to use the product safely. One manufacturer asked the War Production Board to "hold rigid control" over DDT until a greater surplus had accumulated and federal and state officials had developed guidelines for safe and effective use. He feared "chaotic miscellaneous public demand and use" would be dangerous since "we have not yet established the safety controls." On the other hand, "one or two industry representatives" wanted the freedom to sell to civilians all the DDT they could make beyond military requirements.[80]

The DDT Producers Industry Advisory Committee members decided how manufacturers would handle the surplus on July 25, 1945, when they met with representatives of the War Production Board chemicals division and members of the Bureau of Entomology. They knew that entomologists were still not ready to recommend DDT for all uses in agriculture, the market in which producers were most interested. The Department of Agriculture's G. F. McLeod listed four criteria for judging DDT's suitability: the U.S. Bureau of Entomology or experiment station officials should determine that DDT was effective against a given pest; considerable loss should occur if DDT were not used; DDT should "leave no deleterious residue;" and DDT should not poison bees or upset "the biological complex."[81]

The companies wanting to sell won. As soon as "a considerable surplus" existed, the War Production Board would allow companies to sell DDT to anyone in any quantity.[82] Surviving records do not tell us the reasons for the decision, the method used to decide, nor which representatives held which views. But the decision served the interests of the manufacturers who wanted to sell, and it followed more than it broke with regulatory tradition and War Production Board policies.

With that decision, DDT entered its second regulatory phase, in which the market governed DDT sales. (At the beginning of this phase the War Production Board had the authority to limit DDT sales but delegated decisions to companies. Once the board went out of business, no government agency held such authority.) The Bureau of Entomology's Sievert Rohwer tried to impress on industry leaders the significance of this shift in control at the meeting in which they made their decision. He told them that "the producers of DDT will have a great responsibility as well as an opportunity. He expressed the hope that they would use their opportunity wisely. He stressed that there was a great deal that was still unknown on how to formulate DDT insecticides so they could be used safely, effectively, and to the interest of the user and the public good."[83]

Well before the end of World War II, then, American military and civilian leaders were planning for – and arguing about – the shape of the postwar world. A generation later, against the backdrop of another war, many of the same debates would spring into the public arena with a sudden urgency. With evidence of earlier debates hidden (many of the documents used in this chapter were classified), historians and participants in the events of the 1960s could easily see concern about DDT, the balance of nature, chronic poisoning, military research, industrial power, regulatory authority and values, and other elements of the distribution of power among institutions concerned with the control of nature (as well as people) as new. In fact, the debates and resulting actions returned the United States in many ways to where it had been in 1945.

9

War comes home (1945–1950)

When readers picked up the August 27, 1945, issue of *Time* magazine, they saw news of two icons of World War II on the same page. One was the atomic bomb. A series of photographs of the first atomic explosion in New Mexico illustrated the formation of a mushroom cloud. The other was DDT. Beside the bomb photographs was an article announcing the release of DDT to civilians. The "war against winged pests was under way," the magazine reported.[1]

A new era had begun, not simply because World War II had ended but because World War II was coming home. The war already had changed the home front in many ways, but keeping the home fires burning was not the same as having Johnny come through the door. Over the next several years, ideological, technological, and institutional veterans would settle in front of the fire, changing themselves and home life as they did. At times, their military backgrounds dominated their image; at others, it receded out of sight, invisible but not unimportant. The era, it turned out, was Dickensian.

It was a time of hope. If science could create something so powerful as an atomic bomb and so lifesaving as DDT, what could it not do? Small wonder that the two technologies were mentioned in the same breath. In advertisements for DDT and its relatives, Rohm and Haas and Velsicol discussed these powerful new insecticides in text superimposed on full-page photographs of mushroom clouds.[2]

It was a time of gloom. If science could create something so destructive of human life as an atomic bomb, and of nature as DDT, what could it not do? Biologist Orlando Park of Northwestern University warned in October 1945 that humans could annihilate themselves equally well with atomic bombs or insecticides. In both cases, the fates of humans and insects were intertwined. If people killed enough of each other with atomic bombs, "a point will be reached where insect control weakens, and we are no longer the strongest. It should be about here that man begins to fall as a world power, to enter the dusk of biological extinction, from which no previous species has been known to make a complete recovery." (To support his argument, Park cited L. O. Howard's *Insect Menace.*) Conversely, if people killed enough insects with insecticides sprayed from airplanes, the loss of essential species would doom human life as well.[3]

Other critics looked to DDT not so much as a human threat itself but as a model of the atomic threat. In September 1945, Harry D. Gideonse, president of Brooklyn College, told entering freshmen, "The atomic bomb is to humanity what DDT is to fleas and mosquitoes. It has telescoped time and questions that might have called for answers in a decade or so before atomic energy became available are now in an immediate 'do or die' category."[4] Others saw the converse: war against insects was in the "do or die category" and war against humans was in the "stop or die" category. H. L. Haller of the Bureau of Entomology argued that insects would "inherit the earth unless man abandons war and turns his martial interests to killing pests."[5]

Coming full circle, entomologist George C. Decker saw the atomic bomb as a model of the danger posed by DDT and its siblings. He warned in 1950 that people should "not rely entirely upon chemical warfare" to control insects, for "many of the new insecticides can and often do upset the biological balance in an area and while promoting more effective control of one pest we produce an equally more destructive outbreak of some lesser pest.... When properly used insecticides are very valuable tools, but like the 'A' bomb, if unwisely and wrongly used, they may lead us to our doom."[6]

Overall, hope probably outweighed gloom. DDT changed out of uniform and into civilian clothes so fast that an industry journal called the process a "mad scramble." At first, market forces limited sales by leading risk-averse manufacturers (which tended to be the larger companies) to factor in the cost of potential lawsuits and hold off on sales. But smaller companies, apparently less daunted by the risk, went to market. As it turned out, DDT did not produce much visible, short-term damage, and the larger companies followed the small into the market. Sales soared.[7]

Manufacturers ranged from the dozen large companies making DDT for the armed forces (e.g., Du Pont and Merck) to minor players like Walter Steuber. A chemist, Steuber bought chemicals at a drugstore, mixed them in the cellar of his house in Swarthmore, Pennsylvania, and sold DDT to his neighbors for $1.00 a pint.[8] By 1946, DDT had become so popular that some dealers chose to sell only DDT insecticides.[9]

Military dispersal technology helped DDT dominate civilian pest control. By March 1946, twenty-five companies made, or planned to make, aerosol bombs.[10] In 1946, the Oklahoma State Board of Agriculture sent 190 truck-mounted army decontamination sprayers (Chemical Warfare Service machines designed to spread chemicals that counteracted mustard gas) around the state to kill flies.[11] In 1947, thirty-one cities used fog generators (which the Chemical Warfare Service and navy had developed to make screening smokes) in pest control efforts, mainly against flies and mosquitoes.[12] By the end of the decade at least 600 cities in forty-five states used fog machines.[13] One of the most striking contrasts between the 1930s and the late 1940s came from aerial dispersal of insecticides. Surplus military planes, the veterans who piloted them, and DDT powered a steep takeoff for the crop dusting industry (which, like much of agriculture, had stalled during the Depression).[14]

At first, the rhetoric of World War II pervaded the transfer of military technology to civilian pest control. Industrial Management Corporation sold DDT "bug bombs" as "INSECT-O-BLITZ," which alluded to the German term for fast, mechanized warfare and to bombing of English cities. (As *Modern Packaging* noted, "The Bug Bomb derives its name both from its devastating effect on insect life and its appearance.")[15] In an advertisement for DDT, S. B. Penick & Company called for women to join a domestic version of World War II, "the continued battle of the home front" (Figure 9.1). Sherwin-Williams sold DDT in a three-ounce package with a "turret top for squirting dust" and in an eight-ounce "dusting gun for use under stoves, in outdoor areas, swamps, etc."[16]

When companies pasted brand names on containers of DDT, they took pains to describe the contents as the war hero. Industrial Management Corporation summed up the tactic: "It's a sales story that's simple, effective, and *true*. It clears up the confusion in the average person's mind when you tell him – Yes, *INSECT-O-BLITZ is still* exactly the same as supplied to the U.S. Armed Forces."[17] Ads for American Chemical Company's Hot Foot DDT noted that "Deadly 'DDT' was sensationally used by the U.S. Army to kill insects in Europe and Asia." The tactic seemed to work. Sales of Hot Foot jumped 200 percent between January and September 1945. At home and in stores, Americans could hardly escape ads for DDT. Newspapers, magazines, radio shows, farm demonstrations, and in-store displays shouted news of the wonder chemical.

PENICK INSECTICIDAL BASES...

Super Ammunition for the Continued Battle of the Home Front

For the never-ending battle against pests in and about the home, Penick offers a suitable base proven for its "knock-down" and "knock-out" power.

FOR THE HOUSEFLY AND MOSQUITO: PYREFUME SUPER 20—A pure pyrethrum extract guaranteed to assay 2 grams pyrethrins per 100 cc. or expressed by percentage it is 2½% pyrethrins. Light in color it reduces possibility of stain.

FOR ROACHES & OTHER HOUSEHOLD PESTS: PYRETHRUM POWDER—Finely milled and standardized to exact assays. Pyrethrum Powder is available in the following strengths with prices

according to pyrethrum percentages, .8%, .9%, 1.1% and 1.3%. Has great "knock-down" and "knock-out" power.

IMPREGNO—Killing power is immediate as all particles are coated with pyrethrins. Economical —easy to apply.

50% DDT DISPERSIBLE POWDER — Add talc, clay or similar inert material to make a dust containing 1% to 10% DDT. Roach and Flea powders require the higher percentages.

FOR RATS AND MICE — Fortified Red Squill processed to a uniform degree of toxicity which is 500/600 mg/kg. Non-poisonous to domestic animals, it is sure death to mice and rats.

Write For Descriptive Literature

9.1 "Super Ammunition for the Continued Battle of the Home Front." A year after the end of World War II, an insecticide company urged Americans to continue the "battle of the home front" with "super ammunition," including DDT. Unlike battles overseas, this effort would require women to hold the front line. From *SSC* 22 (Aug. 1946): 115.

Imaginative stunts got free publicity. Newspapers around the country reported that Sherwin-Williams had imported 10,000 live flies to Cleveland in the middle of winter for the Mid-America Exposition; there, 150,000 people watched the flies die of "DDT jitters" after landing on screens painted weeks before with DDT.[18]

DDT lived up to its hero's welcome.[19] Cattlemen found that a herd sprayed with one pound of DDT added 1,200 to 2,300 pounds more beef than unsprayed cattle.[20] Potato farmers attributed a 50 percent jump in yield to DDT.[21] Sprayed from the air, DDT killed gypsy moths better than older insecticides at less than a tenth the cost.[22] By 1948, projects to eradicate malaria from Cyprus and Sardinia by killing mosquitoes with DDT appeared "likely to succeed."[23] *House Beautiful* reported in 1949 that "The magic of dry DDT fog can wipe out flies and mosquitoes from the whole community for an entire year for only $2 to $5 a person" but was "harmless to you, your garden, and your house."[24] Paul Muller, the Geigy chemist who developed DDT, received the Nobel Prize for Medicine or Physiology in 1948.[25]

This Nobel Prize winner, among other experts, promoted the idea that DDT made the dream of a pest-free world realistic. In September 1945, Muller and a coworker announced that DDT could "send malaria mosquitoes, typhus lice and other disease-carrying insects to join the dodo and the dinosaur in the limbo of extinct species, thereby ending these particular plagues for all time."[26] Echoing his predecessor as president of the American Association of Economic Entomologists, Clay Lyle called in 1947 for the "complete extermination" of gypsy moths, houseflies, horn flies, cattle grubs, cattle lice, screwworms, and Argentine ants.[27]

Use of DDT against houseflies reinforced these visions. Lyle noted that Idaho had launched the first statewide eradication program in 1946 with the slogan "No Flies in Idaho." The results, according to an organizer, were "so outstanding that it was almost beyond belief." Over two weeks, traps near a slaughterhouse and next to garbage cans caught no flies. The organizer thought the same thing "could probably have occurred in any town in Idaho and on almost any farm."[28] Inspired by "anti-fly wars" in Idaho and elsewhere, the U.S. Junior Chamber of Commerce launched a national campaign for "total annihilation" of flies. Because flies were suspected of carrying polio and other diseases, 1,500 branches of the Jaycees joined 2,000 communities in a "DDT blitz" to improve public health by creating a "fly-free America."[29]

Industry researchers developed related chemicals that joined DDT in the chlorinated hydrocarbon family. One of the first to hit the market was Hercules' Toxaphene, which killed even more species of insects than DDT.[30] Three more chlorinated hydrocarbons – BHC (also known as 666), chlordane, and methoxychlor – soon followed.[31] Companies heralded the arrival of these chemicals with huge advertising campaigns that stressed potency and safety. Chemical Corporation of Colorado ran full-page "editorial-style copy" in 100 Western dailies that said, among other things, that chlordane was strong, safe, and "the greatest discovery since DDT." Dealers sold out their stocks the day the ads appeared. Sales of BHC boomed so high that Commercial Solvents operated its plant twenty-four hours a day.[32]

The organophosphate family of insecticides soon joined the chlorinated hydrocarbons in American farm fields. The U.S. government published intelligence team reports on Gerhard Schrader's insecticide work, insecticide industry journals reported the findings, companies sent samples to university entomologists to test, Monsanto started manufacturing the first organophosphate in the United States (HETP, later called TEPP) in 1946, and competitors soon came out with other organophosphates.[33] Organophosphate manufacturers included Hercules, American Cyanamid, Shell, Niagara, Stauffer, Chemagro, Victor, and Velsicol.[34]

Entomologists and chemical companies had long spoken of insecticides as chemical weapons, but the line between the metaphorical and the literal was hard to see in some of the organophosphates.[35] About the same time that Monsanto and Victor began selling TEPP as an insecticide, the Chemical Warfare Service announced that one pound of TEPP could kill 2 million rats.[36] As *Science News Letter* put it, "In today's paradoxical world.... the line between gas warfare and battling insect pests has become very thin."[37]

Science News Letter published that comment in 1950, after organophosphate insecticides had killed more than a dozen people. Ignorance caused some of these accidents. Container labels did not always make the danger clear, and users did not always read and follow precautions that did appear on labels.[38] But sometimes even experts learned about organophosphate toxicity the hard way. One of America's most important insecticide developers, entomologist Robert Metcalf, received a sample of a compound from American Cyanamid soon after its employees visited I. G. Farben headquarters in Germany. Metcalf thought the compound was innocuous until it poisoned him. Fortunately, he survived.[39]

Cruel misunderstanding caused other accidents. Informed organophosphate users knew, as a 1950 article put it, that they had to "wear a gas mask or die."[40] Unfortunately, some farmers were poisoned while wearing gas masks. The United States had not known about the organophosphate nerve gases until after conquering Germany, and the World War II army surplus masks worn by the farmers dated from before this discovery.[41]

Given the organophosphates' danger, one might wonder why anyone would use them instead of DDT. There were several reasons. DDT did not kill all insects. Parathion, one of the most powerful organophosphates, killed all insect species against which it was tested. Not all forms were equally dangerous; one manufacturer said parathion dusts and powders offered "a rather wide margin of safety."[42] Organophosphates made systemic poisoning of insects possible because plant roots absorbed and translocated the poison to leaves and stems.[43]

Plus, ironically, farmers used organophosphates *because* they used DDT. By killing insect predators along with pests, DDT created pests of formerly minor (because rare) insect species, some of which happened to be immune to DDT. Farmers sprayed organophosphates to kill these so-called "secondary" pests. Although this approach worked by increasing the number of species killed by insecticides, organophosphate publicists described it as a way to "restore a balance in nature" disturbed by DDT.[44]

The arrival of these two families of synthetic chemicals – chlorinated hydrocarbons and organophosphates – marked a new stage in pest control. An assistant dean of agriculture at the University of California commented in 1948, "World War II tipped the scales as far as the insecticidal problem was concerned. DDT was the talisman of modern entomology."[45] Partly the new phase meant replacing older with newer insecticides. By 1947, DDT had replaced 45 percent of the lead arsenate, and almost all of the calcium arsenate, in the United States.[46] The new phase also meant substituting chemical for biological and mechanical methods of pest control. The editor of *Successful Farming* said in 1947 that "chemical warfare against pests has emerged from the primary stage into full scale use, and … agriculture itself has definitely moved out of the mechanical into the chemical phase of its history."[47]

The closer relations that civilian entomologists and industry developed during World War II accelerated these shifts. In 1946, Bureau of Entomology Chief P. N. Annand noted that the "impetus given by the war to the search for new chemicals," and efforts to bring those chemicals to market, had promoted a "cooperative spirit" between government entomologists and industry.[48]

Entomologists and the armed forces also continued their collaboration. The armed forces paid the Bureau of Entomology about half a million dollars a year (most from the army surgeon general) for research, about one-fourth of the bureau's research budget. Along with wanting to control familiar threats such as typhus, the army feared insects that might be deployed in biological warfare. For all its virtues, DDT took hours to kill some species of insects, giving them time to infect soldiers before dying. Fleas, for example, carried plague. A medical officer noted that DDT did "not kill fleas fast enough to give maximum protection to personnel."[49] The bureau continued to devote its Orlando laboratory (where the bureau had developed DDT for the armed forces during World War II) – as well as personnel at other laboratories – to research for the armed forces. The army's interests broadened the bureau's geographical interests and research sites to include not just the United States but the Canadian Arctic, Mexico, and Egypt.[50]

Along with the factories built to make insecticides during the war, plants redirected from weapons production enabled chemical companies quickly to turn out large quantities of DDT and other insecticides. Chemical companies bought some factories and leased others, including chemical warfare plants. Monsanto made DDT in a St. Louis plant leased from the Chemical Corps (the new name of the Chemical Warfare Service).[51] Michigan Chemical Company used the chlorine and lewisite plants at Pine Bluff Arsenal, Arkansas, to make DDT.[52]

Sometimes personnel came along with factories. Julius Hyman founded a new insecticide company at the Chemical Corps's Rocky Mountain Arsenal in Denver, Colorado, developed two powerful new relatives of DDT (aldrin and dieldrin), went into production using equipment set up to make mustard gas, and became the largest chemical company in the Rocky Mountains. The arsenal's former commander, General C. S. Shadle, became a vice president of the company.[53]

"Normal" civilian demand would have absorbed most of this ever-climbing production, but the aftereffects of World War II pushed demand even higher. Fears that Europe might collapse into totalitarianism (possibly of the right, but more likely of the left) after World War II led the United States to push, in the words of Secretary of Agriculture Clinton Anderson, for "a continued all-out [agricultural] production effort to feed hungry and potentially restive populations."[54] Production goals and price supports, set at levels even higher than during World War II, encouraged pesticide use and led to record production levels.[55]

As use soared, questions federal researchers had raised about insecticide safety in World War II continued to plague them – even if they did not trouble many people outside their professions. A continuing concern was the effect of DDT on human health. Wartime experience produced little evidence of acute danger to people, and postwar experience followed that pattern. The open question was chronic damage. The absence of evidence of harm convinced many people, especially those in industry, that DDT was safe. Michigan Chemical noted, "After four years of use by the army, health officials, in agriculture and in the home, there is not a single authenticated case of harmful results from the proper use of DDT."[56]

Within federal regulatory circles, policy makers rued the fact that DDT had become so civilianized that many people had forgotten that its original analyses had been based on military criteria, with civilian safety still an open question when the chemical was released. Calling for reassessment of DDT safety in food in 1949, Food and Drug Commissioner Paul B. Dunbar said that use of DDT in World War II had been a "reasonably calculated military risk" because the "risk of poisoning was less serious than the risk of exposure" to typhus and malaria. But soldiers were exposed to DDT for only short periods, while in the postwar world people might take in small amounts over long periods.[57]

By the time Dunbar made that statement, federal entomologists were trying to limit DDT use in dairy farming. Experimental evidence showed that DDT could be stored in body fat and appear in milk.[58] An industry journal reported in 1945 that, when given large doses of DDT, goats produced milk that killed rats.[59] When DDT showed up in the milk of cows, federal entomologists recommended substituting methoxychlor, a DDT analogue with less persistence, for spraying barns.[60]

Wartime concerns about DDT's effects on wildlife spread to wider audiences. The National Audubon Society held a symposium on DDT in October 1945 that drew experts from the army, navy, other federal agencies, and state agencies. At high enough concentrations, C. H. Curran of the American Museum of Natural History warned, DDT "will kill almost [all], if not all, cold-blooded animals."[61] Curran published an article a month later titled "DDT – The Atomic Bomb of the Insect World," in which he highlighted the reported "devastation" of Saipan by DDT.[62]

Being too devastating was a potential problem for DDT; not being devastating enough was a potential problem for chemical weapons. Leaders of the Chemical Warfare Service feared that the awesome destructiveness of the atomic bomb threatened to make their weapons (and their service) obsolete.[63] Chemical warriors tried to head off post-atomic obsolescence by promoting a strategy of eradicating human enemies while leaving buildings intact. Alden Waitt, who succeeded Porter as chief of the Chemical Warfare Service, said that, unlike atomic weapons, chemical weapons could "incapacitate personnel and make ground, buildings and equipment unusable without demolishing them."[64]

It turned out that World War II did the service a favor by highlighting uses of chemicals other than poison gases, including insecticides. To celebrate the Chemical Warfare Service's twenty-fifth anniversary in 1945, the service selected the theme "Harnessing Chemical Warfare to Peace." Publicity materials listed a number of civilian uses of gases, including seven different insecticide applications. It also noted that decontaminating apparatus could be used to disperse insecticides.[65]

Chemical warfare's role in controlling insects helped the Chemical Warfare Service solidify its position in national defense. Presidents from Coolidge to Roosevelt had opposed chemical warfare because of its "inhumanity." When he vetoed a 1937 bill to make the service into a corps, Roosevelt had said he hoped to abolish the service rather than to "dignify" it with the new name.[66] In 1946, Secretary of War Robert Patterson asked Congress to make the same change.[67] He argued that the service had changed since Roosevelt's 1937 veto. First, "chemical warfare" no longer expressed the service's job. By 1946, the Chemical Warfare Service had developed DDT, incendiaries, and flamethrowers as well as poison gases. Second, the service was "the agency for maintaining and furthering essential relationships between the Military Establishment and the chemical industry." Third, the service researched civilian as well as military uses of chemicals. Patterson offered the use of chemical warfare equipment on boll weevils as an example. Overall, Patterson hoped the name change would "assure a proper conception of its [the Chemical Corps'] purposes among the people of our country."[68] Congress agreed to Patterson's request and converted the Chemical Warfare Service into the Chemical Corps in 1946.[69]

Once the Chemical Warfare Service became the Chemical Corps, it ceased almost all publicity until the defense buildup of 1950. As *Time* noted in 1950, "There are few more controversial, carefully guarded U.S. defense secrets than the weapons of chemical and bacteriological warfare."[70] Two important changes for the Chemical Corps took place with little public fanfare in the intervening years. In 1947, President Truman withdrew the Geneva Protocol from the Senate Foreign Relations Committee, where it had been resting for two decades, signaling that the United States did not intend to ratify it.[71] In 1949, the Chemical Corps's official mission broadened to include all forms of toxicological warfare, including biological and radiological warfare.[72]

One of the Chemical Corps's top research priorities, nerve gases, showed the value of linking research on chemical warfare and pest control. The army brought samples of German gases (the code name, "G" agents, was an abbreviation of "German") to the United States. By November 1946, the Chemical Corps had synthesized five organophosphates and designed a sarin (one of the most powerful nerve gases) pilot plant that overcame problems with the German design.[73] In 1947, it tested G agents at Dugway, Utah.[74] In 1948, Chemical Corps entomologists experimented with G agents and gained data "of fundamental importance" on how G agents affected nerves. In 1948, they also "gassed [insects] with compounds of the G-series and related chemicals, with a view to determining the value of such compounds as fumigants and to explore the possible use of insects as biological indicators in field tests with these compounds."[75]

At least one German scientist worked on organophosphate insecticides and nerve gases for the Chemical Corps. In 1945, the secretary of war approved a plan to employ German scientists and technicians in the United States "to ensure that we take full advantage of those significant developments which are deemed vital to our national security."[76] Freidrich Wilhelm Hoffmann came to the United States in 1947 and worked on insecticides for the Chemical Corps. About a year later, the corps allowed Hoffmann to map and start his own program of classified work on G agents.[77]

Vannevar Bush's vision of a national science foundation encountered a rough road after World War II, and the Chemical Corps joined other branches of the armed forces in funding science in the interim. The Chemical Corps maintained ties with universities and industry created during World War II, often by taking over contracts from the Office of Scientific Research and

Development. In 1946, the corps let more than 100 contracts worth more than $2 million with outside institutions.[78] The proportion of the corps' budget devoted to research and development grew from 10 percent in 1946 to 33 percent in 1949. The expenditure rose to $12 million in 1950.[79]

This emphasis followed the War Department policy to employ universities and industry as much as possible. Chemical Corps officers identified six advantages gained by placing contracts with universities, including access to top researchers, maintenance of a base of scientists for mobilization, goodwill, and favorable publicity.[80] One of the most important outside contracts was with the University of Chicago Toxicity Laboratory, which conducted basic research and tested new compounds as chemical weapons, insecticides, and rodenticides.[81] (The lab discovered TEPP's usefulness as a rodenticide.)[82] The Chemical Corps (and other government agencies) funded research on antidotes to nerve gases and organophosphate insecticides. The scientist who developed one antidote called PAM, Columbia biochemistry Professor David Nachmansohn, used the insecticide TEPP to figure out how nerve gas interfered with nerve cells as a step toward finding an antidote.[83]

Such funding enabled the Chemical Corps (along with other agencies) to put a new scientific field, insect physiology, on its feet. As scientist Vincent Dethier remembered, "the armed forces were supporting all the work that was being conducted in insect physiology because it was hoped that it would provide a chemical panacea."[84]

The careers of Dethier and Glenn Richards illustrated the importance of military interests and funding for insect physiologists. A university entomologist before World War II, Dethier worked on insect control as an officer in the Army's Sanitary Corps during the war. Around the end of World War II, the army assigned Dethier to work as entomologist for the chief of the

Chemical Corps. In that position, he monitored entomological work by the corps and other branches of the armed forces of the United States and other countries. After he left the army and joined the faculty at Johns Hopkins, Dethier worked on "insect chemical senses as they related to the nature of repellency because there was a big effort to develop effective repellents" under contract to the Chemical Corps. Dethier went on to become a member of the National Academy of Sciences.[85] An expert in insect cuticles, Richards was supported by the Office of Scientific Research and Development during World War II. The Chemical Corps sponsored his work from 1945 to 1948. The Army Surgeon General took over funding his work in 1949.[86]

The Chemical Corps also carried out an active program of research on insects in its own laboratories. Chemical Corps scientists screened insecticides and rodenticides, developed new compounds, and created means to disperse insecticides.[87] In 1946–1947, Chemical Corps entomologists studied the mechanism of action of many insecticides "to determine which physiological functions are clearly susceptible to effective attack." It spent $250,000 in 1947 on research on the mechanism of action of insecticides and rodenticides in its own laboratories alone.[88]

Chemical warriors' efforts to keep poison gases secret while publicizing insect control stirred controversy for the Insect Control Committee, which had been created to link chemical warfare and pest control research in the Office of Scientific Research and Development and transferred to the National Academy of Sciences. According to W. D. Reed of the Army Corps of Engineers, Milton C. Winternitz proposed at an April 1946 meeting that the Insect Control Committee be renamed the Clearinghouse for Insect and Rodent Control Information. Reed objected, "We would come in for suspicion if we mislabeled it." Reed suggested that the committee rename itself the Clearinghouse for Chemical and Biological Information and that the Chemical Warfare Service sponsor it because the service had "the primary interest." Colonel Rothchild of the Chemical Warfare Service rebuffed that proposal and suggested, in Reed's words, that "the Surgeon General sponsor the contract on the assumption that the Surgeon General would be above suspicion." After two and a half hours of deliberation, the group agreed to call the center the Clearinghouse for the Coordination of Chemical and Biological Information, which soon became the Chemical-Biological Coordination Center.[89]

The storm passed and the center grew rapidly. In the 1940s, leaders of the center thought they were closing in on scientific breakthroughs by linking chemical warfare, pest control, and related fields. The center set itself two tasks: (1) collecting and assembling information relating chemical structure with biological activity, and (2) facilitating screening of chemicals.[90]

The center did the first task by gathering data on the biological effects of chemicals and publishing reports, abstract bulletins, and reviews. The Orlando insecticide-screening program and the University of Chicago Toxicity Laboratory were two of the main sources of data. Many of the reports came from the Office of Scientific Research and Development, and many of those had formerly been classified. In 1948, the center published a widely circulated review by Robert L. Metcalf titled *The Mode of Action of Organic Insecticides.*[91]

The center did the second task by collecting compounds from organic chemists around the country and forwarding them to screening agencies. The center argued that such a program would provide leads for future research and create a database of information useful to the armed forces in a national emergency. The first screening agencies were the Chemical Corps (chemicals toxic to mammals and plants), National Cancer Institute, Fish and Wildlife Service (rodenticides), and the Bureau of Entomology (insecticides and repellents).[92] By 1949, thirty-one agricultural, medical, and military laboratories were screening chemicals for the center.[93]

By the close of the 1940s, the future of the center looked bright. Membership in subcommittees of the center had grown to eighty-two people.[94] Members of the advisory committee thought the screening program results were "more favorable than had been anticipated." Screening agencies had produced 2,300 reports on 652 compounds. Five of those had shown "outstanding results" as bactericides, herbicides, insecticides, fungicides, and repellents.[95] From screening tests and the general literature, the center had created about 55,000 data sheets on chemical structure and biological activity. It had stored that information on tens of thousands of punch cards that could be sorted mechanically and, the center hoped, reveal unknown correlations.[96]

The center's distant relationship with industry created one of the few clouds over it.[97] Chemical companies (including Du Pont, Hercules, Monsanto, and Abbott) liked the idea of screening but wanted to be sure that they would not lose confidentiality or patent rights.[98] The advisory committee's solution – to accept compounds only if they were "free of all restrictions" and leave resolution of patent issues to screening agencies – did nothing to resolve those concerns.[99] Therefore, Kirner noted, companies were likely to submit only well-tested compounds, not new and promising ones.[100]

Organizers of the center hoped it would appeal to civilian as well as military agencies, with insecticide makers and foundations heading their list of likely donors.[101] But the U.S. Department of Agriculture and the United States Public Health Service turned down appeals for support.[102] (The latter later supported it.) Among civilian organizations, only the American Cancer Society contributed to the center's funding. The army (primarily the Chemical Corps and the Surgeon General's Office), the navy, and the American Cancer Society funded the center.[103]

Unfortunately for the Chemical Corps, the second half of the 1940s opened and closed with a revival of bad publicity about industry-military links. In 1946, a Senate committee investigated charges that contractors and a congressional representative cooperated to defraud the federal government on Chemical Warfare Service contracts. The *New York Sunday News* said (with some exaggeration) that the "fantastic investigation ... threatens to involve half of Congress and the President of the United States."[104] The *Washington Post* called the companies involved a "munitions empire."[105] No one in the Chemical Warfare Service was prosecuted, but the congressional representative lost his bid for reelection and, in July 1947, was convicted with one of the corporate leaders of conspiracy to defraud the government.[106]

In 1949, at Senate hearings on "improper influences" in government, a businessman testified that he received fees for helping clients obtain government contracts. His fees varied, with the highest being Chemical Corps contracts at 15 percent. Other witnesses testified that the businessman claimed close ties with Chemical Corps Chief Alden Waitt. Waitt admitted that he had asked leaders in industry and science to help him get appointed and reappointed as chief. The investigation led to his suspension and sapped agency morale.[107] As always, chemical warfare had had a harder time in peace than in war. The heating up of the Cold War, however, would reinvigorate the agency.

10

Arms races in the Cold War (1950–1958)

When Winston Churchill wanted to evoke the geographical boundary between communism and "Christian civilization," he used a blacksmithing metaphor: an "Iron Curtain" had descended from the Baltic to the Adriatic, he declared at Fulton, Missouri, on March 5, 1946.[1] Later that month, when Churchill wanted to evoke the philosophical boundary between communism and the free world, he turned to insects. On March 18, 1946, in an address at Columbia University, he argued that "our Communist friends should study ... the admirable modern works on the life and the soul of the white ant" to learn about their past and future.[2]

It would take several more years for the American president and his advisers to conclude that the communist threat required a large American mobilization. But when they did, the Cold War repeated the pattern we have seen in earlier wars. Demand for chemicals increased, military and industrial institutions drew closer, the United States added powerful new chemical weapons to its arsenal, demand for agricultural products soared, insecticide use increased, and publicists swapped metaphors between war and pest control.

In this case, though, an important part of the pattern changed: the United States mobilized before and after a shooting war, not just during it. Even before the Korean War broke out, the Truman administration decided that the United States would mobilize on a large scale, something unprecedented in peace. The Korean War helped make the case to the public for mobilization, but it did not initiate it. And after the war, the United States would stay mobilized.[3] As a former president of the Armed Forces Chemical Association noted in 1952, "In the past the military expansion has been made under the urgency of a shooting war with the object of winning the war as soon as possible, and return to a peacetime economy. The job today is bigger, the end not so visible and the white-hot surge of the American people at war is lacking. We are arming today, not necessarily to fight a war but to prevent the most devastating war in all history."[4]

Similarly, pest controllers aimed more and more to prevent insect infestations and thereby head off bigger problems later. In January 1951, W. L. Popham of the Bureau of Entomology said that "preventive entomology" was the new approach to pest control. Popham contrasted preventive entomology with "sandbag control," the reactive effort to control insects once infestations had occurred. New methods of pest control developed over the previous five years, Popham said, made the shift from sandbag to preventive control possible. Preventive entomology would eradicate some insects and head off problems from others through research and planning.[5] In 1952, federal entomologist Clay Lyle declared, "I give an unqualified *yes* to the question, Can insects be eradicated?"[6]

During the Cold War, political and entomological leaders borrowed each other's metaphors freely. They had done so before, but now their emphasis shifted. Previously, they had focused on human and natural enemies as physical threats. The ability of enemy armies to wound or kill, and of enemy insects to transmit disease or destroy food, had been the common denominator. These images continued into the Cold War, but a new emphasis overlay them. Now similarities in the social structures of human and insect enemies took the front row.

Churchill's speech on white ants – known in the United States as termites – sparked a flurry of interest in insect social structures. Churchill had not specified what white ants would teach communists about their past and future, so popular publications took up the issue. The *New York Times* said that "it was assumed" that Churchill alluded to the writings of Jean Henri Fabre and Julian Huxley. These writers described termites as "leading a slavish existence in a completely authoritarian state."[7] A follow-up article in the *Times* elaborated by quoting Maurice Maeterlinck, the poet whom L. O. Howard had cited a quarter-century before to stress the alien nature of insects. But Howard had not emphasized Maeterlinck's comments about social structure, and the *Times* did: "In the terminary the gods of communism become insatiable Molochs. The more they give, the more they require; and they persist in their demands until the individual is annihilated and his misery complete. The appalling tyranny is unexampled among mankind: for while with us it at least benefits the few, in the terminary [*sic*] no one profits. The tyranny there is anonymous, immanent, all persuasive: collective and imperceptible."[8]

Entomologists expanded the discussion beyond termites to include other social insects. The year after Churchill compared communists to termites, Ernest Cory, president of the American Association of Economic Entomologists, titled his 1947 presidential address "Totalitarian Insects." Cory suggested that the lives of bees, termites, and other insects resembled "the totalitarian state in the human world where no individual has personal rights nor any opportunity to improve his position."[9]

Along with highlighting insect social structures, comments about human and insect enemies in the Cold War stressed the vast numbers of enemies facing Americans. The common term for this idea was "hordes." Some Americans had long feared populous Asia, and the "fall" of China to communism reawakened the fear of Asians taking over the free world. In 1950, *Time* magazine published a cover that showed Mao Tse-tung surrounded by a swarm of red locusts. The Red Chinese army had just entered the Korean War and given "the most powerful nation on earth the worst beating in its military history." Although not identified explicitly, the locusts seemed to represent the Red Chinese Army. The cover article described the army as a "horde," which (in Mao's words) acted like "innumerable gnats which, by biting a giant in front and rear, ultimately exhaust him."[10]

"Hordes" was not a new term for insects, but it received a lot of play during the Cold War. In February 1950, Bureau of Entomology Assistant Chief F. C. Bishopp told Congress that federal and state entomologists were trying to control "insect hordes" that caused $4 billion of losses each year.[11] In 1951, the United States rushed a highly publicized load of aldrin to Iran to combat a locust plague. Aldrin's manufacturer, Julius Hyman, noted that its chemicals enabled Iran to "protect its crops from destruction by insect hordes."[12] Byron T. Shaw, deputy administrator of the Agricultural Research Administration of the U.S. Department of Agriculture, told Congress, "I can think of no greater need in time of national emergency than food. And no enemy could disrupt our food supplies so quickly as the hordes of insects within our borders."[13]

To counteract hordes of human enemies, chemical warfare advocates emphasized, Americans would have to rely on superior technology. Weapons that could annihilate enemy soldiers would be especially important. *Armed Forces Chemical Journal* noted that fighting in Korea showed that "our enemies now control or may eventually control countries whose populations add up to a total of almost one billion persons. Such an astronomical number of people can furnish virtually great hordes of military manpower." So "if we are to ... survive, we must employ weapons of mass personnel destruction," including chemical weapons.[14]

The United States did not use poison gases to fight the communist "hordes" in Korea, but it did continue its World War II emphasis on incendiaries. The United States used napalm so heavily – it shipped almost 2 million pounds to Korea in the first four months of the war – that the *New York Herald Tribune* called it the "Number One Weapon in Korea." "Compared with a fire bomb," a colonel commented, "hitting a tank with a rocket or anti-tank gun is like swatting a fly with a lead pencil instead of a fly swatter." The Chemical Corps also developed napalm mines (which covered up to thirty square yards with burning napalm), a napalm satchel charge, and a napalm bunker bomb used to rout entrenched Chinese and North Korean soldiers.[15]

For critics centered in religious circles, eliminating people as efficiently as one eliminated pests bespoke a horrifying attitude. "In Korea," *Christian Century* reported in 1952, "the prevailing tactic, in dealing with a tough village or neighborhood, seems to be to spray it with flaming jellied gasoline – napalm. The Archbishop of York appeals to us to stop. He says that the church should demand an end to 'the use of weapons which indiscriminately destroy, as if they were worthless flies, those for whom Christ died.'"[16]

Chemical warfare advocates found such criticisms unconvincing; they continued to emphasize that, if given the chance, poison gas could eradicate human populations more efficiently than other weapons could. Shortly after the Korean War ended without the use of gas, the Chemical Corps gave Cornelius Ryan (author of the World War II book, *A Bridge Too Far*) unprecedented journalistic access to its facilities. Ryan's resulting piece, a 1953 cover article in *Collier's*, measured the efficiency of gas in two ways. One was dollars. "In World War II, it cost between $10,000,000 and $35,000,000 to *eradicate* people and buildings in one square mile of enemy territory by bombing," Ryan wrote. "Nerve gas could do the same job for one twentieth the amount and leave the buildings and industrial plants intact for an occupying force to take over." Another way to measure efficiency was square miles, specifically the area that one plane could rid of people. A map compared effects of an atomic bomb and GB (sarin nerve gas) on Washington, D.C., and Virginia. It showed that "fumes loosed by seven tons of GB bombs would drift 50 miles, killing everyone in their path. Atom bomb is lethal over only three-mile radius."[17]

American strategy in the Cold War did not rely on weapons alone. American leaders saw pesticide exports, which could help other nations increase food supplies and decrease diseases, as ways of winning allies in the fight against communism. P. H. Groggins, who oversaw agricultural chemical production for the National Production Authority during the Korean War, stressed this point to the National Agricultural Chemicals Association. He said pesticide makers should keep in mind "the motives behind our export programs in improving world conditions and winning friends, as well as markets."[18]

Increased domestic food production was also part of American strategy. High agricultural output advanced defense goals by feeding soldiers, factory workers, and "friendly nations"; building reserves; keeping down inflation; and stemming communism by settling "chaotic conditions" in other countries. The administrator of the U.S. Department of Agriculture's Production and Marketing Administration told Congress in 1951, "As a weapon for defense, food and fiber may not be as spectacular as atomic bombs and guided missiles. But, gentlemen, it is not a matter of which is more important to the defense of the Nation, food or weapons. They are equally important."[19] Director of Defense Mobilization Charles Wilson said in 1952, "We regard agriculture as an essential part of our defense preparedness.... Everything that is humanly possible will be done to keep farm production at a high level."[20]

Pesticides were integral to the effort to increase agricultural production for the defense effort. By 1951, the United States had planted most of its arable land, so it had to rely on chemical inputs to increase yields per acre in order to expand total harvests. The called-for boost in some crops was stunning: 60 percent in cotton, for example, one of the crops most dependent on insecticides.[21] As Agriculture Secretary Charles Brannan told President Truman, the federal government would have to encourage farmers to make more capital investments, especially in "high quality seed, fertilizer, pesticides and feed."[22] The Department of Agriculture encouraged such increases through speeches, production goals, and state and county mobilization committees[23] (Figure 10.1).

Along with rhetoric specific to the Cold War, traditional martial themes helped entomologists define themselves to the public. In 1954, to celebrate 100 years of official entomology in the United States, the Entomological Society of America launched a national public relations campaign under the slogan "Fight Your Insect Enemies" (only a slight modification of the title of L. O. Howard's autobiography, *Fighting the Insects*). The campaign reached the public through newspapers, magazines, radio, television, pamphlets, open houses, and a postage cancellation with the campaign slogan. The cover letter accompanying publicity materials began, "Few people in your public know what would happen if man's ceaseless war on insects was relaxed for even a month. Millions of bushels of wheat ruined, an entire potato crop reduced by half or two-thirds, or every fifth person in a major city mortally ill with plague or yellow fever." The Department of Agriculture issued a bulletin titled *Fighting Our Insect Enemies: Achievements of Professional Entomology, 1854–1954.*[24]

Making the ideological and practical goals of the Cold War possible required increasing the size of, and the links between, a variety of institutions. The Chemical Corps funded extensive research in universities and industry, which, despite some spats, fostered

SAVE THAT COTTON!

During periods of national emergency cotton is vital. It goes into uniforms, gun covers, pup tents, duffle bags and a thousand other items essential to the well equipped soldier. Leave it to the boll weevil and there would not be nearly enough cotton. But cotton we must have in unbelievable quantities and that means death to the weevil.

Benzene Hexachloride is the lethal chemical in most of the dust and spray insecticides which today are destroying these pests and saving cotton for the big defense job.

Whether you have weevil trouble or not, there are many ways in which your own daily life is made safer and more comfortable with chemicals from Tennessee . . . and industry serving all industry.

TENNESSEE
PRODUCTS & CHEMICAL
Corporation
NASHVILLE, TENNESSEE

PRODUCERS OF: FUELS • METALLURGICAL
PRODUCTS • TENSULATE BUILDING PROD-
UCTS • AROMATIC CHEMICALS • WOOD
CHEMICALS • AGRICULTURAL CHEMICALS

10.1 "Save that Cotton!" To save cotton for "the big defense job," this advertisement suggested, farmers should spray invading weevils with BHC (a member of the chlorinated hydrocarbon family of insecticides). From *AC* 6 (Aug. 1951): 16.

close personal relations and synthesis of research objectives. In 1955, the corps had about a third of the civilian consultants employed by the entire army.[25] It held contracts with 373 universities and companies, ranging in value from $5,000 to millions of dollars.[26] In 1956, Alfred C. Benson of the Research Procurement Office of the Chemical Corps said, "We say that for all practical purposes the Research and Development organization of the Chemical Corps includes every trustworthy organization and individual in the United States and in some instances it may include those in other friendly nations of the world."[27] In addition to contracted research, industry shared "millions of dollars worth of research data" with the corps free.[28]

Direct government (including military) funding of research would come to be seen as "natural" by the end of the century, but at mid-century it was still something to get used to. (An exception was research in agriculture, which the federal government had a long history of funding.) "Basic" or "pure" scientists still bridled at government control of their research, and the army often asked the National Academy of Sciences to act as an intermediary. Entomologist A. W. A. Brown once suggested that the army give university presidents "an outline of projects that were important in the national interest," including those on ecology and biological control of insects. A representative of the Army Surgeon General's Office demurred. If the army tried that, he said, it would be "criticized as trying to direct research. Such a suggestion should come from a body such as the National Research Council" of the National Academy of Sciences. In many cases, the academy responded by creating committees of civilian scientists to study military problems.[29] The Chemical–Biological Coordination Center at the National Academy of Sciences continued to supply chemicals and data to the Chemical Corps until, plagued by a variety of problems, it folded in 1957. Its dying act was a bequest to chemical warfare research: it sent its massive data collection to the Chemical Corps.[30]

Over time, though, even "pure" scientists found they could meet their own goals under federal funding, including that from the military. Kenneth Roeder of Tufts University said in 1952 that government sponsors (mainly the army, including the Chemical Corps) and insect physiologists at universities had achieved a "natural fusion" of their research objectives. Roeder declared that university scientists had a "proverbial distrust" of sponsored research, and that research sponsors wanted to solve "purely practical" problems. The atomic bomb and DDT had helped both realize, however, that the same research could aid in solving both "pure" and "applied" problems. The "moral and practical support" of sponsors – including the Army Chemical Corps, which supported Roeder's research – had helped insect physiology enter a period of "steady growth."[31] By 1953, that research had produced so much knowledge that Roeder edited and published a volume of 1,100 pages on insect physiology.[32]

Insect research helped the Chemical Corps learn about the physiology of poisoning. To learn more about nerve gas poisoning, Chemical Corps contractors used, among other things, organophosphate insecticides. In 1953, researchers at Johns Hopkins School of Medicine announced that they had tested nerve gases and parathion on human volunteers as part of a contract with the Chemical Corps Medical Laboratories. Subjects recovered fully from both kinds of poisoning, but recovery could take days. These tests, along with studies of workers severely poisoned in parathion factories, led to recommendations for diagnosis, treatment, and prevention of nerve gas poisoning.[33]

The Chemical Corps and chemical companies took pride in their close cooperation and offered it as a model to other parts of the armed forces. Chemical Corps Deputy Chief Brigadier General Charles E. Loucks said in 1952 that the Chemical Corps was "a combination military-industrial organization."[34] Major General Anthony C. McAuliffe, chief of the Chemical Corps, said, "I believe that our example of seeking to achieve common goals in joint endeavors could very well serve as a model of unification between industry and the military services."[35]

Similarly, corporate leaders and publicists embraced their alliance with government in the war on insects. As Lea Hitchner told Congress when testifying about the role of pesticides in mobilization in 1951, maximum crop production resulted from the cooperation of "the Bureau of Entomology and Plant Quarantine, Bureau of Plant Industry, Soils, and Agricultural Engineering and the Production and Marketing Administration; and with the land grant colleges, the NPA, the OIT, the armed services procurement agencies, and the industry."[36] Insecticide companies likewise depended on universities for research. Carlos Kampmeier of Rohm & Haas (and chair of the National Agricultural Chemicals Association Information Committee) said in 1951 that "industry, colleges and experiment stations are partners in a 'hot war' against insect and disease pests that cost farmers ten billion dollars a year."[37] Government field trials, funded by taxes, brought many insecticides to market; without that subsidy, an industry journal said, many insecticides would not have been sold.[38]

Defense mobilization accelerated chemical company growth. By mid-1952, with military procurement still growing, chemical production was leaping 20 to 25 percent per year. The federal government fueled this expansion by creating demand and providing tax breaks. The federal Defense Production Administration issued accelerated tax amortization certificates for $20 billion in industrial expansion – including plants to make fifty or more chemicals essential to national defense – by July 1952. An industry executive estimated that 70 percent of the growth in the chemical industry in the early 1950s was "related directly to defense" and financed by tax amortization. Subsidies continued through the rest of the decade. Between 1954 and 1959, the federal government issued amortization certificates worth $3 billion to boost military chemical production alone.[39]

Sometimes fault lines broke out in the military-industrial rela-
tionship, in which case the lack of a declared war put the Chemical
Corps at a disadvantage. When the Korean War began, the
Chemical Corps's industrial chief wanted the Julius Hyman
Company to move out of Rocky Mountain Arsenal so that the
corps could make chemical weapons and maintain security.[40]
Hyman enlisted Colorado Senators Johnson and Millikin, Claude
Pepper, and Charles E. Shadle (a retired general and former com-
mander of Rocky Mountain Arsenal working for Hyman) to lobby
on their behalf. According to a Chemical Corps branch chief,
Shadle claimed that he had control over construction at Rocky
Mountain Arsenal by virtue of his position with the Defense
Production Authority and "went to great length to explain that it
is absolutely essential" that Hyman retain its facilities. The issue
rose to the secretary of the army, who decided that Hyman could
use the arsenal's facilities until "a *military need actually exists for
them.*" Citing Hyman's "numerous contacts" and the secretary of
the army's statement, the chief of the Chemical Corps's materiel
division gave up.[41]

Hyman stayed and soon became a division of Shell Chemical.[42]
Because the Chemical Corps could not use its machinery at Rocky
Mountain Arsenal to make a key chemical (dichlor), it had to buy
it from contractors, including Shell. Shell made dichlor at Rocky
Mountain Arsenal on a "cost plus fixed fee" contract, the fixed fee
being guaranteed profit. The contract was worth an estimated
$1.125 million per year.[43]

The Cold War also sparked tremendous growth in the Chemical
Corps. At the start of the Korean War, the corps had under way
one construction project worth $233,000. By the end of 1952, it
had begun projects worth almost 1,400 times that amount – 361
projects at a cost of more than $323 million.[44]

The Korean War catalyzed the rapid entry of organophosphate
nerve gases into the American arsenal. The United States had
tested nerve gases since the end of World War II, but it had not set-

tled on a standard gas or designs for bombs to disperse it. In a crash program, the Chemical Corps built one plant at Muscle Shoals, Alabama, to make nerve gas intermediates, and another at Rocky Mountain Arsenal to convert intermediates into nerve gas, fill bombs with it, and store the bombs. The Chemical Corps chose GB (sarin, one of the gases developed by Gerhard Schrader) as its standard nerve gas in April 1951. It launched a massive effort to make nerve gas cluster bombs, shells (for howitzers, mortars, and guns), and warheads. In 1953, the United States began filling bombs with nerve gases. A 1954 analysis judged that the corps had telescoped seven or eight years of work into four.[45] After the Korean War, the Chemical Corps continued to build up its arsenal. In 1954, the Chemical Corps's Rocky Mountain Arsenal manufactured nerve gas twenty-four hours a day, seven days a week.[46]

At first, the public got a confused idea of nerve gas, seeing it as some magical, harmless material spread like DDT. The impression came from journalists who read too much into a 1950 comment from Chemical Corps Chief General Anthony C. McAuliffe. The "military concept of annihilating the enemy's military might, and destroying his industrial potential, has radically changed since the end of the recent conflict," McAuliffe said. Chemical and biological weapons, such as nerve gas, provided the opportunity to "reduce a potential enemy's will to resist and thereby obtain victory without the destruction of his economy."[47] Journalists took the optimistic view and assumed that nerve gas would paralyze rather than kill. *Time* reported in 1950, "Presumably [nerve gas] would be sprayed over enemy cities by planes in the same way that whole areas are sprayed with mosquito-killing DDT, paralyzing the whole population. Then the attacking army, equipped with protective masks, would march in and take over."[48]

After the war, however, the fatal power of nerve gas became clear, and chemical weapons joined nuclear weapons as up-to-date symbols of mass annihilation. The Chemical Corps aided this shift by opening its arsenals to Cornelius Ryan and other journalists. In March 1954, when two Colorado newspapers disclosed that Rocky Mountain Arsenal made nerve gas, comparisons to the atomic bomb stood front and center. "Potential military value of GB gas," said the *Denver Post*, "is greater in some respects than even the atomic weapons.... An invader can wipe out life in a city and take it over intact – its industries, utilities, transportation and power plants ready to be used again in a few hours, instead of being ruined and radioactive." Picking up the story, the *New York Times* led with this line: "A new weapon in the horror class with atomic and hydrogen bombs is being made and stored at the Rocky Mountain arsenal."[49]

Throughout the 1950s, the Chemical Corps saw the United States in a chemical arms race with the Soviet Union.[50] In 1951, the chief of the U.S. corps announced that the United States needed to "keep ahead" of Soviet developments in chemical and biological weapons.[51] In 1957, Chief William M. Creasy quoted Soviet Defense Minister Georgi Zhukov's statement that "any new war will be characterized by mass use of airpower, various types of rocket, atomic, thermo-nuclear, chemical, and biological weapons."[52] In 1960, the army estimated that chemical weapons made up one-sixth of the Soviet stockpile.[53] General Arthur G. Trudeau, chief of research and development for the army, said at the end of the decade that the United States and the Soviet Union were still in a "weapons race for military superiority."[54]

At the same time, pest controllers found themselves in another chemical arms race. Right after World War II, entomologists around the world noticed that DDT and its relatives clobbered pests for a few years and then failed.[55] Species of the most dangerous disease-carrying insects – lice, flies, and mosquitoes – all resisted DDT and its relatives by 1952.[56] Other chlorinated hydrocarbons had the same problem. In 1949, Phoenix controlled flies with a new DDT relative, dieldrin. In 1950, the same chemical "had no measurable effect on the fly population at all."[57] Worldwide, the problem worsened every year.[58]

Pest controllers and journalists framed insecticide resistance using military metaphors. Entomologist Robert L. Metcalf said, "It is clear that these chemicals [DDT and other post-World War II insecticides] have won only a battle, not the war, against insects."[59] Ralph Bunn of the Army Surgeon General's Office complained, "We may win a battle, as we did with the introduction of DDT, but insects rapidly develop effective defensive measures and the war still goes on."[60] *Popular Science* reported, "The battle between the wonder insecticide, DDT, and the housefly has been won by the fly."[61] Some journalists explicitly compared the situation to an arms race. "A world-wide armaments race is under way between chemists and insects," *Science News Letter* lamented. "The chemists develop new insecticides, but the insects create their own special defenses against these insecticides within two to three years."[62]

Chemists countered resistance with a stream of new chemicals.[63] Roy Hansberry of Shell concluded in 1954 that control of resistant insects "must depend on an endless development of new insecticides of greater variety and specification."[64] The ability of new chemicals to kill insects resistant to older chemicals became a selling point, especially when the new family of organophosphates entered the market. American Cyanamid noted that malathion "even kills flies resistant to DDT and other chlorinated hydrocarbon insecticides."[65]

The idea that resistance was inevitable gained steam when insects began standing up to the organophosphates. In 1956, entomologists concluded that houseflies and mites had developed this trait.[66] The solution was to add a new family of insecticides – carbamates – to the chlorinated hydrocarbons and organophosphates. In 1957, Union Carbide announced that its new carbamate, sevin (also known as carbaryl) was "safe, inexpensive, stable, and of relatively broad spectrum effectiveness."[67] Sevin was about half as acutely toxic to rats as DDT.[68] By 1961, Union Carbide was selling millions of pounds of sevin, and Hercules, Dow, and Bayer were developing other carbamates.[69] Major targets included dieldrin-resistant sugar cane frog hoppers and BHC and toxaphene-resistant cattle ticks.[70]

The race for stronger insecticides apparently put a new, deadlier type of nerve gas into the American arsenal. About 1954, ICI introduced a new type of organophosphate insecticide but withdrew it because the compound was highly toxic to people. The British chemical warfare research station at Porton brought this chemical and its relatives to the attention of the United States, which named the compounds V agents.[71] V agents were so toxic that small quantities on the skin, including in aerosol form, could cause casualties. Even troops wearing gas masks would suffer "30% casualties with 50% deaths," the army estimated. Direct fire, mortar, artillery, guided missiles, tactical air, and mines all might deliver V agents.[72] The United States began construction of a plant to make a V agent (VX) in 1959.[73]

The evolutionary arms race with insects had implications for military medicine as well as chemical warfare. DDT, the wonder worker against lice in World War II, failed to kill lice in Korea. The army called in federal entomologists, who recommended other chemicals in place of DDT (including, ironically, the pyrethrum powder that DDT had replaced in World War II).[74] Switching insecticides solved the army's problem in the short run, but it raised a haunting specter. If lice could resist DDT, could other insects do the same? The answer, reports from around the world soon showed, was yes. This was a serious problem: among methods of pest control, only insecticides offered the speed and universality of coverage needed to control diseases on battlefronts. As an army medical officer put it, "Insecticides would always be necessary for use by the Army overseas."[75]

The army took the lead in countering resistance with research. With funding from the armed forces, federal entomologists wrote the first two reviews of resistance in 1949 and 1951. The entomologists concluded that no one understood resistance, almost no one was trying to understand it, and everyone had better understand it soon. Resistance would "make headlines as big as those concerning the new atomic bomb, if only the significance of the matter were properly understood," noted the second review.[76] For its part, the Bureau of Entomology tried to find new chemicals to replace those becoming obsolete. By July 1952, the Orlando lab had screened 11,000 compounds for the army. Of these, 237 insecticides killed lice for a month or more, and thirty-five compounds killed 95 to 100 percent of mosquito larvae at one part per 100 million.[77]

But searching for an endless stream of new chemicals struck the Army Surgeon General's Office as an inadequate solution to the problem. It asked the National Research Council to organize the first conference on resistance.[78] The council organized a meeting in December 1951 in Cincinnati. Sixty-three researchers in entomology, economic entomology, genetics, and ecology attended.[79] The army committed $100,000 for 1952 and $300,000 a year for 1953 and 1954 for research on the topics recommended by the conference. University researchers took the bait. By June 1952, before the army even solicited proposals, researchers had submitted seven applications[80] and the army immediately funded most of them.[81] A National Academy of Sciences committee later noted that few articles on resistance had been published before 1949. By 1956, 147 scientific articles on resistance appeared. The committee judged that the "increase was largely a consequence of the interest engendered by the Cincinnati meeting."[82]

The most cogent explanation for resistance came from evolutionary biologists, who put forward the troubling prediction that resistance was inevitable. At the 1951 meeting on resistance, evolutionary biologist Theodosius Dobzhansky argued that resistance was an example of natural (or perhaps artificial) selection.[83] Some insects happened to be immune to an insecticide; they survived spraying and reproduced while their susceptible conspecifics did not; and, in a few generations, most members of a population were resistant. The next five years bore out Dobzhansky's prediction as more and more species developed resistance to more and more pesticides.[84]

Chemists thought Dobzhansky unduly pessimistic and continued to believe that they could find a magic bullet.[85] Chemist Milton S. Schechter said he and his colleagues were not ready to concede defeat: "I am a chemist, and after hearing all the entomologists, insect physiologists, and so on, paint a very black picture, I would like to say that perhaps there is a little note of optimism with the chemists.... Perhaps some work can be directed toward other chemicals which do not build up such high resistance."[86]

But over the next five years, no one produced a practical way to solve the resistance problem (aside from continually introducing new chemicals). So the Army Surgeon General's Office asked the National Academy of Sciences to organize a second conference. Military speakers posed the problem for the 1956 conference: how could the military continue to control insects with chemicals, especially under combat conditions, when the insects of most concern to the army (flies, mosquitoes, and lice) were all developing resistance?[87] The 1956 conferees had no answer. They could only call for more research, especially in ecology.[88]

The free market seemed to offer companies the wrong incentives to address this problem. At a 1959 conference on resistance, George R. Ferguson of Geigy suggested that more specific chemicals (those that killed few species of pests) should be the direction of research in the future. Unfortunately, as Ferguson and Dow's W. E. Ripper noted, market incentives (and thus industrial research foci) went in the opposite direction. The more species a chemical could kill, the greater the potential market. Few companies would want to invest in research on a chemical that killed few species.[89]

At the same 1959 meeting, some entomologists argued that the solution to the resistance problem was a broader approach to insect control. E. F. Knipling of the Bureau of Entomology, who had overseen the Orlando laboratory when it developed DDT during World War II, took industry to task for its response to resistance. "Substitute insecticides are not a satisfactory solution to the resistance problem," he said. Knipling advocated a variety of methods – chemical, biological, cultural, and varietal – to handle pest problems.[90] Knipling himself had developed a creative way to eradicate an important cattle pest, the screwworm, when he and other researchers sterilized and released male screwworms. The sterilized males mated with females but no progeny resulted, leading to eradication of the insect from some places.[91]

Meanwhile, the scale of insecticide application continued to soar. In 1958, with a fleet consisting almost entirely of surplus military aircraft, about 5,000 planes were treating 200 different crops with 100 million gallons of liquid sprays and over 800 million pounds of insecticide dusts, seeds, and fertilizers. The area was enormous: over 100 million acres were treated from the air – one-sixth of the cultivated land in the United States.[92] The reason for this growth was simple: cost. A study of charges in Oregon in 1956 found that dusting and spraying were significantly cheaper when done by air than on the ground.[93]

Although the atomic bomb was *the* icon of the Cold War, nations never deployed the bomb in combat after World War II. But, as in World War II, they did rely on chemistry as the workhorse science during the Cold War. On the battlefronts of Korea, napalm was the most important weapon for aerial attack and personnel destruction. Insecticides protected soldiers from insect-borne diseases. On the home front, insecticides became the first choice among weapons for the fight against insects. Discussing the key role of chemicals in the Cold War, a vice president of American Cyanamid called the chemical industry the "minutemen of mobilization." But today's minutemen did not wield a plow *or* a gun. They wielded both. Ernest Hart, president of the National Agricultural Chemicals Association, said, "Agricultural chemicals are of course weapons in this day of total warfare."[94] Or as the vice president of American Cyanamid summed up the difference, the Cold War erased "the lines of demarcation between war and peace."[95] As the 1950s turned the corner to the 1960s, however, sentiment was growing among Americans that they would be better off if some of the lines were restored.

11

Backfires (1958–1963)

When moviegoers streamed into theaters in 1954 to see the new
science-fiction film *Them!* they were treated to the sight of giant
ants created in the New Mexico desert by fallout from the first
atomic blast. Under great secrecy, two federal entomologists flew
in to advise local police, the Federal Bureau of Investigation, and
the army on how to conquer these beasts. This team used traditional weapons (rifles and grenades) to kill off the biggest threat, a
queen that had escaped into the sewers of Los Angeles. But they
used chemical weapons – poison gas and flamethrowers – to kill
most of the ants in their nest.[1]

Them! presaged a period of intense focus on fallout. Fears grew
over the next half decade as knowledge of the extent and dangers of
radiation increased. The same year *Them!* appeared, the unfortunate crew of a Japanese fishing boat (ironically named *The Lucky
Dragon*) found itself downwind of an atomic test in the Pacific.
Fallout sickened and killed crew members, making the dangers of
radiation highly visible. Something too small to see threatened
human health, it was clear, and radiation from tests was spreading
around the world. Physicists, the most prominent members of a
post-World War II scientific movement concerned with atomic

weapons, found their ranks reinforced with scientists from biology, chemistry, medicine, and other fields. Biologist Barry Commoner spearheaded efforts to publicize the biological dangers of fallout, and chemist Linus Pauling lobbied for a ban on above-ground nuclear testing (for which he received the Nobel Peace Prize in 1962). At the same time, several examples of chemical disasters hit the headlines. Thalidomide poisoning (which caused grotesque birth defects) was one of the most heart-wrenching.[2]

By 1959, when Alfred Hitchcock produced *North by Northwest,* the public was ready for a new image of terror. In *Them!,* entomologists had used chemical weapons to save Americans from an entomological threat. Now, much like nuclear weapons, chemicals seemed to threaten ordinary citizens. In *North by Northwest,* hero Roger Thornhill (Cary Grant) disembarked from a bus in a rural area. An airplane appeared and began "dustin' crops where there ain't no crops." Then the plane turned toward Thornhill, who stood, in the words of the script, "wide-eyed, rooted to the spot.... There are two men in the twin cockpits, goggled, unrecognizable, menacing.... Desperately he drops to the ground and presses himself flat as the plane zooms over him with a great noise, almost combing his hair with a landing wheel.... He gets to his feet, looks about, sees a cornfield about fifty yards from the highway ... and decides to make a dash for the cover of the tall-growing corn.... Skimming over the top of the cornstalks, the plane ... lets loose thick clouds of poisonous dust which settle down into the corn. WITHIN THE CORNFIELD, THORNHILL, still lying flat, begins to gasp and choke as the poisonous dust envelops him. Tears stream from his eyes but he does not dare move as he HEARS THE PLANE COMING OVER THE FIELD AGAIN. When the plane zooms by and another cloud of dust hits him, he jumps to his feet and crashes out into the open, half blinded and gasping for breath."[3]

Hitchcock had a talent for transforming familiar objects – birds, rope, and neckties in other movies – into symbols of menace. But he had less work to do with the crop duster. When researchers first dusted crops from the air in the 1920s, they learned that clouds of poison streaming from the sky terrified people caught unaware below. In the 1920s, 1930s, and 1940s, publicists used airplanes' dropping gas on civilians as icons of total war.

But in the 1950s, the threat came home to people in their own homes. At the same time that their fear of chemicals themselves grew, homeowners found themselves with less control over insecticide spraying. During the 1950s, crop dusters sprayed ever more acres – along with suburbanites moving into agricultural areas. In 1958, federal eradication projects sprayed enormous square miles of the Northeast and the South in efforts to eradicate insect pests. A flood of scathing publicity followed. Then *North by Northwest* appeared. At the same time, the Chemical Corps increased public fears of chemicals by, ironically, launching a major public relations drive designed to make chemical weapons more appealing. Chemical weapons soon joined hydrogen bombs in public and expert discussions as symbols of "terror."

The Chemical Corps's publicity campaign grew out of a study committee's report. In 1955, Secretary of the Army Wilber M. Brucker approved a report from a civilian advisory board that called for a larger role for chemical warfare in national defense. The board urged the Chemical Corps to start a public relations campaign to bring about "a more candid recognition of the proper place of chemical and biological warfare" because they had "unique potential in warfare without associated destruction of facilities and the attendant problems of rehabilitation."[4] The *New York Times* reported that unnamed military officials decided "as a matter of policy, that public support was required to make possible further developments of some promising and rather astounding chemical warfare techniques."[5]

The *Reporter*, a magazine specializing in journalism, summed up key features of the campaign:

- High military officers make speeches to specially selected groups.
- Officers testify at Congressional hearings (closed to the press), and carefully screened material is then released with some fanfare. Such hearings are also the occasion for "spectacular" demonstrations of the effects of various drugs on animals.
- Articles by retired officers, who cannot be held accountable, appear in magazines.
- Word is passed around among writers who specialize in scientific and military subjects that formerly classified material is now available to them for stories; or sometimes a writer will be given a tip on where classified material may be found in non-classified publications.
- Writers are also informed that certain high military officers are now receptive to interviews.
- Writers and editors are privately briefed by some civilian with a pipeline to difficult-to-obtain data who uses opportunities for exclusive stories as bait.[6]

A typical piece in this campaign appeared in *Harper's* in 1959. General J. H. Rothschild, a retired chemical officer, argued that germs and gas were "as potent" as nuclear weapons but possibly "both more effective and more humane." Rothschild complained that the army and State Department muzzled the Chemical Corps by allowing public discussion only of defensive measures. "But surely everyone who thinks about it must realize that we are working on offensive weapons as well as defense against them," Rothschild admitted. "The Department of Defense would be impossibly incompetent if it were not." Rothschild concluded by urging abandonment of Roosevelt's no-first-use policy and considering chemical and biological weapons "among the normal, usable means of war."[7]

Along with trying to persuade the public, the corps tried to persuade Congress. In 1958, Chief Chemical Officer William Creasy testified to Congress that the public saw chemical weapons as "too horrible to even think about." In fact, Creasy argued, chemical, biological, and radiological weapons were the "most effective and humane way to wage warfare." Two examples buttressed his point. One was that the United States could have saved 25,000 American casualties on Iwo Jima had it used these weapons. Second, and this was the spectacular part, the corps had developed chemicals that would temporarily incapacitate troops but not permanently harm them. Creasy called these weapons "psychochemicals." (An industry journal reported that Creasy "was especially high on psychochemicals.") Creasy concluded that the United States should put chemical warfare "in exactly the same category that we put the atom bomb and all other things," rather than following a no-first-use policy. He added that the country should increase funding for Chemical Corps research.[8]

A follow-up to Creasy's testimony probably garnered more headlines than any other single event in the publicity campaign. To illustrate how psychochemicals would make bloodless war possible, the army released a film in December 1958. In it, a cat chased and caught a mouse, inhaled an unnamed gas, and then cowered from another mouse. Two television networks showed the film. *Life* magazine and newspapers around the country published still photographs.[9] Within days, judged a chemical warfare journal, "about everyone in the country" was familiar with the film.[10] In November 1959, *Newsweek* revealed the name of the chemical administered to the cat: LSD-25. It also reported that LSD-25 had been tested on people. When administered to army volunteers, "alert, well-trained soldiers completely ignored the barked orders of a drill sergeant." LSD-25 even prompted a Pentagon joke: to end interservice rivalry, "release LSD-25 in the Pentagon air-conditioning system."[11]

The campaign seemed to increase the chances for reversal of the United States' no-first-use policy. Along with statements about Soviet advances in unconventional weapons, reports about psychochemicals impressed the Pentagon brass as well as Congress and the public. Echoing early reports about nerve gas, army leaders said it might "be possible to direct such gases against entire cities, preparing the way for their seizure without damage to the buildings and with no harmful after-effects upon the population."[12]

Some journalists suggested that this campaign was arguing for a policy change that already had been made in secret. Publicly, the United States adhered to Roosevelt's policy to use chemical weapons only in retaliation. Journalist Walter Schneir noted, however, that the transcript of Creasy's 1958 testimony to a Congressional committee raised questions:

General Creasy: "First I will start off with the national policy." [Discussion off the record.]

Representative Gerald R. Ford, Jr. *(D., [sic] Michigan):* "May I ask how long that policy has been in effect?"

General Creasy: "Since about October 1956, about a year and a half ago. The national policy has been implemented by a Department of Defense Directive." [Off the record.][13]

The publicity campaign helped increase Chemical Corps funding and status within the armed forces. Stressing the value of psychochemicals, the army requested $40 million in research funds. But Pentagon authorities were reportedly "so impressed … that they proposed that the Army budget for such purposes be doubled to $80,000,000."[14] In its 1962 budget request, the army asked for $85 million for chemical and biological warfare.[15] The Pentagon's research chief announced that the United States should rely more heavily on chemical weapons and less on atomic weapons.

Chemical weapons were cheaper, could be tailored to a small conflict, were more acceptable to world opinion, and could be used to control millions of people by killing or putting them to sleep, as the United States wished.[16]

The campaign succeeded in increasing public awareness but backfired by making chemical weapons (aside from LSD-25) look at least as threatening to civilians as hydrogen bombs. When *U.S. News and World Report* carried news of Creasy's testimony before Congress, its headline read, "New Worry for World? If Nuclear Weapons Are Banned, Something Worse in their Place?" The magazine reported that chemical and biological weapons would be directed against "masses of people" if used in war in order to destroy people but not buildings.[17] The civil defense committee of the American Chemical Society announced that one plane-load of nuclear bombs would damage thirty-six square miles; the same plane carrying chemical weapons could eradicate people from an area almost three times as large (100 square miles).[18]

The campaign also backfired by leading antinuclear scientists to expand their concerns to chemical and biological weapons. In 1959, the Society for Social Responsibility in Science passed a resolution deploring the Chemical Corps's efforts to promote chemical and biological weapons to the public. The same year, the Pugwash Conference focused on chemical and biological weapons. The *Bulletin of the Atomic Scientists* printed a special symposium issue on chemical and biological warfare in 1960. When the Society for Social Responsibility in Science held a forum on chemical and biological warfare at Harvard in October 1960, 400 people attended and the two main presidential candidates sent statements. Richard Nixon called research and development in this area essential; John Kennedy called for international control and eventual disarmament.[19]

By 1961, chemical and biological weapons had joined atomic weapons as well-recognized weapons of mass destruction.

Longtime atomic critic and *Saturday Review* editor Norman Cousins criticized nerve gas by comparing it to DDT. He wrote that nerve gas GB "acts like a super-insecticide against human beings. Like DDT, its effect is widespread and almost instantaneous. Exposure to GB in gas form is lethal in a matter of seconds." Nor did Cousins find the psychochemicals humane. The ability to "twist a man's character all out of shape and control his thoughts ... in the name of national security" struck him not as an advance, but as a way of ending life. In his magazine and in a 1961 book, Cousins summed up his argument: "Man is in possession today of almost total power but his instruments of control over that power are unscientific and indeed primitive." These technologies had created, Cousins believed, a "crisis of power without control."[20]

The threat of "power without control" also motivated one of the more surprising critics of defense policy, Dwight Eisenhower. After eight years of overseeing the American armed forces, he chose his farewell address as president to warn Americans of the domestic costs of permanent mobilization. Four of his points are most relevant here.

First, he affirmed that the United States had gained extraordinary power through post-World War II technology. Without naming specific weapons, he said that the country had gained the power to "utterly destroy this civilization." Second, he rued the maldistribution of power over that technology brought on by permanent mobilization. In one of his most famous phrases, he warned against a vast "military-industrial complex" that influenced every level of government and endangered "our liberties and democratic processes." Third, he criticized the power of money to direct research in universities, once "the fountainhead of free ideas and scientific discovery." Finally, he offered balance – between private and public economy, between costs and benefits, between short- and long-term planning – as the solution to these problems. In one paragraph alone, he used "balance" seven times.[21]

With this speech, Eisenhower made it respectable for centrists to criticize defense policy. (Ever after, critics of the "military-industrial complex" took care to cite Eisenhower as the source of the phrase.) The Cold War was not yet over, but even the commander in chief was having second thoughts about the price of waging it. Democracy itself, along with the physical well-being of its citizens, was threatened.

At the same time that news of fallout, nerve gas, and the military-industrial complex drifted into homes, so did pesticides. As more Americans took up gardening and yard care, pesticide manufacturers increased their marketing to this group of consumers. Several factors increased this market: movement to the suburbs, shorter work weeks, longer vacations, and daylight savings time.[22] A bevy of advertisements escorted insecticides onto the home market. When Union Carbide introduced its Eveready insecticide line, it announced that it would take out "full page color advertisements in *Better Homes & Gardens, Flower Grower* and *Popular Gardening,* as well as network spots on Union Carbide's Omnibus TV program. This national advertising program will be backed up in certain test areas by radio announcements and local newspaper space. In another move to attract attention to the new pesticide line, a series of awards will be offered for the 'Gardener of the Year.' Garden clubs are being asked to nominate entries to compete in the contest, which will involve answering 100 questions about pesticides and gardening." Awards included a trip to New York.[23]

Insecticide company leaders also devoted more publicity to the home market because the post-World War II synthetics had "won over" most government entomologists to pesticides. As an industry journal put it, "There is no longer any need for the industry to explain the benefits of chemical insecticides to extension workers and the Department of Agriculture. The thinking of the industry and the department is very close on the subject of chemical insecticides. The same time and effort formerly spent in meetings of the industry and the Department of Agriculture will bring a lot more results if the public can be ... kept informed of new pest control developments."[24]

Unfortunately, chemical companies sold the same products for home use that they sold for agricultural use, which meant wide spectrum and relatively toxic chemicals. The "logical toxicants for use in home garden pesticides would be pyrethrum, rotenone, ryania and similar materials which are essentially nontoxic to human and warm blooded animals," *Agricultural Chemicals* noted in 1953. But many companies entered the home market to expand sales of existing products, not to tailor-make new ones. So "the common toxicants in home garden products are DDT, chlordane, lindane, and methoxychlor." Only the most toxic chemicals – such as parathion – had stayed off the market. The journal suggested that insecticide formulators probably would have sold these lethal chemicals to home gardeners too, had the primary producers not decided "to keep such materials out of the hands of amateur applicators."[25] But poisonings still resulted, such as when an infant handling a mixture of parathion and DDT died in 1951.[26]

Although they may have been holding something toxic, homeowners had some control over house and garden insecticides. They had little control over agricultural and public health spraying. The exodus from city to suburb placed citizens near agricultural fields across the nation, increasing the frequency with which crop dusters sprayed people in homes and schools.[27] At the same time, two major government eradication programs sharply increased the number of people and area of private lands sprayed from the air.[28]

One program was against the gypsy moth in the Northeast. In 1958, J. I. Rodale noted that the gypsy moth program "was the first time that the highly populated northeastern area of the United States had dramatized to its populace the extent to which the chemical industry is today influencing our environment."[29] In 1957, the

U.S. Department of Agriculture, New Jersey, Pennsylvania, New York, and Michigan responded to the spread of the gypsy moth by spraying 3 million acres with DDT from the air. The short-term goal was to eradicate gypsy moths from the periphery of the infested area and suppress them in the center. The longer-term goal was to contain the gypsy moth east of the Berkshires and the Green Mountains of New England, and then to eradicate it completely. To federal entomologists, the 1957 effort was "simply an extension of the principles used in forest insect control for the past 12 years," and the increased area sprayed that year (a jump from 1 million to 3 million acres) was "hardly a gamble."[30]

In the second program, the Department of Agriculture took on the fire ant in the South. Planners expected to spray dieldrin or heptachlor (both chlorinated hydrocarbons) over 20 to 30 million acres in eight to ten southern states from the air and ground in 1958. "The objective," *Agricultural Chemicals* reported, "is to clean up areas completely and keep them clean as the program moves forward."[31]

The eradication programs alarmed gardeners. In March 1958, concern about the "danger to our natural resources as a result of the increased programs of mass spraying" led the Garden Clubs of America to sponsor a panel discussion on aerial pest control. Representatives from the Department of Agriculture and the National Agricultural Chemicals Association spoke in favor of mass spraying, while biologist Robert Cushman Murphy accused aerial applicators of being "trigger happy."[32]

Conservationists, who believed that the programs threatened wildlife, protested in even more venues. In December 1957, Assistant Secretary of the Interior Ross Leffler wrote Secretary of Agriculture Ezra Taft Benson to urge limits on aerial spraying and warn that dieldrin would threaten fish and wildlife. In early 1958, the Audubon Society asked the secretary of agriculture to suspend the fire ant spray program. The society went on record as opposing "all insect control programs in which highly toxic chemicals are broadcast unless incontrovertible evidence becomes available that no serious damage to human and wildlife resources will result."[33]

The struggle escalated a notch in mid-1958, when the Alabama Department of Conservation called on federal and state authorities to halt the spray program until they developed ways to protect people, fish, and wildlife. The department made this demand after surveying 100 sprayed acres and finding six dead rabbits, three dead quail, and forty-eight dead songbirds. "Hedgerows, fencerows, and small woods areas reeked with the odor of decaying bodies," the department reported. The department's director said, "There is even critical danger to citizens of Alabama who may get the insecticides from vegetables, milk, or other everyday necessities of life." Publications of national conservation organizations – such as the National Wildlife Federation and the Audubon Society – broadcast news of Alabama's action across the country and reported that "conservation groups all over the country are rallying to support of Alabama's position."[34]

That same year, *Field and Stream* carried an article whose title captured the special fear induced by aerial spraying: "Poison from the Air." It reported, "A recent magazine article created the impression that grave danger threatened vast areas of the country if total war was not declared at once on the fire ant." But once that "war began" with aerial spraying, the magazine warned, wildlife experts started to worry. One of the biggest problems was that "this big control program got off the ground *with no provision for finding out*" what the effects would be on wildlife. The tally of wildlife damage made for "grim reading" and included dead rabbits, foxes, a house cat, a skunk, birds, snakes, frogs, and birds.[35]

More members of the public took notice when conservationists' arguments spread to influential newspapers. The *New York Times* slammed the fire ant program in January 1958, when it editorialized that the Department of Agriculture's fire ant "cure … may well be infinitely worse than the fire ant's burn. It is rank folly for the Government to embark on an insect-control program of this scope without knowing precisely what damage the pesticide itself will do to both human and animal life, especially over a long period." The money spent on spraying, the editorial said, would be better spent on "studying just what the spread of toxic chemicals from the air will do to bird and animal life and reproduction, and to human health."[36]

Widely read magazines also spread news of the dangers of aerial spraying. In a 1959 article titled "Backfire in the War Against Insects," *Reader's Digest* reported a prediction by George J. Wallace, a zoologist at Michigan State University: "If this and other pest-eradication programs are carried out as now projected, we shall have been witnesses, within a single decade, to a greater extermination of animal life than in all the previous years of man's history on earth." The article concluded, "This may be a wildly pessimistic view. Nobody knows. But why risk it?"[37] In 1961, the *Saturday Evening Post* editorialized that "it is doubtful that the [fire ant] program justifies the slaughter of million of birds, fish and small game." Too often, it said, powerful pesticides were "broadcast by airplane in vast quantities and without due care."[38] On the heels of that piece came a critical article in the *Police Gazette*. ("Of all publications," *Agricultural Chemicals* groaned.)[39] In 1962, *Life* criticized pesticides in an article titled "War Against the Insects."[40] In 1960, *Sports Illustrated* published an article called "The Deadly Spray." "Man's chemical warfare against his insect enemies has at last reached the point where it threatens the well-being of man himself," the magazine charged.[41]

The reception of aerial spraying contrasted with that of fogging after World War II for several reasons. One was the publicity of other threats at the same time, including fallout, thalidomide, and chemical weapons. Another was that not everyone perceived the gypsy moth or the fire ant as a large threat. One of the leaders of the gypsy moth program noted that opposition was highest in areas where the gypsy moth was uncommon. There, citizens saw the eradication program as "a gigantic experiment making guinea pigs of an unsuspecting populations."[42]

Increased fear of insecticide toxicity also played an important role. All through the 1950s, insecticide makers saw themselves as embattled victims of alarmist critics, and especially those worried about residues on food. In 1951, the editor of *Agricultural Chemicals* complained about "this everlasting barrage of investigations, hearings, proposed legislation, and general harassment by obviously unqualified or prejudiced persons or agencies which makes the insecticide and fungicide business more of a nightmare with each passing day.... To summarize the whole thing bluntly, agricultural chemical producers are thoroughly disgusted."[43] One focus of disgust was Congress, specifically Representative James J. Delaney, who led hearings on insecticides beginning in 1950.[44] Although many witnesses testified about the benefits of pesticides at the hearings, some – such as physician M. S. Biskind and organic gardener J. I. Rodale – stressed their dangers. Delaney seemed to find testimony about dangers compelling. He published an article in *American Magazine* titled "Peril on Your Food Shelf."[45] The majority of the Delaney committee called for new legislation to protect the public from residues; a minority recommended no change in insecticide laws.[46]

Poisoning from residues was, if it occurred, a slow and subtle process. But acute poisoning, mainly of farm workers by organophosphates, was another matter. The number of insecticide poisoning cases rose as use of the organophosphates increased. The most dangerous organophosphate was parathion, which killed scores of farmers, crop dusters, and insecticide factory workers by 1957.[47] (To fight this trend, organophosphate insecticide factories used a blood test developed by the Chemical Corps for nerve gases. When parathion accidents did happen, the Chemical Corps used the resulting data to develop recommendations for diagnosing and treating nerve gas exposure. For both nerve gas and insecticide exposure, the treatment was the same: atropine injections and artificial respiration.)[48] The dangers of parathion were so great that the ability to decontaminate people and factories became a selling point. In 1959, parathion maker Victor Chemical advertised that it had "4 decontamination squads at your disposal 24 hours a day, 7 days a week, at 4 strategic locations."[49]

Scale was also important in leading to shifts in views. When *Agricultural Chemicals* challenged *Reader's Digest* on its apparent switch from support to criticism of insecticides, the latter replied that its criticism focused on large-scale spraying. "The whole question of massive aerial spraying of insecticides – and this rather than carefully evaluated spot eradication is the topic being discussed – remains hotly controversial."[50]

Control turned out to be one of the most important factors. Commenting on a mosquito spray program in Michigan, Alfred G. Etter wrote in 1959, "I can remember using flit and bug bombs and yellow bulbs. I had some control over them." Aerial spraying, on the other hand, made people "the poorer and the closer to slavery for this thundering monster with its cloud of poison spray that sends my dog and me cowering into the house."[51] J. I. Rodale argued that "hundreds of people would have felt that their rights were being infringed even if they were sprayed with pure water. Americans are like that, and because the chemical industry has failed to realize it, it is getting deeper and deeper into trouble."[52] In 1957, Wilhelmine Kirby Waller spoke out against the gypsy moth spray program at the National Audubon Society's convention by saying, "It seems to me that there is something in the air that smacks of dictatorship – a type of government never heretofore associated with our American way of life."[53]

Finally, being sprayed from the air was simply scary. Even proponents described aerial spraying as aerial combat, and it was not hard for the people below to feel like targets. *Agricultural Chemicals* said in 1958 that "flying a big aerial spray project is about the nearest thing one finds in civilian life to the operation of an aerial combat team in wartime. There are the same problems of logistics, the advance planning and strategy, briefing, reconnaissance and many of the same elements of hazard."[54] Not to mention metaphors. Diamond Chemicals advertised in February 1958 that "airplane applicators get a fast shot at the enemy. The successful ones make sure their ammunition is dependable."[55] R. E. Monroe, the assistant executive director of the National Aviation Trades Association, said in 1958 that agricultural aviation was "biological warfare" that demands "better ammunition, guns, and gunnery."[56]

The feeling of helplessness increased when citizens failed to halt spraying through a lawsuit. In a well-publicized case, thirty Long Island residents sued to stop aerial spraying of DDT. Witnesses for the plaintiffs in the 1958 trial included biologist Robert Cushman Murphy and Malcolm Hargraves, a hematologist at the Mayo Clinic. Hargraves suspected that DDT – which he compared to atomic radiation – and other chlorinated hydrocarbons caused leukemia, Hodgkin's disease, aplastic anemia, and other diseases. On the other hand, a key defense witness, Wayland J. Hayes of the U.S. Public Health Service, testified that tests on prisoners and industrial workers showed no harm from DDT.[57] The judge found the testimony of Hayes and other defense witnesses persuasive. Citing a lack of proof of harm, Judge Walter Bruchhausen ruled that "mass spraying has a reasonable relation to the public objective of combating the evil of the gypsy moth and thus is within the proper exercise of the police power by the designated officials."[58]

Some leading entomologists recognized that the large eradication projects gave entomology a black eye. Robert Metcalf, president of the Entomological Society of America, said at the society's 1958 annual meeting that "adverse publicity such as lawsuits

against widespread programs give nothing in return but bad publicity. Blanket aircraft applications of pesticides over highly populated areas represents the least selective approach to insect control
and should be employed with extreme caution."[59]

Proponents of the eradication programs responded to criticism with large public relations campaigns of their own. The U.S.
Department of Agriculture announced that domestic tomcats
posed a greater danger to birds than did the spray program. Its
own tests found no evidence that dieldrin posed danger to mammals or birds. The chemical would, however, kill fire ants for
three years. Paradoxically, the department also said, "It is far
safer to administer these poisons under federally supervised controls than to have them used by individual farmers who perhaps
may understand their efficiency but are not fully familiar with
their residual effects."[60] The department produced a film, *The
Fire Ant on Trial,* which summarized the case for the spray
campaign.[61]

Pesticide makers also counterattacked. The "pesticide industry
will take major steps to combat the series of complaints against
community-wide eradication programs," reported *Agricultural
Chemicals* in 1958. "Several individual companies are putting their
top management and public relations skills into the fray. NAC
[National Agricultural Chemicals Association] is sparking a drive
with industry and government to report more facts to the public."[62] As part of this effort, insecticide advocates argued that only
experts were qualified to judge pest control programs. *Agricultural
Chemicals* wrote *Reader's Digest* to criticize the qualifications of
the journalist who wrote the article critical of mass aerial spraying.
"Our own feeling is that when you get a public health problem
such as this, with its entomological background and scientific
overtones, the writing should be done by someone with specific
training in the particular science under discussion," the industry
journal argued.[63]

Opponents of aerial spraying often asserted the rights of individuals to be free of government intrusion; proponents argued for utilitarianism. The Department of Agriculture's L. S. Curl said that Americans must choose between "living with a new pest, its damages and costs of control, or taking measures to contain or eliminate it. To preserve our way of life, we have no choice other than to accept a limited calculated risk to a small portion of our natural resources here and there, in order to preserve the whole."[64] *Agricultural Chemicals* wrote, "The United States Department of Agriculture is in the best possible position to decide what action is needed to protect the interests of all of us, and to make its decision on the basis of the 'greatest good for the greatest number.'"[65]

Looking for analogies, the editors of *Agricultural Chemicals* turned to public health and national defense: "Much commotion has been raised by one particular New York newspaper ... about the right of a citizen to be free from the possible hazard involved in mass aerial spraying. We wonder if these bellicose members of the press would be equally vociferous and indignant in defense of a handful of moral objectors who might refuse to be inoculated when plague threatened, or a band of conscientious objectors refusing to share in national defense in time of emergency. We see all three cases as essentially parallel."[66]

Nature writer Rachel Carson also saw similarities between insecticide spraying and national defense programs, but from the opposite point of view. The Long Island DDT trial rekindled an old interest in the impact of pesticides on wildlife. Drawing largely on evidence presented at the trial, she authored a book detailing her criticisms. Her search for a framing metaphor led her to war. In 1961, she wrote a friend, "I told you that a possible opening sentence had drifted to the surface of my mind recently. It was – 'This is a book about man's war against nature, and because man is part of nature it is also and inevitably a book about man's war against himself.' Very plain and simple, but I thought perhaps it went to the heart of it. [Editor Paul Brooks] agrees. Out of our discussion of that came a couple of possible book titles – *The War against Nature,* or *At War with Nature.*"[67]

For reasons that are unclear, Brooks later suggested titling the book *Silent Spring.* An immediate blockbuster, the book sold half a million copies in hard cover, rode the best-seller list for thirty-one weeks, received glowing reviews, stimulated a presidential inquiry and congressional hearings, and helped make pesticides into powerful symbols of dangerous modern technologies.[68] *Silent Spring* also aroused hatred. Several scientists wrote scathing reviews, chemical companies mounted publicity counter-campaigns, and some readers thought the argument overwrought. H. Davidson of San Francisco wrote the *New Yorker,* which published excerpts from *Silent Spring,* to say, "As for insects, isn't it just like a woman to be scared to death of a few little bugs! As long as we have the H-bomb, everything will be O.K."[69] Davidson's praise for the H-bomb was ironic, because Carson relied on comparisons of pesticides to atomic fallout to help make her case. All the same factors that influenced the reaction against the eradication programs, plus a large base of research and eloquent writing, helped the book resonate with the public.

Lurking in the background was the Cold War. *Silent Spring* gave voice to the same sentiments that drove Dwight Eisenhower's farewell address in 1961. The war against communism and the war against insects, in their minds, created similar problems in human society.[70] We have no evidence that either party recognized similarities, but Carson's main points mirrored Eisenhower's.[71] First, the United States had gained extraordinary power through post-World War II technology. The cover of one edition of Carson's book described it as about "man-made pollutants that threaten to destroy life on this earth." Second, she rued the maldistribution of power over powerful technology brought on by the war against insects. She thought bad technology arose from "an era dominated by industry," especially when paired with "authoritarians" in government. Third, she criticized the power of money to direct research in universities. Industry used research funding to woo university scientists away from sensible biological control research in favor of more profitable chemical methods, she argued. And fourth, she offered balance – between private citizens and government, between people and nature, and within nature itself – as the solution to these problems.[72]

In making this argument, Carson relied on literal and metaphorical similarities between chemical warfare and pest control. She wrote that synthetic insecticides came from chemical warfare research during World War II, when "insects were widely used to test chemicals as agents of death for man." She went on to describe aerial spraying in the United States as chemical warfare that caught people and nature in its crossfire. Surplus airplanes from World War II produced "'an amazing rain of death' upon the surface of the earth." Carson talked of this rain as "chemical war," "chemical battle," "chemical barrage," "all-out chemical assault," "all-out chemical war," and "chemical death rain."[73]

This rhetoric helped *Silent Spring* act as a mirror in more ways than one. In its similarities to Eisenhower's critique, the book reflected a growing unease about the distribution and use of power in the United States. In its comparisons to chemical weapons, the book reversed the image of pesticides cultivated over the preceding decades. Yes, Carson's metaphors implied, pesticides were powerful weapons, just as publicists had been saying. But no, these weapons were not aimed just at insects: they were also aimed at her readers. In her words, "heedless and unrestrained use of chemicals is a greater menace to ourselves than to the targets"[74] (Figure 11.1).

At the same time, a conflict in a small Asian country called Vietnam mirrored the developments – technological, political, and ideological – on which Eisenhower and Carson focused. And, like

"ANOTHER SUCH VICTORY AND I AM UNDONE."

11.1 "Another Such Victory and I Am Undone." In this 1962 cartoon, Bill Mauldin suggested that Rachel Carson had reversed public perceptions of pesticides. Long portrayed as weapons in the war on insects, insecticides now looked like potentially lethal threats to their users. From Yale Collection of American Literature, Beinecke Rare Book and Manuscript Library, reprinted with special permission from the *Chicago Sun-Times*, Inc. @ 1999.

Silent Spring, Vietnam reversed the image of pesticides and the people who wielded them.

One touchpoint was the use of another class of miracle pesticides from World War II, phenoxyacetic herbicides. Prior to World War II, chemical herbicides were few and inefficient. Then research sponsored by the Office of Scientific Research and Development found that certain compounds (phenoxyacetic acids) killed plants at low concentrations. In 1944, the Chemical Warfare Service incorporated research on herbicides, including a promising phenoxyacetic chemical called 2,4-D, into its program. Scientists believed their discoveries made it realistic to starve enemy civilians by destroying their food supply. According to the head of the research program, George Merck, "Only the rapid ending of the war prevented field trials in an active theater of synthetic agents that would, without injury to human or animal life, affect the growing crops and make them useless."[75]

During World War II, Chemical Warfare Service officers also envisioned another wartime use for herbicides. After seeing chemical officers direct aerial DDT spraying in the Pacific, future chief Alden Waitt filed a report in which he suggested using chemicals "for tree-defoliation (to eliminate foliage screening Japanese positions)."[76] The British had the same idea in Malaya, where they thought herbicides would be useful to kill crops and reveal hiding places used by communist guerrillas.[77]

The United States considered the same two-pronged strategy in Vietnam. In 1962, a South Vietnamese official announced that the United States and South Vietnam would spray herbicides to destroy food crops and foliage relied on by communist guerrillas. The plan to destroy crops was dropped, but the jungle spraying program became the huge, well-known Operation Ranch Hand.[78] At home, the American chemical industry saw parallels between this program and the aerial pesticide sprayings that had stirred up such a public hornet's nest. Spray planes in Vietnam dropped pamphlets "assuring farmers that the chemicals were harmless to humans and animals." In February 1962, *Agricultural Chemicals* suggested, "Perhaps this would be a public relations move suitable for use in the United States when large-scale spray programs must be carried on near populated areas. Not over a community that is touchy about 'litter bugs,' however."[79]

At the same time the herbicide spray program got under way, a chemical house-that-Jack-built sequence undermined the American cause. American DDT was sprayed to kill malaria-carrying mosquitoes, cats disappeared from sprayed areas, and field rats (thought to have been kept under control by the cats) devastated crops in six South Vietnamese provinces. "As a result," reported *Agricultural Chemicals*, "the hungry, rural population is tending to support the communist insurgents because they believe (however erroneously) DDT to be responsible for the disaster."[80]

Industrial publicists sensed a public relations disaster in the offing. Within a month, *Agricultural Chemicals* reversed course. "'I didn't raise my pesticide to be a soldier' could be adopted as the theme of the pesticide industry, and with just cause," wrote *Agricultural Chemicals* in March 1962 when it reported on the DDT and herbicide controversies. "It might be well in the future for a country planning to use pesticides as a weapon of war to consider the side effects and the very good chance that there will be adverse publicity. The Vietnamese operations may have set an unfortunate precedent to which aggressors of the future can point while waging 'germ' warfare."[81]

For liberals and conservatives alike, chemical warfare became a benchmark of the severity of the war. Liberals thought the war too severe. In 1963, *The New Republic* charged that the "silent war in South Viet-Nam (or should one say: silenced)" had entered a new phase with the use of defoliants. The Pentagon's denial of using poison gas "is true only if one postulates an essential difference between something poisonous and something highly toxic," it argued. A defoliant "hits the hapless peasants – men, women, and children – caught up in the midst of this murderous war."[82] The same year, Bertrand Russell wrote that use of napalm bombs and defoliants "constitutes and results in atrocities, and points to the fact that this is a war of annihilation."[83] For conservatives, the war was not severe enough. Echoing arguments made during the Korean War, *National Review* countered, "The best way for the United States to achieve its military aims in Southeast Asia would be to rely on chemical warfare" because it drew on "our real strength: the production of weapons that can effectively counter a very numerous foe."[84]

What a different world from the one Tocqueville had described. In his view, nature protected American democracy by shielding the country from human enemies. Nature's free defense kept the army and the state (the two biggest threats to democracy) small. Now oceans no longer sufficed for national defense. Technology had made the world smaller, increasing the interests of Americans overseas and the vulnerability of the country to attack. The country became permanently mobilized, ensuring a large army and state (often called the National Security State). The rise of total war, in which technology substituted for soldiers, joined permanent mobilization in creating a large civilian interest group permanently concerned just as intimately with war as were the army and the state. Eisenhower argued for the historical novelty of this arrangement, saying, "This conjunction of an immense military establishment and a large arms industry is new in the American experience."[85]

Tocqueville had offered a second reason why nature advanced American democracy. By creating a bounty available to all, nature created a large middle class that quelled agitation by upper and lower classes. In the perception of Eisenhower and Carson, this too had changed. Tocqueville's nature, like Turner's frontier, had been physical, and the federal government had transferred it rapidly to private individuals. In theory, the endless frontier of Vannevar Bush did the same: pioneer scientists pushed the frontier back, and the rest of the citizenry followed in their footsteps to reap the rewards. In many ways they did. But Bush's frontier struck Eisenhower and Carson as less democratic than Turner's or Tocqueville's. The new pioneers were an educated class, a "scientific-technological elite" that wielded disproportionate economic and political power because of their ability to control nature.

In mobilizing against human and natural enemies, Eisenhower and Carson argued, members of this elite class all too easily lost sight of what they were ostensibly trying to protect. In Eisenhower's words, "We must never let the weight of this combination endanger our liberties or democratic processes."[86] The fight to save people and crops from insects, Carson argued, had led to "contamination of man's total environment."[87] Officially at peace, Eisenhower and Carson argued, the United States bore the burdens usually associated with war. It was waging peaceful war.

12

Epilogue

For the rest of the twentieth century, Americans looked at many of the events described here as mirrors of their hopes, fears, and ideas. When asked in the 1980s why they worked on nuclear weapons, scientists at Los Alamos and Sandia National Laboratories relied most often on the philosophy of deterrence and the history of DDT. The interviewer summarized their interpretation of the latter this way: "DDT was trumpeted as a great discovery. It promised only beneficial outcomes: malaria a thing of the past, increased crop yields, large victories for humans in their competition with insect species. Who could have predicted what would happen as the miracle chemical worked its way up the food chain?"[1] The reasoning was sophistry, but it illustrated the enduring links between weapons of mass destruction and pest control.

Insecticides appeared regularly in the headlines through the turn of the century. In the short run, *Silent Spring* helped set off a national reconsideration of pesticides and pesticide policy. Pushed along by the rise of environmental groups, this effort had one of its most prominent effects when the U.S. Environmental Protection Agency banned most domestic uses of DDT in 1972. Soon after, the agency banned several of DDT's relatives. They included aldrin and dieldrin, the twin compounds manufactured by Shell at the Chemical Corps's Rocky Mountain Arsenal.[2] Along with other factors, *Silent Spring* helped stimulate research on new approaches to pest control. One of the most popular, integrated pest management, foreswore the idea that all insects in a field were enemies in need of extermination. Instead, practitioners of this system sprayed only when insect populations crossed a threshold that made spraying economical.[3] In 1999, when *Time* magazine named "the 100 most influential people" of the twentieth century, Carson (along with Einstein, Freud, Salk, and Keynes) appeared on the magazine's cover.[4]

But farmers, public health officials, the armed forces, and homeowners continued to rely heavily on insecticides, and insects continued to evolve resistance. By 1986, at least 447 species of insects and mites resisted insecticides (along with at least 100 species of plant pathogens and forty-eight species of weeds).[5] A similar pattern held with antibiotics. The Centers for Disease Control and Prevention announced in 1995 that doctors were prescribing expensive, wide spectrum drugs rather than cheaper, narrowly targeted drugs, contributing to an evolution of drug-resistant microbes. Resistance was thought to contribute to the 60,000 deaths each year in the United States from hospital-acquired infections.[6]

Chemical weapons also hit the headlines regularly through the turn of the century. In 1969, President Richard Nixon renounced the first use of chemical weapons, as well as the use of biological weapons altogether, and asked the Senate to ratify the Geneva Protocol of 1925 because "mankind already carries in its own hands too many of the seeds of its own destruction."[7] The Senate ratified the Geneva Protocol (along with the Biological Weapons Convention, the first post-World War II agreement to eliminate an entire class of weapons), and Gerald Ford signed both in 1975.[8] In 1997, after negotiations under Republican and Democratic presidents alike, the U.S. Senate ratified a new Chemical Weapons Convention. In contrast to its earlier stance, the American Chemical Society supported the treaty. (Among other things, the treaty would have restricted trade by chemical companies based in countries that did not ratify the treaty.)[9]

By the 1990s, the idea that war had a major impact on the environment had percolated into public consciousness. Journalists and scholars raised warning flags about "ecological warfare" throughout the Persian Gulf War. The clouds created when Iraq set Kuwaiti oil wells alight became powerful symbols of Iraq's misdeeds. When researchers examined military bases inside the United States, they found an expensive toxic legacy of military activities. In 1995, the Congressional Budget Office estimated that the United States would have to spend $30 billion to clean up contaminated military bases, in addition to the $11 billion already spent by that year.[10] But war still provided a powerful incentive to ignore environmental concerns. In last-minute negotiations in Tokyo over greenhouse emissions in 1997, the United States successfully inserted a provision allowing countries to emit greenhouse gases without limit during overseas operations.[11]

The Persian Gulf War also revived public awareness of chemical weapons. In 1997, the Pentagon estimated that 27,000 American troops could have been exposed to gas, including sarin, when the United States blew up an Iraqi depot in 1991.[12] (Metaphorical links between war and pest control also continued. A pest control company ran an advertisement, in the wake of the Gulf War, in which an exterminator targeted and attacked pests in the same way smart missiles targeted and attacked Iraqi targets.)[13] The potential for chemical sabotage became all too clear in 1995, when a Japanese cult killed twelve people (and wounded some 5,000 more) by releasing sarin gas in the Tokyo subway system.[14] In 1997, Secretary of State Madeleine K. Albright said that "the most overriding security interest of our time" was the spread of chemical and biological weapons in the Middle East and Persian Gulf.[15] Defense Secretary William Cohen warned, "The front lines are not longer overseas" because criminal organization, cults, and foreign countries could release chemical and biological weapons inside the United States. Cheaper to make and easier to disperse than nuclear weapons, such weapons were "the poor man's atomic bomb."[16]

The end of the Cold War shed some light on the history of chemical weapons in the United States. The General Accounting Office reported in 1994 that the army had tested chemicals on about 3,500 army and air force personnel. Some of the chemical agents could cause diseases, such as leukemia, emphysema, and cancer, years after exposure. Defense officials said that researchers had not followed all of the 1947 Nuremberg Code of Ethics, which set out rules for tests on human beings (and which the secretary of defense had ordered the armed forces to follow). Among other things, subjects had not been able to exercise informed consent to tests in the 1950s and 1960s.[17]

Looking back, we can see similarities in efforts to control human and insect enemies. Wars on human and insect enemies both focused on enemies, especially enemies that did not respect *boundaries*. Once erected, international borders, fence rows, and the walls of homes created the rights of citizens, farmers, and homeowners to protect their land and homes against "invading" enemies – including, ironically, some longtime residents. American farmers referred to insects in fields as "invaders" and "trespassers" although most insects had arrived long before the farmers.[18] The emphasis on protection against outsiders helps to explain the popularity of "extermination," or driving beyond boundaries, as a term for dealing with both human and insect enemies.[19]

Like physical structures, mental divisions between human beings and nature created useful boundaries, especially because one could move human beings and animals from one side of the boundary to the other. Describing insects as national enemies on par with Japanese soldiers elevated "bugs" from the category of "nuisance" to national threat. This did not always imply exaggeration. In the Pacific, for example, malaria-carrying mosquitoes caused more casualties than enemy soldiers, making them important dangers for armies. Movement of people into the category of "animal" had consequences of far more horrifying significance. Wouk emphasized that the ability to redefine a human being as an insect was an "asset beyond price" in a military setting, but an asset that resulted in "massacres."

Not coincidentally, human beings developed similar technologies to kill human and insect enemies. In some cases, farmers and armies used identical chemicals (chloropicrin and hydrogen cyanide) to kill their enemies. In others, closely related chemicals (arsenicals and organophosphates) served both purposes. In yet another, use of a relatively innocuous chemical to human beings (DDT) relied on chemical warfare equipment on airplanes to place, in the words of a historian, "the attack against mosquitoes on an entirely different plane."[20] For chemical warriors, at least, these similarities came as no surprise. As previously mentioned, Major General William Porter, chief of the Chemical Warfare Service, noted in 1944, "The fundamental biological principles of poisoning Japanese, insects, rats, bacteria and cancer are essentially the same."[21]

The development of common technologies relied on alliances, usually organized by nation-states, between civilian and military institutions. The world wars and the Cold War forged especially close links between military and scientific institutions, and efforts to maintain such links became hallmarks of the post-World War II era. Against both kinds of enemies, it turned out, the army became the institution most interested in research to find new solutions to problems raised when opponents evolved ways to counter new technology.

Although linked metaphorically, technologically, and institutionally, wars on insects and human beings differed in several respects. First, control of poisons rested in different hands. Almost anyone could use insecticides, but chemical weapons remained the purview of military (or terrorist) institutions. Second, insecticides and poison gases followed different trajectories in American war efforts. Insecticides became "miracle chemicals" used widely to halt insect-borne diseases. Whether because of the Geneva Protocol of 1925 or for other reasons, however, combatants (with the probable exception of Japan) did not use poison gas on battlefields. But another kind of chemical weapon, the incendiary bomb, proved efficient at this task. Third, morality usually did not enter discussions of killing insects, while it often figured in debates about human warfare. In fact, moral concerns help to explain the popularity of insect metaphors for human enemies. Western thought has long regarded conquest of nature as a moral duty, rather than a moral dilemma, and conquest of insects offered an especially useful metaphor for human warfare. The implicit appropriateness of eliminating natural enemies entirely, exemplified in the lack of moral connotations of the term "extermination," suggests that ideas about complete conquest of nature contributed to the ideology of war on human beings.

The rhetoric of exterminating or annihilating enemies – whether insect or human – antedated the twentieth century. What set that century apart were the technology and bureaucratic organizations that enabled nations to carry out extermination campaigns on a far larger scale. The growth of technology and institutions, often under the sponsorship of nation-states, made it feasible to kill enemies with chemical compounds more quickly, and over a wider area, than ever before. Annihilation of national and natural enemies had become realistic on a large scale, a reality both comforting and disturbing to people who lived in the post-World War II era. The twin insecurities raised by military and civilian technology illustrated that war and environmental change were not separate endeavors, but rather related aspects of life in the twentieth century.

One of the best places to see these linkages made concrete was at Rocky Mountain Arsenal. There, using the same equipment, Shell made insecticides and the Chemical Corps made chemical weapons. By 2000, Rocky Mountain Arsenal no longer produced either kind of chemical, but the residues of both remained. In 1987, extensive soil and water contamination led the Environmental Protection Agency to place Rocky Mountain Arsenal on its National Priorities List for toxic cleanup.[22]

Rocky Mountain Arsenal was an environmental disaster, but it was also a symbol of hope. Toxic chemicals contaminated about 15 percent of the arsenal's twenty-seven square miles, but the rest had stood "off limits" for decades for security reasons and provided ideal wildlife habitat.[23] So too with other military sites. The demilitarized zone of Korea became one of the most bountiful nature preserves in Asia, providing homes to endangered species and migratory birds. Peace, environmentalists worried, would destroy the sanctuary by opening it to suburbanization.[24] In the United States, the army turned over pieces of Illinois prairie, Maine woods, California beaches, and northern Virginia meadows to other agencies, such as the U.S. Fish and Wildlife Service, to manage as wildlife refuges or parks. By 2000, the army had transferred as much as 100,000 acres.[25] So war, in its many guises, helped as well as harmed the environment. Such was the nature of life in the most ironic of centuries.

Primary sources

This study relied as much as possible on primary sources. Records of the Preventive Medicine Service are part of the collection of the Office of the Surgeon General (Record Group 112) of the National Archives and Records Administration. The records were housed at the Washington National Records Center in Suitland, Maryland, when I examined them. They later moved to the National Archives building in College Park, Maryland. The most important series for understanding the service's efforts to control typhus was that of the USA Typhus Commission (Entry 343). The most important series for understanding the service's efforts to control malaria in the Pacific were General Subject File (Entry 29), Security Classified General Subject File (Entry 30), and World War II Administrative Records.

The Chemical Warfare Service is a difficult agency to study. Its records remain heavily classified (especially as one moves closer to the present), and its declassified records are scattered and incompletely indexed. The National Archives and Records Administration's collection for the Chemical Warfare Service (Record Group 175) was housed in Suitland, Maryland and then in College Park, Maryland. I examined them in both locations. The most important records for this study were in the Historian's

Background Files, R&D Case Files, Miscellaneous Series Correspondence (Entry 2B), and Assistant Chief for Materiel, Technical Division, General Administrative Series, 1942–1945 (Entry 4L). Archivists in College Park suggested that I use a hand-written list, apparently created for the move, as a finding aid, which guided me to records in the series 67A4900. The hand-written list did not use the entry number system employed in most National Archives finding aids, and it was unclear how long archivists would continue to rely on it. I have cited records as they were categorized when I examined them. The important Historian's Background Files and R&D Files were included under that entry, which I had not encountered in Suitland. Unfortunately, archivists were unable to locate some items on the list (including parts of the Historian's Background Files). The Chemical Warfare Service's journals – *Chemical Warfare, Chemical Warfare Bulletin, Chemical Corps Journal,* and *Armed Forces Chemical Journal* – were very useful; they published a great deal of information unavailable in archival records.

Allied intelligence reports on the German chemical warfare program, including the overlapping research on organophosphates and insecticides, are in the Library Project Files (often called the P file) of the Assistant Chief of Staff (G-2) Intelligence, Administrative Division, U.S. Army (Record Group 319) at the National Archives. I examined these records in Suitland, but they were later moved to College Park.

Research in the archives of the National Academy of Sciences in Washington, D.C., was critical. As described in this book, the Office of Scientific Research and Development created an umbrella committee to bring together research on chemical warfare and pest control in World War II. This committee transferred to the National Academy of Sciences/National Research Council near the end of the war, and its records transferred with it. (Other records of the Office of Scientific Research and Development went to the National Archives.) Most of the records are found under Committee on Insect Control or Insect Control Committee (both names were used). Records of various other committees of the National Research Council were also useful, especially Chemical-Biological Coordination Center, Committees on Military Medicine, Committee on Sanitary Engineering and Environment, and Advisory Board on Quartermaster Research and Development.

To study federal entomologists, I used National Archives records of the Bureau of Entomology/Bureau of Entomology and Plant Quarantine (Record Group 7) in Suitland and the Office of the Secretary of Agriculture (Record Group 16) in Washington. Both have since moved to College Park. Records are plentiful through the end of World War II but thin considerably thereafter. I also interviewed entomologists who worked on pest control in World War II: Vincent G. Dethier, September 18, 1992, Edward F. Knipling, September 10 and 16, 1992, Robert Metcalf, November 3, 1992, and Curtis Sabrosky, June 20, 1991. To get a systematic sense of research emphases in entomology, I analyzed the indexes for every fifth year of *Journal of Economic Entomology,* as well as the table of contents of all books on entomology in the National Agricultural Library in Beltsville, Maryland. This analysis enabled me to chart the relative importance of chemical, biological, and cultural methods of pest control over time.

Public relations offices of chemical companies and industry groups did not respond to requests for information and refused permission to reprint advertisements. Two journals provided excellent coverage of the industry, *Soap and Sanitary Chemicals* and *Agricultural Chemicals.* Neither is indexed, so I looked at all issues of the former from 1926 (when it began publication) through World War II and the latter from 1946 (when it began publication) to 1962. Other chemical industry journals, indexed in the *Industrial Arts Index,* were also useful. The *AIFA Newsletter* (for Agricultural Insecticides and Fungicides Association, which became the National Agricultural Chemicals Association after World War II) was useful for understanding World War II; the newsletter is in the National Agricultural Library in Beltsville, Maryland. In the National Archives, records of the War Production Board (Record Group 179) are especially important.

To trace the way institutions portrayed themselves to the public, and the way journalists and others viewed those institutions, I relied most heavily on the *Reader's Guide to Periodical Literature,* the *New York Times Index,* and congressional hearings and speeches.

Books and journals were also important primary sources but, because they are relatively easy to locate and too numerous to list, they are not discussed here. The notes identify the most important.

Abbreviations

AC	*Agricultural Chemicals*
AFCJ	*Armed Forces Chemical Journal*
GPO	U. S. Government Printing Office
NARA	National Archives and Records Administration, Suitland, Maryland, Washington, D.C., and College Park, Maryland
NAS	National Academy of Sciences, Washington, D.C.
NMAH	National Museum of American History, Smithsonian Institution, Washington, D.C.
NRC	National Research Council, NAS
NYT	*New York Times*
RG 7	Bureau of Entomology/Bureau of Entomology and Plant Quarantine, U.S. Department of Agriculture, NARA
RG 16	Office of the Secretary of Agriculture, NARA
RG 92	Office of the Quartermaster General, U.S. Army, NARA
RG 112	Office of the Surgeon General, U.S. Army, NARA
RG 175	Chemical Warfare Service/Chemical Corps, U.S. Army, NARA
RG 179	War Production Board, NARA
RG 227	Office of Scientific Research and Development, NARA

RG 319   Assistant Chief of Staff (G-2) Intelligence, Admin-
         istrative Division, U.S. Army, NARA
SSC   *Soap and Sanitary Chemicals*
TL   Truman Library, Independence, Missouri
WNRC   Washington National Records Center, Suitland,
         Maryland

Notes

1 "Nature Abounds in Shadow of Lethality," *Washington Post,* 9 Oct. 1996; William Cronon (ed.), *Uncommon Ground* (New York: W. W. Norton, 1996), 28, 59; Rocky Mountain Arsenal, "Wildlife at the Refuge," n.p., viewed 18 Nov. 1999 *(http://www.pmrma.army.mil/htdores/refuge/wildrma.html).*

2 "Nature Abounds."

3 William Booth, "Ecosystem Paradoxically Glows at Former Atomic Bomb Factory Site," *Washington Post,* 26 May 1996; Mary Jordan, "New Rallying Cry: Save the DMZ," *Washington Post,* 8 Oct. 1997.

4 Isaiah 2:4.

5 Karl von Clausewitz, *On War,* (O. J. Matthijs Jolles, trans.) (Washington: Combat Forces Press, 1953), 5, 85 (emphasis added).

6 On humans and nature, see Keith Thomas, *Man and the Natural World: A History of the Modern Sensibility* (New York: Pantheon Books, 1983). "Quanta" from Joseph A. Wildermuth, letter to *Washington Post Book World,* 20 Feb. 1994, 14. David Noble suggests that neoclassical economics (which views the military as an "externality") and "the peculiarly American blindness to the presence of the military" contribute to the view that civilian and military enterprises are separate endeavors. David F. Noble, "Command Performance: A Perspective on the Social and Economic Consequences of Military Enterprise," in Merritt Roe Smith (ed.), *Military Enterprise and Technical Change: Perspectives on the American Experience* (Cambridge, Mass.: MIT Press, 1985), 329–346, see 330–331.

Historians of insecticides have shown, however, that efforts to control human and natural enemies have not proceeded independently. Emory Cushing, Vincent Dethier, Thomas Dunlap, and John Perkins have pointed out that manufacturing of explosives in World War I produced a by-product called paradichlorobenzene (PDB), which entomologists then developed into an insecticide; that entomologists often used military metaphors; that World War II stimulated development of DDT; and that some insecticides were related to nerve gases. Historians of chemical weapons, too, have noted this last point. John H. Perkins, *Insects, Experts, and the Insecticide Crisis: The Quest for New Pest Management Strategies* (New York: Plenum, 1982), 4–10; John H. Perkins, "Reshaping Technology in Wartime: The Effect of Military Goals on Entomological Research and Insect-Control Practices," *Technology and Culture* 19 (no. 2, 1978): 169–186; Thomas R. Dunlap, *DDT: Scientists, Citizens, and Public Policy* (Princeton: Princeton University Press, 1981), 36–37, 59–63; Emory C. Cushing, *History of Entomology in World War II* (Washington: Smithsonian Institution, 1957); V. G. Dethier, *Man's Plague? Insects and Agriculture* (Princeton: Darwin Press, 1976), 112; and Stockholm International Peace Research Institute, *The Problem of Chemical and Biological Warfare: A Study of the Historical, Technical, Military, Legal, and Political Aspects of CBW, and Possible Disarmament Measures*, vol. 1: *The Rise of CB Weapons* (New York: Humanities Press, 1971), 70–75.

[7] For overviews of military history, see Peter Paret, "The New Military History," *Parameters* 21 (autumn 1991): 10–18, and the special issue of *Journal of Military History* 57 (Special Issue, Oct. 1993). On links between military and civilian endeavors, see William H. McNeill, *The Pursuit of Power: Technology, Armed Force, and Society Since A. D. 1000* (Chicago: University of Chicago Press, 1982); Lewis Mumford, *Technics and Civilization* (New York: Harcourt, Brace & World, 1963); Lewis Mumford, *The Myth of the Machine*, vol. 2: *The Pentagon of Power* (New York: Harcourt Brace Jovanovich, 1970); and John U. Nef, *War and Human Progress: An Essay on the Rise of Industrial Civilization* (New York: W. W. Norton, 1968).

For overviews of environmental history, see Carolyn Merchant (ed.), *Major Problems in American Environmental History* (Lexington, Mass.: D. C. Heath, 1993); Donald Worster (ed.), *The Ends of the Earth: Perspectives on Modern Environmental History* (New York: Cambridge University Press, 1988); Kendall E. Bailes (ed.), *Environmental History: Critical Issues in Comparative Perspective* (Lanham, Md.: University Press of America, 1985); Lester J. Bilsky (ed.), *Historical Ecology: Essays on Environment and Social Change* (Port Washington, N.Y.: Kennikat Press,

1980); the roundtable in *Journal of American History* 76 (Mar. 1990): 1087–1147; John Opie, *Nature's Nation: An Environmental History of the United States* (Fort Worth: Harcourt Brace College Publishers, 1998).

For overviews of environmental and military issues in the history of technology, see Jeffrey K. Stine and Joel A. Tarr, "Technology and the Environment: The Historians' Challenge," *Environmental History Review* 18 (spring 1994): 1–7; Smith, *Military Enterprise*; Barton C. Hacker, "Military Institutions, Weapons, and Social Change: Toward a New History of Military Technology," *Technology and Culture* 35 (no. 4, 1994): 768–834; and Alex Roland, "Technology and War: The Historiographical Revolution of the 1980s," *Technology and Culture* 34 (Jan. 1993): 117–134.

Works on war and culture include Elaine Tyler May, *Homeward Bound: American Families in the Cold War Era* (New York: Basic Books, 1988); John Morton Blum, *V Was for Victory: Politics and American Culture During World War II* (New York: Harcourt Brace Jovanovich, 1976); Paul Boyer, *By the Bomb's Early Light: American Thought and Culture at the Dawn of the Atomic Age* (Chapel Hill: University of North Carolina Press, 1994); Paul Fussell, *The Great War and Modern Memory* (New York: Oxford University Press, 1975).

Works on war and the environment include Susan D. Lanier-Graham, *The Ecology of War: Environmental Impacts of Weaponry and Warfare* (New York: Walker and Company, 1993); Michele Stenehjem Gerber, *On the Home Front: The Cold War Legacy of the Hanford Nuclear Site* (Lincoln: University of Nebraska Press, 1992); Seth Shulman, *The Threat at Home: Confronting the Toxic Legacy of the United States Military* (Boston: Beacon Press, 1992); J. P. Robinson, *The Effects of Weapons on Ecosystems* (Oxford: Pergamon Press, 1979); Arthur H. Westing and Malvern Lumsden, *Threat of Modern Warfare to Man and His Environment: An Annotated Bibliography Prepared Under the Auspices of the International Peace Research Association* (Paris: UNESCO, 1979); Ralph H. Lutts, "Chemical Fallout: Rachel Carson's *Silent Spring,* Radioactive Fallout, and the Environmental Movement," *Environmental Review* 9 (fall 1985): 210–225; Avner Offer, *The First World War: An Agrarian Interpretation* (Oxford: Clarendon Press, 1989); Alfred W. Crosby, *Ecological Imperialism: The Biological Expansion of Europe, 900–1900* (New York: Cambridge University Press, 1986); William H. Durham, *Scarcity and Survival in Central America: Ecological Origins of the Soccer War* (Stanford: Stanford University Press, 1979); Roy A. Rappaport, *Pigs for the Ancestors: Ritual in the Ecology of a New Guinea People* (New Haven, Conn.: Yale University Press, 1984); Arthur H. Westing (ed.), *Explosive Remnants of War: Mitigating the Environmental Effects* (London: Taylor and Francis, 1985).

8 Bernard S. Schlessinger and June H. Schlessinger (eds.), *The Who's Who of Nobel Prize Winners 1901–1995,* 3rd ed. (Phoenix: Oryx Press, 1996), 110–111.

9 This book approaches ideology, especially metaphorical links between war and pest control, in much the same spirit as Arthur Lovejoy. He wrote, "There are, first, implicit or incompletely explicit *assumptions,* or more or less *unconscious mental habits,* operating in the thought of an individual or a generation. It is the beliefs which are so much a matter of course that they are rather tacitly pre-supposed than formally expressed and argued for, the ways of thinking which seem so natural and inevitable that they are not scrutinized with the eye of logical self-consciousness, that often are most decisive of the character of a philosopher's doctrine, and still oftener of the dominant intellectual tendencies of an age." Arthur O. Lovejoy, *The Great Chain of Being: A Study of the History of an Idea* (Cambridge: Harvard University Press, 1936), 7 (emphasis in original). For arguments on imagination and war in the twentieth century similar to those here, see Craig M. Cameron, *American Samurai: Myth, Imagination, and the Conduct of Battle in the First Marine Division, 1941–1951* (Cambridge: Cambridge University Press, 1994); and Michael S. Sherry, *The Rise of American Air Power: The Creation of Armageddon* (New Haven, Conn.: Yale University Press, 1987).

On the key role of metaphor in thought and communication, see David E. Leary, "Psyche's Muse: The Role of Metaphor in the History of Psychology," in *Metaphors in the History of Psychology,* ed. David E. Leary (Cambridge: Cambridge University Press, 1990), 1–78; Robert J. Sternberg, *Metaphors of Mind: Conceptions of the Nature of Intelligence* (Cambridge: Cambridge University Press, 1990); George Lakoff and Mark Johnson, *Metaphors We Live By* (Chicago: University of Chicago Press, 1980); George Lakoff, *Women, Fire, and Dangerous Things: What Categories Reveal About the Mind* (Chicago: University of Chicago Press, 1987); Howard Margolis, *Patterns, Thinking, and Cognition: A Theory of Judgment* (Chicago: University of Chicago Press, 1987); Mary B. Hesse, *Models and Analogies in Science* (Notre Dame, Ind.: University of Notre Dame Press, 1966); Andrew Ortony (ed.), *Metaphor and Thought* (Cambridge: Cambridge University Press, 1979); Max Black, *Models and Metaphors: Studies in Language and Philosophy* (Ithaca: Cornell University Press, 1962); and Susan Sontag, *Illness as Metaphor* (New York: Farrar, Straus, and Giroux, 1978).

10 Alden H. Waitt, *Gas Warfare* (New York: Duell, Sloan and Pearce, [1942]), 7–8.

11 Leo P. Brophy, Wyndham D. Miles, and Rexmond C. Cochrane, *The Chemical Warfare Service: From Laboratory to Field* (Washington: Office of the Chief of Military History, 1959), 27; Waitt, *Gas Warfare,* 11.

12 James B. Scott (ed.), *The Hague Conventions and Declarations of 1899 and 1907* (New York: Oxford University Press, 1915), 225–226; Calvin Dearmond Davis, *The United States and the First Hague Peace Conference* (Ithaca: Cornell University Press, 1962), 119.

13 Davis, *First Hague Peace Conference,* 119.

14 Seth Low, "The International Conference of Peace," *North American Review* (Nov. 1899): 625–639, see 629.

15 James Brown Scott (ed.), *Reports to the Hague Conferences of 1899 and 1907* (London: Clarendon Press, 1917), 131, 177.

16 Scott, *The Hague Conventions and Declarations of 1899 and 1907,* 116, 232, 236.

17 E. C. Holton, "Insecticides and Fungicides," *Industrial and Engineering Chemistry* 18 (Sept. 1926): 931–933, see 931.

18 Quoted in James Whorton, *Before Silent Spring: Pesticides and Public Policy in Pre-DDT America* (Princeton: Princeton University Press, 1974), 15.

19 E. O. Essig, *A History of Entomology* (New York: Macmillan, 1931), 442–448; Herbert Leopold, "Pyrethrum – A Long-Range View of Production and Markets in Japan," *SSC* 14 (Sept. 1938): 86; John Powell, "Pyrethrum 1917–1931," *SSC* 7 (Oct. 1931): 93.

20 Powell, "Pyrethrum 1917–1931," 95.

21 Alfred Weed, "Pyrethrum – Its Agricultural Future," *SSC* 6 (Nov. 1930): 107ff.

22 Dunlap, *DDT,* 18–19.

23 Holton, "Insecticides and Fungicides."

24 *Oxford English Dictionary,* 2nd ed.

25 James J. Walsh, *The Thirteenth: Greatest of Centuries* (New York: Catholic Summer School Press, 1910).

26 Geoffrey Lean, Don Hinrichsen, and Adam Markham, *Atlas of the Environment* (New York: Prentice-Hall, 1990), 17, 19, 25.

27 "Millennium of Wars," *Washington Post,* 13 Mar. 1999.

28 Alexis de Tocqueville, *Democracy in America,* vol. 1 (New York: Vintage, 1945), 301–302.

29 Alexis de Tocqueville, *Democracy in America,* vol. 2 (New York: Vintage, 1990), 268–269, 285.

30 Tocqueville, *Democracy,* 2:252–254, 264.

31 Tocqueville, *Democracy,* 2:268, 277, 281, 285.

32 Tocqueville, *Democracy,* 1:452.

[33] William Cronon, "A Place for Stories: Nature, History, and Narrative," *Journal of American History* 78 (Mar. 1992): 1347–1376.

CHAPTER 2. THE LONG REACH OF WAR (1914–1917)

[1] William H. Nichols, "The War and the Chemical Industry," *Science* 41 (8 Jan. 1915): 37–47, see 38. Nichols founded the Nichols Copper Company (later Phelps Dodge Refining Corp.). Williams Haynes, *American Chemical Industry*, vol. 3: *The World War I Period: 1912–1922* (New York: D. Van Nostrand Company, Inc., 1945), 81.

[2] L. H. Baekeland, "Chemistry and Preparedness," *World's Work* 32 (Sept. 1916): 499–512, see 499–500; James R. Withrow, "The American Chemist and the War's Problems," *Science* 43 (16 June 1916): 835–842, see 836.

[3] "American Chemical Industry Leaps Forward under the Spur of War," *Current Opinion*, Nov. 1917, 349–350, see 349.

[4] Benedict Crowell, *America's Munitions, 1917–1918* (Washington: GPO, 1919), 104.

[5] Haynes, *American Chemical Industry*, 3:202.

[6] James Q. Du Pont, "The Du Pont Company and National Defense," *AFCJ* 10 (Mar.–Apr. 1956): 20ff., see 45.

[7] Withrow, "American Chemist," 842; Charles Baskerville, "Our Chemical Industries after the War," *American Review of Reviews* 59 (June 1919): 618–622, see 618.

[8] Fred Aftalion, *A History of the International Chemical Industry* (Philadelphia: University of Pennsylvania, 1991), 102–104, 115–116; Haynes, *American Chemical Industry*, 3:214; Nichols, "War and the Chemical Industry," 41.

[9] L. F. Haber, *The Chemical Industry, 1900–1930: International Growth and Technological Change* (Oxford: Clarendon Press, 1971), 185.

[10] James B. Conant, *My Several Lives: Memoirs of a Social Inventor* (New York: Harper and Row, 1970), 44–45.

[11] Haber, *Chemical Industry*, 187–188, 210; John H. Perkins, *Insects, Experts, and the Insecticide Crisis: The Quest for New Pest Management Strategies* (New York: Plenum Press, 1982), 4.

[12] R. Wolcott Hooker, "The Story of Hooker Electrochemical Company," *AFCJ* 10 (Jan.–Feb. 1956): 22ff., see 23–24.

[13] Haynes, *American Chemical Industry* 3:210–212, 229, 247–253; Haber, *Chemical Industry*, 187–188, 210; Perkins, *Insects, Experts*, 4.

[14] Baekeland, "Chemistry and Preparedness," 499.

[15] Charles H. Herty, "The Expanding Relations of Chemistry in America," *Science* 44 (6 Oct. 1916): 475–482, see 481–482.

16 W. D. Hunter, *The Boll Weevil Problem, Bulletin 512, Department of Agriculture* (Washington: GPO, 1912), 45.

17 Haynes, *American Chemical Industry,* 3:109–110; Douglas Helms, "Technological Methods for Boll Weevil Control," *Agricultural History* 53 (1979): 286–299, see 291.

18 Haynes, *American Chemical Industry,* 3:110.

19 F. C. Cook, R. H. Hutchison, and F. M. Scales, *Further Experiments in the Destruction of Fly Larvae in Horse Manure, Bulletin 245, Department of Agriculture* (Washington: GPO, 1915); A. B. Duckett, *Para-dichlorobenzene as an Insect Fumigant, Bulletin 167, Department of Agriculture* (Washington: GPO, 1915); W. Moore, "Fumigation of Animals to Destroy their External Parasites," *Journal of Economic Entomology* 9 (1916): 71–78; all cited in E. B. Blakeslee, *Use of Toxic Gases as a Possible Means of Control of the Peach-Tree Borer, Bulletin 796, Department of Agriculture* (Washington: GPO, 1919), 4.

20 L. O. Howard, *The House Fly: Disease Carrier* (New York: Frederick A. Stokes Company, 1911), xvii.

21 H. H. Johnston, "Next War: Man Versus Insects," *Living Age* 68 (21 Aug. 1915): 476–482, see 478, 480, 482.

22 Johnston, "Next War," 477–478, 482.

23 L. O. Howard, "Stephen Alfred Forbes, 1844–1930," in Stephen Alfred Forbes, *Ecological Investigations of Stephen Alfred Forbes* (New York: Arno Press, 1977), 3–54, see 3–4.

24 Stephen A. Forbes, "The Ecological Foundations of Applied Entomology," *Annals of the Entomological Society of America* 8 (Mar. 1915): 1–19, see 2, 6, 12.

25 Forbes, "Ecological Foundations of Applied Entomology," 2, 6, 12.

26 Stephen A. Forbes, "Fifty Billion German Allies Already in the American Field," *Chicago Herald,* 3 June 1917.

27 A. L. Melander, "Can Insects Become Resistant to Sprays?" *Journal of Economic Entomology* 7 (1914): 167–172.

28 The reaction to Melander's theory is recounted by one of his students in an oral history interview brought to my attention by Pamela Henson: John Frederick Gates Clarke, "Interview 1," 26 Feb. 1986, 13–14, 24, Record Unit 9555, Smithsonian Institution Archives, Washington, D.C.

29 Frank N. Egerton, "Changing Concepts of the Balance of Nature," *Quarterly Review of Biology* 48 (1973): 322–350.

30 *Everybody's* 34 (April 1916): 528–529, cited in *Readers' Guide to Periodical Literature,* 4:1031.

31 *Sterlingworth Bug Book,* 2.

32 Johnston, "Next War," 477–478, 482.

[33] Friedrich Prinzing, *Epidemics Resulting from Wars* (Oxford: Clarendon Press, 1916).

[34] Hans Zinsser, *Rats, Lice, and History* (London: George Routledge & Sons, 1935), 152.

[35] Prinzing, *Epidemics*, 5.

[36] Zinsser, *Rats, Lice, and History*, 296–299, see 298.

[37] Hugh R. Slotten, "Humane Chemistry or Scientific Barbarism? American Responses to World War I Poison Gas, 1915–1930," *Journal of American History* 77 (Sept. 1990): 476–498; Robert Harris and Jeremy Paxman, *A Higher Form of Killing: The Secret Story of Chemical and Biological Warfare* (New York: Hill and Wang, 1982); L. F. Haber, *The Poisonous Cloud: Chemical Warfare in the First World War* (Oxford: Clarendon Press, 1986); Daniel Patrick Jones, "The Role of Chemists in Research on War Gases in the United States During World War I" (Ph.D. diss., University of Wisconsin, 1969).

[38] Gen. von Deimling, *Reminiscences* (Paris: Montaigne, 1931), in Hanslian, *The German Gas Attack*, 9, quoted in Frederic J. Brown, *Chemical Warfare: A Study in Restraints* (Westport, Conn.: Greenwood Press, 1968), 41.

[39] "Moral Aspects of Asphyxiation," *Literary Digest* 50 (12 June 1915): 1393.

[40] 1899 Convention II, article 23a, and 1907 Convention IV, article 23a, in James B. Scott (ed.), *The Hague Conventions and Declarations of 1899 and 1907* (New York: Oxford University Press, 1915), 116, 230, 236.

[41] French in *Manchester Guardian*, 1915, quoted in "Moral Aspects of Asphyxiation," 1393.

[42] H. S. Villard, "Poison Gas, 1915–1926: German Atrocity – American Necessity," *Nation* 124 (12 Jan. 1927): 32.

[43] Augustin M. Prentiss, *Chemicals in War: A Treatise on Chemical Warfare* (New York: McGraw-Hill, 1937), 129–219.

[44] Harris and Paxman, *Higher Form*, 22–23, 34.

[45] Karl von Clausewitz (O. J. Matthijs Jolles, trans.), *On War* (Washington: Combat Forces Press, 1953), 138.

[46] H. G. Wells, *The World Set Free: A Story of Mankind* (New York: Dutton, 1914), 69; Michael Howard, "Men Against Fire: The Doctrine of the Offensive in 1914," in Peter Paret (ed.), *Makers of Modern Strategy: From Machiavelli to the Nuclear Age* (Princeton: Princeton University Press, 1986), 510–526, see 510–515.

[47] *Oxford English Dictionary*.

[48] H. G. Wells, *War and the Future: Italy, France, and Britain at War* (London: Cassell, 1917), 151.

[49] E. I. Du Pont de Nemours & Company, *Du Pont: The Autobiography of an American Enterprise* (New York: Charles Scribner's Sons, 1952),

75–77, quoted in Du Pont, "The Du Pont Company and National Defense," 45.

50 Withrow, "American Chemist," 840.

51 Herty, "Expanding Relations of Chemistry," 477–478.

52 President Woodrow Wilson later made the National Research Council a permanent organization. Rexmond C. Cochrane, *The National Academy of Sciences: The First Hundred Years, 1863–1963* (Washington: National Academy of Sciences, 1978), 208–209, 235–236.

53 Wells, *War and the Future*, 151.

54 Charles E. Heller, "The Perils of Unpreparedness: The American Expeditionary Forces and Chemical Warfare," *Military Review* 65 (Jan. 1985): 12–25, see 15–17; H. L. Gilchrist, *A Comparative Study of World War Casualties from Gas and Other Weapons* (Washington: GPO, 1931), 23.

55 Mary Beth Norton, David M. Katzman, Paul D. Escott, Howard P. Chudacoff, Thomas G. Paterson, and William M. Tuttle, Jr., *A People and a Nation: A History of the United States* (Boston: Houghton Mifflin, 1994), 688.

56 George Sylvester Viereck, *Spreading Germs of Hate* (New York: Horace Liveright, 1930), facing 120, 160.

57 Wells, *War and the Future*, 12. Rudyard Kipling said in 1915, "There are only two divisions in the world to-day – human beings and Germans." *London Morning Post*, 22 June 1915, quoted in Harold D. Lasswell, *Propaganda Technique in the World War* (New York: Knopf, 1927), 91.

58 On views of enemies, see Sam Keen, *Faces of the Enemy: Reflections of the Hostile Imagination* (San Francisco: Harper & Row, 1986), 60–64; Peter Paret, Beth Irwin Lewis, and Paul Paret, *Persuasive Images: Posters of War and Revolution from the Hoover Institution Archives* (Princeton: Princeton University Press, 1992); and J. Glenn Gray, *The Warriors: Reflections on Men in Battle* (New York: Harper & Row, 1970).

59 H. G. Wells, *What Is Coming? A Forecast of Things After the War* (London: Cassell, 1916), 220.

60 Gilson Gardner, "Feeding the War Ring," *Harper's Weekly*, 13 Mar. 1915, 244–247, see 247.

61 Quoted in John E. Wiltz, *In Search of Peace: The Senate Munitions Inquiry, 1934–36* (Baton Rouge: Louisiana State University Press, 1963), 4–5.

62 Quoted in Earl A. Molander, "The Emergence of Military-Industrial Criticism: 1895–1915," in Gregg B. Walker, David A. Bella, and Steven J. Sprecher (eds.), *The Military-Industrial Complex: Eisenhower's Warning Three Decades Later* (New York: Peter Lang, 1992), 237–267, see 264 n. 15.

63 David M. Kennedy, *Over Here: The First World War and American Society* (New York: Oxford University Press, 1980), 12.

CHAPTER 3. JOINING THE CHEMISTS' WAR (1917–1918)

1 Alexis de Tocqueville, *Democracy in America,* vol. 2 (New York: Vintage, 1945), 268.

2 Charles E. Heller, "The Perils of Unpreparedness: The American Expeditionary Forces and Chemical Warfare," *Military Review* 65 (Jan. 1985): 12–25, see 21.

3 *Who's Who in the Chemical and Drug Industries, 1928* and *Who's Who in Engineering … 1922–1923* (Biographical microfilm collection, University of Virginia Library).

4 U.S. Congress, Senate, Committee on Military Affairs, *Reorganization of the Army,* part 1, 66th Cong., 1st sess. (Washington: GPO, 1919), 352–353.

5 H. L. Gilchrist, *A Comparative Study of World War Casualties from Gas and Other Weapons* (Washington: GPO, 1931), 7, 18a; Augustin M. Prentiss, *Chemicalsin War: A Treatise on Chemical Warfare* (New York: McGraw-Hill, 1937), 674.

6 Gilchrist, *World War Casualties: A Treatise on Chemical Warfare,* (New York: McGraw-Hill, 1937).

7 Fries to J. D. Law, 16 Aug. 1919, General Fries's File, RG 175.

8 B. C. Goss to Maj. Gen. Sibert, 18 Jan. 1918, Chief—CWS, General Fries's File, 1918–20, RG 175.

9 Text accompanying John Singer Sargent's *Gassed* in Imperial War Museum, London, viewed in 1996.

10 Quoted in Victor Lefebure, *The Riddle of the Rhine: Chemical Strategy in Peace and War* (London: W. Collins Sons, 1921), 237.

11 Amos A. Fries and Clarence J. West, *Chemical Warfare* (New York: McGraw-Hill, 1921), 90.

12 Senate Committee on Military Affairs, *Reorganization,* part 1, 414.

13 Peyton C. March, *The Nation at War* (Garden City, N.Y.: Doubleday, Doran & Company, 1932), 333–334.

14 Fries and West, *Chemical Warfare,* 89–90.

15 Edward B. Clark, *William L. Sibert: The Army Engineer* (Philadelphia: Dorrance and Company, 1930), 12, 159–160.

16 Fries and West, *Chemical Warfare,* 36.

17 C. H. Foulkes, *Gas! The Story of the Special Brigade* (Edinburgh: William Blackwood & Sons, 1934), 107; Henry F. Thuillier, *Gas in the Next War* (London: Geoffrey Bles, 1939), 68; L. F. Haber, *The Poisonous Cloud: Chemical Warfare in the First World War* (Oxford: Clarendon, 1986), 174.

18 Haber, *Poisonous Cloud,* 174; Frederic J. Brown, *Chemical Warfare: A Study in Restraints* (Westport, Conn.: Greenwood Press, 1968), 39.

[19] "United States Chemical Warfare Service," part 1, *Scientific American* 120 (29 Mar. 1919): 318ff., see 318.

[20] Amos A. Fries, "The Future of Poison Gas," *Current History* 15 (Dec. 1921): 419–422.

[21] Daniel P. Jones, "The Role of Chemists in Research on War Gases in the United States During World War I" (Ph.D. diss., University of Wisconsin, 1969), 122.

[22] Jones, "Role of Chemists," 105–106; Leo P. Brophy, Wyndham D. Miles, and Rexmond C. Cochrane, *The Chemical Warfare Service: From Laboratory to Field* (Washington: Office of the Chief of Military History, 1959), 4–5; Rexmond C. Cochrane, *The National Academy of Sciences: The First Hundred Years, 1863–1963* (Washington: National Academy of Sciences, 1978), 231–232.

[23] Hydrogen cyanide is also called hydrocyanic acid and prussic acid. In practice, hydrogen cyanide dispersed in open air too quickly to kill soldiers effectively. Although many nations researched hydrogen cyanide as a chemical weapon, only the French persisted in using it during World War I. To kill insect pests in orchards, fumigators enclosed trees in tents before releasing the gas. Haber, *Poisonous Cloud,* 62–63, 117–118; Brophy, et al., *From Laboratory to Field,* 55–56; Williams Haynes, *American Chemical Industry,* vol. 3: *The World War I Period: 1912–1922* (New York: D. Van Nostrand, 1945), 111–112.

[24] L. O. Howard, "Entomology and the War," *Scientific Monthly* 8 (Jan.–June 1919): 109–117.

[25] James G. Hershberg, *James B. Conant: Harvard to Hiroshima and the Making of the Nuclear Age* (New York: Alfred A. Knopf, 1993), 46–47; James B. Conant, *My Several Lives: Memoirs of a Social Inventor* (New York: Harper and Row, 1970), 48–49.

[26] Conant, *My Several Lives,* 49.

[27] Senate Committee on Military Affairs, *Reorganization,* part 1, 412.

[28] Fries to George E. Chamberlain, 16 Sep. 1919, Chamberlain—Senator, General Fries's File, RG 175.

[29] Brown, *Chemical Warfare,* 28–30.

[30] Jones, "Role of Chemists," 120–121.

[31] Brophy et al., *From Laboratory to Field,* 12–13; Cochrane, *National Academy of Sciences,* 232; Jones, "Role of Chemists," 121.

[32] B. C. Goss to W. Sibert, 18 Jan. 1918, Chief—CWS, General Fries's File, RG 175.

[33] Prentiss, *Chemicals in War,* 195.

[34] General Electric Company, *The Story of the Development Division, Chemical Warfare Service* (n.c.,n.p., 1920), 182.

[35] Benedict Crowell, *America's Munitions, 1917–1918* (Washington: GPO, 1919), 303–307, see 307.

[36] Mark Clodfelter, "Pinpointing Devastation: American Air Planning before Pearl Harbor," *Journal of Military History* 58 (Jan. 1994): 75–101, see 76–81.

[37] Richard Barry, "America's Most Terrible Weapon," *Current History* 9 (Jan. 1919): 125–128, see 127–128.

[38] Brown, *Chemical Warfare*, 45, n. 98.

[39] Barry, "America's Most Terrible Weapon," 127–128.

[40] Will Irwin, *The Next War: An Appeal to Common Sense* (New York: Dutton, 1921), 66.

[41] "Destroy this Mad Brute," H. R. Hopps, Imperial War Museum PC 0248 Cat. No. IWM PST 0243, London.

[42] George Creel, *How We Advertised America: The First Telling of the Amazing Story of the Committee on Public Information that Carried the Gospel of Americanism to Every Corner of the Globe* (New York: Harper & Brothers, 1920).

[43] Stephen A. Forbes, "Fifty Billion German Allies Already in the American Field," *Chicago Herald*, 3 June 1917.

[44] "Warfare," quoted in Howard, "Entomology and the War," 117; L. O. Howard, "Entomology as a National Defense," *Entomological News* 28 (1917): 229.

[45] Howard, "Entomology and the War," 109, 111, 117; Gustavus A. Weber, *The Bureau of Entomology: Its History, Activities, and Organization* (Washington: Brookings Institution, 1930), 50.

[46] Stanhope Bayne-Jones, "Typhus Fevers," in U.S. Army Medical Service, *Preventive Medicine in World War II*, vol. 7: *Communicable Diseases: Arthropodborne Diseases Other Than Malaria* (Washington: GPO, 1964), 175–274, see 182; E. C. Cushing, *History of Entomology in World War II* (Washington: Smithsonian Institution, 1957), 23; Hans Zinsser, *Rats, Lice, and History* (London: George Routledge & Sons, 1935), 298–299.

[47] Surviving records do not indicate whether experimenters tested gases on human beings in chambers. W. Dwight Pierce to L. O. Howard, [n.d.], and "Report on Experiments Conducted on October 16, 1918, Testing the Effect of Certain Toxic Gases on Body Lice and Their Eggs," Correspondence and Reports Relating to a Study of Body Lice 1918, RG 7.

[48] Haynes, *American Chemical Industry*, 3: 111; R. C. Roark, *A Bibliography of Chloropicrin, 1848–1932* (Washington: GPO, 1934), 1–2.

[49] The Bureau of Chemistry, Bureau of Plant Industry, and the Federal Horticultural Board helped the Bureau of Entomology conduct research at

Chemical Warfare Service laboratories at American University. "The Chemical Warfare Service in Peace," [n.d.], 029.0611 Articles and Speeches—Peacetime Activities, Station Series 1942–1945 Security Classified, RG 175; I. E. Neifert and G. L. Garrison, *Experiments on the Toxic Action of Certain Gases on Insects, Seeds, and Fungi* (Washington: GPO, 1920); and Haynes, *American Chemical Industry,* 3:111. Quotation is from the abstract of "Killing Weevils with Chloropicrin," in Roark, *Bibliography of Chloropicrin,* 3.

50 Brophy et al., *From Laboratory to Field,* 16–17.

51 Quoted in Jones, "Role of Chemists," 89.

52 Frederick Jackson Turner, "The Significance of the Frontier in American History," in *History, Frontier, and Section: Three Essays by Frederick Jackson Turner* (Albuquerque: University of New Mexico Press, 1993), 59–91.

CHAPTER 4. CHEMICAL WARFARE IN PEACE (1918–1934)

1 Henry Jervey to Chief of Engineers, 21 Feb. 1919, attached to Fries to George E. Chamberlain, 22 Sept. 1919, Chamberlain—Senator, General Fries's File, RG 175; U.S. Congress, Senate, Committee on Military Affairs, *Reorganization of the Army,* part 1, 66th Cong. 1st sess. (Washington: GPO, 1919), 280.

2 Fries to J. D. Law, 16 Aug. 1919, Law Capt. J. D., General Fries's File, RG 175.

3 March's views were summarized by Senator Chamberlain in Senate Committee on Military Affairs, *Reorganization,* part 1, 317.

4 Fries to J. L. Clarkson, 20 Sept. 1919, Clarkson Major J. L., General Fries's File, RG 175.

5 "Resolution," n.d., Resolutions re CWS, General Fries's File, RG 175.

6 Fries to E. J. Atkisson, 25 Sept. 1919, Atkisson Col. E. J.; William H. Chadbourne to Fries, 1 Nov. 1919, Chadbourne Maj. Wm.; M. T. Bogert to Fries, 10 Nov. 1919, Bogert Col. M.T.; Fries to G. N. Lewis, 23 Sep. 1919, Lewis Col. G. N.; Hildebrand to Julius Kahn, 4 Aug. 1919, Hildebrand Lt. Col.; Levering to Julius Kahn, 15 Jan. 1920, Kahn—Hon. Julius M. C.; all in General Fries's File, RG 175.

7 Fourteen articles in this series are cited in Gilbert F. Whittemore, Jr., "World War I, Poison Gas Research, and the Ideals of American Chemists," *Social Studies of Science* 5 (1975): 135–163, see 157, 159.

8 Senate Committee on Military Affairs, *Reorganization,* part 1, 409–411.

9 Secretary, American Chemical Society, to Newton Baker, 26 June 1919, General Fries's File, RG 175.

[10] Leo P. Brophy, Wyndham D. Miles, and Rexmond C. Cochrane, *The Chemical Warfare Service: From Laboratory to Field* (Washington: Office of the Chief of Military History, 1959), 28; Daniel P. Jones, "The Role of Chemists in Research on War Gases in the United States During World War I" (Ph.D. diss., University of Wisconsin, 1969), 212; Frederic J. Brown, *Chemical Warfare: A Study in Restraints* (Westport, Conn.: Greenwood Press, 1968), 77–85.

[11] Harry S. Knapp, "Treaty No. 2 of the Washington Conference (Relating to Submarines and Noxious Gases)," *Political Science Quarterly* 39 (June 1924): 201–217.

[12] Quoted in "Problems to Be Attacked by the Conference," *Literary Digest* 71 (12 Nov. 1921): front cover.

[13] Robert V. Hudson, *The Writing Game: A Biography of Will Irwin* (Ames: Iowa State University Press), 130–132.

[14] Will Irwin, *The Next War: An Appeal to Common Sense* (New York: Dutton, 1921), 28.

[15] Irwin, *Next War*, 27, 35–43, see 35.

[16] Irwin, *Next War*, 28–30, 33–34.

[17] Quoted in Irwin, *Next War*, 46, 108.

[18] "Disarmament and Poison Gas," *Illustrated World* 36 (Nov. 1921): 353ff., see 354.

[19] "Chemical Warfare" (reprinted from editorial, *Army and Navy Register*, 7 Jan. 1922), *Chemical Warfare* 8 (no. 1, 1922): 20–21, see 20; see also "Gas in Warfare" (reprinted from *Cleveland Topics*, 1 Jan. 1927), *Chemical Warfare* 13 (no. 3, 1927): 57–59, 65, see 59.

[20] Fries, "Future of Poison Gas," *Current History* 15 (Dec. 1921): 419–422, see 421–422.

[21] A. A. Fries and C. J. West, *Chemical Warfare* (New York: McGraw-Hill, 1921), vii.

[22] "Editorial Comment," *Chemical Warfare* 6 (no. 8, 1921): 1.

[23] Theodore M. Knappen, "Chemical Warfare and Disarmament," *Independent* 107 (22 Oct. 1921): 73–74, see 74.

[24] "'Viper' Weapons," *Literary Digest* 71 (24 Dec. 1921): 8–9, see 9.

[25] Quoted in "'Viper' Weapons," 8–9.

[26] *Seattle Times* paraphrased and other newspapers quoted in "'Viper' Weapons," 8–9; see also "Poison Gas Propaganda," *Nation*, 21 Sept. 1921, 311–312.

[27] Quoted in Knapp, "Treaty No. 2," 213–214.

[28] Quoted in "'Viper' Weapons," 8–9.

[29] The resolution became Article V of the "Treaty Relating to the Use of Submarines and Noxious Gases in Warfare" (*Foreign Relations, 1922*

[Washington: GPO, 1922], 1:269); Daniel P. Jones, "American Chemists and the Geneva Protocol," *Isis* 71 (Sept. 1980): 426–440, see 428; "Role of Chemists," 187; Brown, *Chemical Warfare,* 67.

30 "Chemical Warfare Making Swords into Plowshares," *Chemical Warfare* 8 (no. 2, 1922): 2–5, see 2.

31 Daniel P. Jones, "From Military to Civilian Technology: The Introduction of Tear Gas for Civil Riot Control," *Technology and Culture* 19 (1978): 151–168; Leo Finkelstein and C. G. Schmitt, *History of Research and Development of the Chemical Warfare Service in World War II (1 July 1940–31 December 1945),* vol. 19, part 1: *Insecticides, Miticides, and Rodenticides* (Army Chemical Center, Maryland: Technical Command, 7 Dec. 1949), 1; "Gas for Golf Green Worm," *NYT,* 15 July 1923; "Chemical Warfare Making Swords into Plowshares"; Amos A. Fries, "Extracts from the Annual Report of the Chief of the Chemical Warfare Service (Brigadier General Amos A. Fries) to the Secretary of War," *Chemical Warfare* 10 (no. 12, 1924): 9–12, see 9–10.

32 "Army Invents Mask against All Poisons," *NYT,* 8 Apr. 1923.

33 Quoted in "Its Greater Service to Peace: From *Gazette Times,* Pittsburgh, Pa., November 24, 1924," *Chemical Warfare* 11 (no. 2, 1925): 22.

34 "Peacetime Attainments of Chemical Warfare Service," *Chemical Warfare* 9 (no. 2, 1923): 21–22.

35 Harry L. Gilchrist, "Chlorine Gas — Its Uses a Hundred Years Ago, Its Uses Today as a Therapeutic Agent in Certain Respiratory Diseases with Report of 900 Cases," *Wisconsin Medical Journal* 23 (Oct. 1924): 234–242.

36 "United States Chemical Warfare Association," *Chemical Warfare* 11 (no. 1, 1925): 13–16. See also Amos A. Fries, "Extracts from the Annual Report of the Chief of the Chemical Warfare Service."

37 Gilchrist, "Chlorine Gas," 235; "What the Army Does in Peace: *Chicago Tribune,* December 31, 1922," *Chemical Warfare* 9 (no. 1, 1923): 17.

38 E. B. Vedder and H. P. Sawyer, "Chlorin as a Thereapeutic Agent in Certain Respiratory Diseases," *Journal of the American Medical Association* 82 (8 Mar. 1924): 764; E. B. Vedder and H. P. Sawyer, "The Treatment of Certain Respiratory Diseases by Chlorin," *Journal of the American Medical Association* 84 (31 Jan. 1925): 361, both cited in Harold S. Diehl, "Value of Chlorin in the Treatment of Colds," *Journal of the American Medical Association* 84 (30 May 1925): 1629–1632, see 1629.

39 "War's Deadly Gas Is Used by Science to Help Humanity," *New York World,* 8 June 1924.

40 "United States Chemical Warfare Association," *Chemical Warfare* 11 (no. 1, 1925): 13–16; "Poison Gases of War to Cure Human Ills," *Popular Mechanics* 42 (Sept. 1924): 353–354, see 353.

41 Diehl, "Value of Chlorin," 1632.

42 "Chemical Warfare Making Swords into Plowshares," 3.

43 "Chemical Warfare: Editorial in *Army and Navy Register,* January 7, 1922," *Chemical Warfare* 8 (no. 1, 1922): 20–21.

44 "Use Poison Gases to Fight Mosquito," *NYT,* 9 Feb. 1923.

45 F. J. Brinley, "Insecticidal Value of Certain War Chemicals as Tested on the Tent Caterpillar," *Journal of Agricultural Research* 33 (15 July 1926): 177–182, see 177.

46 Finkelstein and Schmitt, *Research and Development of the Chemical Warfare Service,* 1–2; I. E. Neifert and G. L. Garrison, *Experiments on the Toxic Action of Certain Gases on Insects, Seeds, and Fungi,* USDA Bulletin No. 893 (Washington: GPO, 1920).

47 "Extracts from the Annual Report of the Chief of the Chemical Warfare Service," 11.

48 "Edgewood Seeking Boll Weevil Poison," *Chemical Warfare* 9 (1924): 14. The allocation was in Military Appropriations Act (Public Law No. 213, 68th Congress). Finkelstein and Schmitt, *Research and Development of the Chemical Warfare Service,* 2.

49 H. W. Walker and J. E. Miles, "Progress Report of Work of the Chemical Warfare Service on the Boll Weevil, *Anthonomus grandis,*" *Journal of Economic Entomology* 19 (1926): 600–601; H. W. Walker, "A Brief Resume of the Chemical Warfare Service Boll Weevil Investigation," *Chemical Warfare* 13 (no. 12, 1927): 231–237; H. W. Walker and J. E. Miles, "Chemical Warfare Service Boll Weevil Investigation Progress Report," *Industrial and Engineering Chemistry* 19 (1927): 703–711; Finkelstein and Schmitt, *Research and Development of the Chemical Warfare Service,* 1–5.

50 Harry A. Mount, "Peace-Time Jobs for Poison Gas," *Scientific American* 126 (May 1922): 326–327; "Harnessing War Gases for Peace-Times," *Popular Mechanics* 44 (Sept. 1925): 451–457.

51 "Peacetime Uses," *Chemical Warfare* 8 (no. 11, 1922): 10.

52 "Gassing the Boll-Weevil: Editorial from *Boston Transcript,* September 19, 1922," *Chemical Warfare* 8 (no. 10, 1922): 11. This argument was also used in later years. In 1928, Fries argued, "It is believed that the contribution of the Chemical Warfare Service to industry alone have more than amply justified the sums devoted to research, to say nothing of the tremendous progress made in the protection of our Army and Nation against enemy chemical warfare in any future emergency." Amos A. Fries, "By-Products of Chemical Warfare," *Industrial and Engineering Chemistry* 20 (1928): 1079–1084, see 1084.

53 "Gas for the Boll Weevil," *NYT,* 13 Sept. 1922.

54 Samuel P. Huntington, *The Soldier and the State: The Theory and Politics of Civil-Military Relations* (Cambridge: Harvard University Press, 1957).

55 "War Gas Found Useful to Fight Farmers' Pests," *Chemical Warfare* 9 (no. 1, 1923): 14.

56 "Gassing the Boll-Weevil," 11.

57 "Chemistry and War: The Following Was Printed in a Pamphlet Issued Under the Auspices of the National Research Council," *Chemical Warfare* 6 (no. 6, 1921): 13–15, see 14.

58 Amos A. Fries, "Address before Chemical Industries Exposition, New York City," 12 Sept. 1922, 029.0611 Articles & Speeches – Peacetime Activities, Station Series Security Classified, RG 175.

59 Walker, "A Brief Resume of the Chemical Warfare Service Boll Weevil Investigation," 232–233.

60 "The Blessings of Chemical Warfare," *Literary Digest* 95 (29 Oct. 1927): 59.

61 "Guarding the Secrets of Chemical Warfare" *Current Opinion* 72 (May 1922): 653–654, see 654.

62 "Against Use of Poison Gas," *NYT*, 8 Jan. 1922.

63 *Foreign Relations, 1925* (Washington: GPO, 1925), 1:27, 89–90.

64 "Chemists Protest Ban on Poison Gas," *Chemical Warfare* 11 (nos. 8–9 1925): 13; Jones, "American Chemists and the Geneva Protocol," 433–438; Jones, "The Role of Chemists in Research on War Gases," 191; Kevin Takashi Fujitani, "The United States and Chemical Warfare: The 1925 Geneva Gas Protocol and Its Legacy" (M.A. thesis, University of Hawaii, 1991), 88–89.

65 Quoted in Jones, "American Chemists and the Geneva Protocol," 427–428, 437.

66 Jones, "American Chemists and the Geneva Protocol," 438.

67 Jones, "American Chemists and the Geneva Protocol," 427.

68 Brown, *Chemical Warfare*, 116–123, see 122; Augustin M. Prentiss, *Chemicals in War: A Treatise on Chemical Warfare* (New York: McGraw-Hill, 1937), 693–695.

69 "The Next War: Annihilation," *Catholic World* 142 (March 1936): 646–649, see 646; "When Death Strikes from the Sky," *Literary Digest* 120 (28 Sept. 1935): 14–15, see 14; "Paris Prepares for Gas," *Scientific American* 156 (May 1937): 302–303, see 303.

70 Edward C. McDowell, "Poison Gas: Myth and Menace," *Current History* 44 (July 1936): 59–64, see 59.

71 Alden H. Waitt, "No Super War Gas!" *Scientific American* 153 (Dec. 1935): 293–297, see 296.

[72] Adrian St. John, "Will Gas Destroy Populations in the Next War?" *Literary Digest* 117 (3 Mar. 1934): 17.

[73] Prentiss, *Chemicals in War*, 680.

[74] C. E. Brigham, "How Serious Is This Gas Menace?" *Saturday Evening Post*, 10 July 1937, 10ff., see 10–11.

[75] "Dealing Death from the Air Three Drops at a Time," *Current Opinion* 71 (Aug. 1921): 246–247; Waitt, "No Super War Gas!" 294.

[76] Prentiss, *Chemicals in War*, 34.

[77] *The Public Papers and Addresses of Franklin D. Roosevelt*, Samuel I. Rosenman (ed.), vol. 5, *The People Approve, 1936* (New York: Random House, 1938), 289.

[78] Roosevelt, *Chemical Warfare Service – Veto Message*, U.S. Congress, Senate, Document 90, 75th Cong., 1st sess. (Washington: GPO, 1937), 1.

CHAPTER 5. MINUTEMEN IN PEACE (1918–1937)

[1] L. O. Howard, "On Some Presidential Addresses;" the War Against the Insects," *Science* 54 (30 Dec. 1921): 641–651, see 642.

[2] Howard, "On Some Presidential Addresses," 642.

[3] Howard, "On Some Presidential Addresses," 650–651.

[4] Howard identified the 1921 address as a turning point in his representation of insects and hoped that appreciation for the "insect war" would lead to support for entomology. L. O. Howard, *The Insect Menace* (New York: Century, 1931), ix; Howard, "U.S. Wages Insect War," *Science News-Letter* 10 (20 Nov. 1926): 127; R. C. Roark, "Household Insecticides," *SSC* 11 (Nov. 1935): 117 (emphasis added); and Thomas R. Dunlap, *DDT: Scientists, Citizens, and Public Policy* (Princeton: Princeton University Press, 1981), 37.

[5] William Crowder, "Insects and Human Destiny," *Century Magazine* 104 (May 1922): 142–148, see 142–143, 148.

[6] William Atherton Du Puy, "The Insects Are Winning," *Harper's Magazine*, Mar. 1925, 435–440.

[7] Howard, *Insect Menace*, 156–157; L. O. Howard, *Fighting the Insects: The Story of an Entomologist* (1933; New York: Arno Press, 1980).

[8] Maidl quoted in Howard, *Insect Menace*, 201; Albert Dickman, "In Defense of Insects," *Scientific American* 153 (Sept. 1935): 124–126.

[9] Howard, "On Some Presidential Addresses," 642, 647–649, see 647–648; Howard, "The War Against Insects: The Insecticide Chemist and Biologist in the Mitigation of Plant Pests," *Chemical Age* 30 (1922): 5–6.

[10] Corley McDarment, "The Use of Airplanes to Destroy the Boll Weevil," *McClure's Magazine* 57 (Aug. 1924): 90–102, see 91–92; Eldon W. Downs

and George F. Lemmer, "Origins of Aerial Crop Dusting," *Agricultural History* 39 (1965): 123–135, see 124, 127.

11 McDarment, "The Use of Airplanes to Destroy the Boll Weevil," 91–92; Downs and Lemmer, "Origins of Aerial Crop Dusting," 124, 127.

12 G. B. Post, *Boll Weevil (Anthonomus grandis) Control by Airplane,* Georgia Agricultural College Bulletin 301 (Athens, 1924), abstracted in Ina L. Hawes and Rose Eisenberg (eds.), *Bibliography on Aviation and Economic Entomology,* USDA Bibliographical Bulletin No. 8 (Washington: GPO, 1947), 6.

13 Hawes and Eisenberg, *Bibliography on Aviation,* 8–9; Downs and Lemmer, "Origins of Aerial Crop Dusting," 130–32, see 130; Douglas Helms, "Technological Methods for Boll Weevil Control," *Agricultural History* 53 (Oct. 1979): 286–299.

14 B. R. Coad, E. Johnson, and G. L. McNeil, *Dusting Cotton from Airplanes,* USDA Bulletin No. 1204 (Washington: GPO, 1924), 36; McDarment, "The Use of Airplanes," 96.

15 McDarment, "The Use of Airplanes," 102;" Aerial Warfare – on Insects – Up to Date," *Literary Digest* 83 (13 Dec. 1924): 61–62.

16 L. O. Howard, "The Needs of the World as to Entomology," *Smithsonian Institution Annual Report, 1925* (Washington: GPO, 1926), 355–372, see 370; Howard, *Insect Menace,* 283; R. C. Roark, *A Bibliography of Chloropicrin, 1848–1932* (Washington: GPO, 1934).

17 C. N. Myers, Binford Throne, Florence Gustafson, and Jerome Kingsbury, "Significance and Danger of Spray Residue," *Industrial and Engineering Chemistry* 25 (1933): 624–628.

18 "Insect War Aided," *Business Week,* 26 June 1943, 56, 60.

19 H. E. Howe, "The Service of the Chemist: War Credits," *Scientific American* 120 (19 Apr. 1919): 406ff., see 406.

20 Charles Frederick Carter, "Growth of the Chemical Industry," *Current History* 15 (Dec. 1921): 423–428, see 424; see also Charles Baskerville, "Our Chemical Industries after the War," *American Review of Reviews* 59 (June 1919): 618–622, see 618.

21 Alfred D. Chandler, Jr., *The Visible Hand: The Managerial Revolution in American Business* (Cambridge: Belknap Press, 1977), 375; Davis Dyer and David B. Sicilia, *Labors of a Modern Hercules: The Evolution of a Chemical Company* (Boston: Harvard Business School Press, 1990), 187–189, 204; Dan J. Forrestal, *Faith, Hope and $5,000: The Story of Monsanto* (New York: Simon and Schuster, 1977), 73; Williams Haynes, *American Chemical Industry,* vol. 4, *The Merger Era* (New York: D. Van Nostrand, 1948), xvii; David A. Hounshell and John Kenly Smith, Jr., *Science and Corporate Strategy: Du Pont R&D, 1902–1980* (Cambridge: Cambridge University Press, 1988), parts 2 and 3; Carter, "Growth of the

Chemical Industry," 427; Floyd L. Darrow, "The New Age of Chemistry," *St. Nicholas* 55 (May 1928): 551ff., see 551.

22 David M. Kennedy, *Over Here: The First World War and American Society* (New York: Oxford University Press, 1980), 139; see also Williams Haynes, *American Chemical Industry*, vol. 3, *The World War I Period: 1912–1922* (New York: D. Van Nostrand, 1945), 192–202, 257; Howe, "The Service of the Chemist," 408.

23 Haynes, *American Chemical Industry*, 3:464; Forrestal, *Faith, Hope and $5,000*, 51; see also Dyer and Sicilia, *Labors of a Modern Hercules*, 183.

24 Haynes, *American Chemical Industry*, 4:342.

25 John H. Perkins, *Insects, Experts, and the Insecticide Crisis: The Quest for New Pest Management Strategies* (New York: Plenum Press, 1982), 5.

26 Carbide and Carbon Chemicals Corporation marketed the latter under the name Carboxide (Haynes, *American Chemical Industry*, 4:343).

27 "Insect War Aided," 56, 60.

28 "This War May Never End," *Hercules Mixer* (Sept. 1941): 288–291, see 289.

29 In 1940, *National Petroleum News* described the period before 1930 as the "racket era" of insecticides: "The mixtures were often of indifferent toxic quality and the odorous oils left oily residues on draperies and furniture." "'Swat the Fly' Campaign Made a Profitable Market for Some Oil Companies," *National Petroleum News* 32 (8 May 1940): 25ff., see 28; "The Address of President Hoyt," *SSC* 1 (Dec. 1925): 43ff., see 45; G. R. Rinke, "The New Era in Household Insecticides," *SSC* 1 (Apr. 1926): 47; John Powell, "Pyrethrum, 1917–1931," *SSC* 7 (Oct. 1931): 93ff., see 115; Williams Haynes, *American Chemical Industry*, vol. 5: *Decade of New Products* (New York: D. Van Nostrand, 1954), 318.

30 "The Extermination of Ants," *SSC* 1 (Nov. 1925): 41–43, see 41; see also Charles Southern, "Insecticide Sales – Up or Down?" *SSC* 12 (Mar. 1935): 107ff., see 109.

31 Rinke, "The New Era in Household Insecticides," 47.

32 M. A. Reasoner, "Insect Borne Diseases," *SSC* 1 (Feb. 1926): 47–49, see 47.

33 "Insects More Deadly Than Bullets," *SSC* 1 (May 1926): 51.

34 "A Cross-Section of the Quebec Meeting," *SSC* 1 (July 1926): 49ff, see 49, 51.

35 Dunlap, *DDT*, 36–37.

36 "Flit Newspaper Campaign Moves North with Warm Weather," *Printers' Ink* 139 (16 June 1927): 149–150, see 150.

37 "What's So Funny about Flit?" *Advertising and Selling* (9 July 1930).

38 Information Age Exhibit, National Museum of American History, Smithsonian Institution, Washington, D.C., viewed 28 Dec. 1998.

39 Victor Froelicher, "The Story of DDT," *SSC* (Jul. 1944): 115ff.

40 Robert Harris and Jeremy Paxman, *A Higher Form of Killing: The Secret Story of Chemical and Biological Warfare* (New York: Hill and Wang, 1982), 57; Stockholm International Peace Research Institute, *The Problem of Chemical and Biological Warfare,* vol. 1, *The Rise of CB Weapons* (New York: Humanities Press, 1971), 71–72; British Intelligence Objectives Subcommittee, "Development of New Insecticides and Chemical Warfare Agents, Report No. 714," [n. d.], 23, Library Projects File, RG 319; Robert L. Metcalf, "The Impact of Organophosphorous Insecticides Upon Basic and Applied Science," *Bulletin of the Entomological Society of America* 5 (1959): 3–15.

41 Combined Intelligence Objectives Subcommittee, "A New Group of War Gases, No. 23–7," 23 Apr. 1945, 3–7, Library Projects File, RG 319; Harris and Paxman, *Higher Form,* 58–59, see 58.

42 The patent claimant announced in 1932 that he had developed a mantle to protect "troops against the raining down [of gases] by airmen." Wickham Steed, "The Future of Warfare," *Nineteenth Century* 16 (Aug. 1934): 129–140, see 132–133; see also Wickham Steed, "Aerial Warfare: Secret German Plans," *Nineteenth Century* 116 (July 1934): 1–15; Wickham Steed, "Mr. Steed's Rejoinder," *Nineteenth Century* 16 (Sept. 1934): 337–339.

43 Robert S. Allen, "Chemical Warfare, a New Industry," *Nation* 124 (12 Jan. 1927): 33.

44 Norman Hapgood, *Professional Patriots* (New York: Albert & Charles Boni, 1927), vi–vii, 1–6, see 6.

45 U.S. Congress, House, Committee on Foreign Affairs, *Hearings on H. J. Res. 183, A Joint Resolution to Prohibit the Exportation of Arms, Munitions, or Implements of War to Belligerent Nations,* 70th Cong., 1st sess. (Washington: GPO, 1929), 21–26, 39.

46 "Arms and the Men," *Fortune* 9 (Mar. 1934): 53ff., see 53, 55.

47 "Arms and the Men," 53, 55.

48 John E. Wiltz, *In Search of Peace: The Senate Munitions Inquiry, 1934–36* (Baton Rouge: Louisiana State University Press, 1963), 21.

49 George Seldes, *Iron, Blood and Profits: An Exposure of the World-Wide Munitions Racket* (New York: Harper and Brothers, 1934), 8, 162; H. C. Engelbrecht and F. C. Hanighen, *Merchants of Death: A Study of the International Armament Industry* (New York: Dodd, Mcad, 1934), 3–6, 10, 143, 147, 173–178.

50 Wiltz, *In Search,* 21, Roosevelt quoted on 23.

51 Poem from undated clipping from *Minneapolis Tribune* in Nye Papers, quoted in Wiltz, *In Search,* 17.

[52] Wiltz, *In Search*, 24–37; Matthew W. Coulter, *The Senate Munitions Inquiry of the 1930s: Beyond the Merchants of Death* (Westport, Conn.: Greenwood, 1997).

[53] Irenee du Pont believed newspapers were more responsible for causing wars than arms makers were. Stephen and Joan Raushenbush, *War Madness* (Washington: National Home Library Foundation, 1937), 11; H. C. Engelbrecht, *"One Hell of a Business"* (New York: Robert M. McBride, 1934), 45; Wiltz, *In Search*, 72–73, 148–153, see 73.

[54] U.S. Congress, Senate, Special Committee on Investigation of the Munitions Industry, *Munitions Industry*, Report No. 944, part 3, 74th Cong., 2d sess. (Washington: GPO, 1936), 19–20.

[55] Quoted in Wiltz, *In Search*, 224.

[56] Senate, *Munitions Industry*, 19–27, 171, 274.

[57] Amos Fries to Irenee du Pont, 7 Feb. 1928, in U.S. Congress, Senate, Special Committee Investigating the Munitions Industry, 1935, 2840, cited in Senate, *Munitions Industry*, 143.

[58] Senate, *Munitions Industry*, 12.

[59] Many observers credited the Nye hearings with stimulating passage of neutrality legislation (Wiltz, *In Search*, 227–231); Senate, *Munitions Industry*, 1–2, 15, 17.

[60] "The Next War: Annihilation," *Catholic World* 142 (Mar. 1936): 646–649, see 646, 649; Raushenbush and Raushenbush, *War Madness*, Foreword [no p.]; Frank C. Hanighen, "Poison Gas and the Civilian Front," *New Republic* 87 (5 Aug. 1936): 373–374, see 374.

CHAPTER 6. TOTAL WAR (1936–1943)

[1] Quoted in Mark E. Neely, Jr., "Was the Civil War a Total War?" *Civil War History* 37 (no. 1, 1991): 5–28, see 9.

[2] Quoted in Russell F. Weigley, *The American Way of War: A History of United States Military Strategy and Policy* (New York: Macmillan, 1973), 207.

[3] Erich Ludendorff, *Der Totale Krieg* (Munich: Ludendorffs Verlag, 1935); Erich Ludendorff, *The "Total" War* (London: Friends of Europe, 1936).

[4] Michael S. Sherry, *The Rise of American Air Power: The Creation of Armageddon* (New Haven: Yale, 1987), 69–75.

[5] W. F. Kernan, "The Airplane in Future War," *Commonweal* 27 (1 Apr. 1938): 621–622.

[6] P. X. English, "Chemical Warfare Intelligence Summary No. 1," 17 Apr. 1941, attached to Ralph C. Smith to Chief, CWS, 25 Apr. 1941, OCCWS

Correspondence Cross Reference 1941, Historian's Background Files, RG 175.

7 "United States Now at War with Germany and Italy," *NYT,* 12 Dec. 1941.

8 Albert Hirst to editor, *NYT,* 9 Dec. 1941.

9 H. G. Nicholas (ed.), *Washington Despatches, 1941–1945* (Chicago: University of Chicago Press, 1981), 558.

10 Quoted in Craig M. Cameron, *American Samurai: Myth, Imagination, and the Conduct of Battle in the First Marine Division, 1941–1951* (New York: Cambridge University Press, 1994), 1.

11 Robert Baker to editor, *NYT,* 9 Dec. 1941.

12 Remarks by Reps. Alben Barkley and Robert L. F. Sikes, *Congressional Record,* Appendix 89 (Washington: GPO, 1943), A4171, A2024. The importance of these experiences came to the fore in the conflict over a scuttled Smithsonian exhibit on the atomic bombing of Japan. [Ken Ringle, "Enola Gay, at Ground Zero," *Washington Post,* 26 Sept. 1994; Martin Harwit, *An Exhibit Denied: Lobbying the History of the Enola Gay* (New York: Copernicus, 1996); Robert Jay Lifton and Greg Mitchell, *Hiroshima in America: Fifty Years of Denial* (New York: G. P. Putnam's Sons, 1995).] On Japanese treatment of prisoners, see Ronald H. Spector, *Eagle Against the Sun: The American War with Japan* (New York: Vintage, 1985), 396–400. On killing airmen and the view that the Japanese wanted to exterminate Americans, see Robert L. Scott, Jr., *God Is My Co-Pilot* (New York: Charles Scribner's Sons, 1943), 253.

13 Robert Sherrod, *On to Westward: War in the Central Pacific* (New York: Duell Sloan and Pearce, 1945), 15, quoted in Spector, *Eagle against the Sun,* 410; T. Grady Gallant, *On Valor's Side* (New York: Doubleday, 1963), 288.

14 H. H. Arnold, speech, Detroit, 8 Nov. 1944, binder 5, Speech File, box 226, Papers of Henry Harley Arnold, Library of Congress, Washington, quoted in Sherry, *Air Power,* 245.

15 Quoted in Thomas B. Buell, *Master of Sea Power* (Boston: Little, Brown, 1980), 357.

16 Advertisement for Rohm and Haas, *SSC* (May 1945): 110.

17 Advertisement for Hudson, *SSC* (May 1945): 108.

18 Margaret Bourke-White, *Portrait of Myself* (New York: Simon and Schuster, 1963), 199–200, emphasis in original. I thank Randall Bond for bringing the Flying Flitgun to my attention.

19 Leo P. Brophy, Wyndham D. Miles, and Rexmond C. Cochrane, *The Chemical Warfare Service: From Laboratory to Field* (Washington: Office of the Chief of Military History, 1959), 196, 266–268, 342–343.

20 J. Enrique Zanetti, "The Forgotten Enemy," *Independent Journal of Columbia University* 3 (10 Jan. 1936): 1ff., see 1, 4.

[21] Zanetti, "The Forgotten Enemy," 1, 4.

[22] J. Enrique Zanetti, "Strategy of Incendiaries," *Chemical Warfare Bulletin* 27 (Apr. 1941): 41–44, see 42.

[23] Brophy et al., *From Laboratory to Field*, 342; Brooks E. Kleber and Dale Birdsell, *The Chemical Warfare Service: Chemicals in Combat* (Washington: GPO, 1966), 617.

[24] Brophy et al., *Laboratory to Field*, 196, 266–268, 342–343.

[25] James Phinney Baxter 3rd, *Scientists Against Time* (Boston: Little, Brown and Company, 1946), vii–ix, 3–25.

[26] Louis F. Fieser, *The Scientific Method: A Personal Account of Unusual Projects in War and in Peace* (New York: Reinhold, 1964), 14–16, 26–27; William H. Baldwin, "Front Lawn Laboratory," *Chemical Warfare Bulletin* 31 (Jan.–Feb. 1945): 10–11.

[27] Fieser, *Scientific Method*, 49–50.

[28] Baxter, *Scientists Against Time*, 292; Baldwin, "Development of Incendiary Bombs," 7, quoted in John W. Mountcastle, "Trial by Fire: U.S. Incendiary Weapons, 1918–1945" (Ph.D. dissertation, Duke University, 1979), 148 (and 149–150 for other cited information).

[29] Baxter, *Scientists against Time*, 292–293; Bush to Arnold, 13 Oct. 1944, 373.2 Report of Operations – General, Records of the Headquarters Twentieth Air Force, RG 18, Army Air Forces, NARA, quoted in Sherry, *American Air Power*, 230; "Special Fire Bomb Used to Set Blazes in Japan," *NYT*, 11 Mar. 1945; "Chemical Warfare Service Celebrates Silver Anniversary," *Chemical and Engineering News* 23 (25 Sept. 1945): 1612–1615, see 1613–1614.

[30] Fieser, *Scientific Method*, 130–134.

[31] W. A. Noyes, Jr., "Relationships of NDRC to the Armed Services and to Allied Countries in Chemical Warfare," in Noyes (ed.), *Chemistry: A History of the Chemistry Components of the National Defense Research Committee, 1940–1946* (Boston: Little, Brown, 1948), 141–154, see 146.

[32] Noyes, "Relationships of NDRC to the Armed Services and to Allied Countries in Chemical Warfare," 146–147; Office of the Chief, CWS, "Report of Activities of the Technical Division During World War II," 1 Jan. 1946, 81, in envelope: History—World War II—Rough Draft, Assistant Chief for Materiel Technical Division General Administrative Series, RG 175.

[33] Baxter, *Scientists against Time*, 299.

[34] W. N. Porter to Paul Pritchard, 28 Mar. 1945, 425, #228.01, HC-EA, quoted in Mountcastle, "Trial by Fire," 146.

[35] Frederic J. Brown, *Chemical Warfare: A Study in Restraints* (Westport, Conn.: Greenwood Press, 1968), 205.

[36] M. E. Barker to Chief, CWS, 18 Feb. 1942, B3.1d/2 Technique for High Altitude Spray, R and D Case Files, RG 175.

37 Secretary of Navy to Secretary of State, 15 Jan. 1942, notes from the files of Dale Birdsell, 740.00116 Pacific War 3, quoted in Brown, *Chemical Warfare,* 199.

38 Marshall to Commanding Gen., Bobcat, 25 Apr. 1942, Chemical Warfare Service 470.6/2711-2754, Adjutant General's Office, Edgewood Arsenal Historical Office, quoted in Brown, *Chemical Warfare,* 205. Brown notes that "similar messages were sent to all field commanders" (*Chemical Warfare,* 205 n. 38).

39 Alden H. Waitt, "Poison Gas in This War," *New Republic,* 27 Apr. 1942, 563–565.

40 "The Last Weapon," *Time,* 25 May 1942, 71–72; Alden H. Waitt, "Gas Attacks from the Air," *Popular Science,* June 1942, 102ff., see 102; Alden H. Waitt, *Gas Warfare* (New York: Duell, Sloan and Pearce, [1942]), 3–6.

41 Barton J. Bernstein, "Why We Didn't Use Poison Gas in World War II," *American Heritage* 36 (no. 5, 1985): 40–45, see 43.

42 L. J. Livingston to Chiefs, News Division, et al., n.d., 000.7 Chemical Warfare Service, Miscellaneous Series Correspondence, RG 175.

43 Samuel I. Rosenman (ed.), *The Public Papers and Addresses of Franklin D. Roosevelt,* vol. 12: *1943: The Tide Turns* (New York: Harper, 1950), 243; see also John Ellis van Courtland Moon, "Chemical Weapons and Deterrence: The World War II Experience," *International Security* 8 (Spring 1984): 3–35.

44 "History of the War Department Civilian Protection Schools," 15 Aug. 1943, 8–12, Standing Operating Procedure for Protection of the Office of the Chief, Chemical Warfare Service, War Department Civilian Protection School Series, RG 175.

45 Mary Petty, *New Yorker,* 18 July 1942, cover; reprinted with commentary by Lee Lorenz, "Petty Thoughts," *New Yorker,* 14 Apr. 1997, 58–59, see 58.

46 "Insect Saboteurs," *Science News Letter* 44 (9 Oct. 1943): 238.

47 The difference can be seen in *New York Times Index* for 1941 ("Japanese beetle," 1141) and 1942 ("Jap beetle," 734).

48 W. E. Dove, "Preparation of a Booklet Illustrating Species of Insects Affecting Dairy Products," 16 June 1945, USDA National Defense—History of Defense and War Efforts (Semi-Annual) Jan. 1–June 30, 1945, History of Defense and War Activities 1941–50, RG 7.

49 "Insects: An All-Out Attack on Fifth Columnists in the Garden," *House and Garden,* Jan. 1943, 53.

50 Chief, Chemicals Section, to D. P. Morgan, 3 Jan. 1942, Priorities 9, Insecticides-Fungicides-Disinfectants-Herbicides, Office of Agricultural Defense Relations/Office for Agricultural War Relations, RG 16.

51 P. H. Groggins to T. M. Patterson, 7 July 1942, attached to Patterson to Groggins, 10 July 1942, Insecticides 2 Arsenicals July 1–July 20, Office of

Agricultural Defense Relations/Office for Agricultural War Relations, RG 16.

[52] R. C. Roark to P. N. Annand, 6 Jan. 1945, History of Development—Bureau of Entomology and Plant Quarantine—World War 2 1945, History of Defense and War Activities 1941–50, Correspondence and Reports, RG 7.

[53] P. H. Groggins to W. E. Anderson, 23 June 1942, Insecticides 2 Arsenicals June 15 to June 30, General Correspondence 1941–1943, Office of Agricultural Defense Relations/Office for Agricultural War Relations, RG 16.

[54] J. G. Horsfall to R. G. Griggs, 5 May 1942, Committee on War Biology, Biology and Agriculture, NAS-NRC Central File, NAS; Emory C. Cushing, *History of Entomology in World War II* (Washington: Smithsonian Institution, 1957), 94.

[55] P. H. Groggins to L. S. Hitchner, 1 Sept. 1942, Insects, General Correspondence 1941–1943, Office of Agricultural Defense Relations/Office for Agricultural War Relations, RG 16; see also Denis Hayley, *The Catalyst: The First Fifty Years of NACA* (Washington: National Agricultural Chemicals Association, 1983), 19.

[56] Stanley B. Freeborn, "The Malaria Control Program of the United States Public Health Service Among Civilians in Extra-Military Areas," *Journal of the National Malaria Society* 3 (Mar. 1944): 19–23, see 19.

[57] W. A. Hardenbergh to Chief, Division of Preventive Medicine, 24 Feb. 1942, 725.11 Prevention and Restriction 1941–42, General Subject File, RG 112; William A. Hardenbergh, "Control of Insects," in United States Army Medical Service, *Preventive Medicine in World War II*, vol. 2: *Environmental Hygiene* (Washington: GPO, 1955), 179–232, see 191, 197; Blanche B. Armfield, *United States Army Medical Service: Organization and Administration in World War II* (Washington: GPO, 1963), 102.

[58] Paul A. Harper, Wilbur G. Downs, Paul W. Oman, and Norman D. Levine, "New Hebrides, Solomon Islands, Saint Matthias Group, and Ryukyu Islands," in U. S. Army Medical Service, *Preventive Medicine in World War II,* vol. 6: *Communicable Diseases: Malaria* (Washington: GPO, 1963), 399–496, see 425–426, 435; P. A. Harper, E. T. Lisansky, and B. E. Sasse, "Malaria and Other Insect-Borne Diseases in the South Pacific Campaign," *American Journal of Tropical Medicine* (supplement) 27 (no. 3, 1947): 1–67, see 10.

[59] P. F. Russell, "Introduction," in U.S. Army Medical Service, *Preventive Medicine in World War II,* 6: 1–10, see 3.

[60] J. M. Roamer to various recipients, 25 Mar. 1944, OCCWS Correspondence Cross Reference 1944, Historian's Background Files, RG 175.

61 Harper et al., "Malaria and Other Insect-Borne Diseases in the South Pacific Campaign," see 3, 36.

62 Quoted in Mary Ellen Condon-Rall, "Allied Cooperation in Malaria Prevention and Control: The World War II Southwest Pacific Experience," *Journal of the History of Medicine and Allied Sciences* 46 (1991): 493–513, see 497.

63 Oliver R. McCoy, "War Department Provisions for Malaria Control," in U. S. Army Medical Service, *Preventive Medicine in World War II*, vol. 6: 11–60, see 14–16; Paul F. Russell, "Lessons in Malariology from World War II," *American Journal of Tropical Medicine* 26 (1946): 5–13, see 11; Condon-Rall, "Allied Cooperation in Malaria Prevention and Control," 502–506.

64 McCoy, "War Department Provisions for Malaria Control," 48–51.

65 "War Department Training Circular No. 16," 14 Apr. 1945, HD 725 Insect Control—Directives, War Department Training Circulars, WWII Administrative Records, RG 112.

66 McCoy, "War Department Provisions for Malaria Control," 52.

67 Office of the Surgeon General, Circular Letter no. 44, "Tropical Diseases no. 4," 15 Feb. 1943, Correspondence, Committees on Military Medicine, Division of Medical Sciences, NRC.

68 Harper et al., "Malaria and Other Insect-Borne Diseases in the South Pacific Campaign," 31.

69 "Miss Mosquito Junction of 1943," SSC (Jan. 1944); McCoy, "War Department Provisions for Malaria Control," 52.

70 Harper et al., "Malaria and Other Insect-Borne Diseases in the South Pacific Campaign," 36.

71 Press release, General Headquarters, Southwest Pacific Area, 4 June 1944, 725 Insect Control 1945 SWPA (PI), WWII Administrative Records, RG 112.

72 Press release, General Headquarters, Southwest Pacific Area, 4 June 1944; McCoy, "War Department Provisions for Malaria Control," 51.

CHAPTER 7. ANNIHILATION (1943–1945)

1 E. F. Knipling, "Insect Control Investigations of the Orlando, Fla., Laboratory During World War II," in *Annual Report of the Board of Regents of the Smithsonian Institution, 1948* (Washington: GPO, 1948), 331–348, see 337; Bureau of Entomology and Plant Quarantine, "Insecticides and Insect Repellents Developed for the Armed Forces at the Orlando, Fla., Laboratory," Report No. 100, 1 July, 1945, 22, Division of Medical Sciences 1940–1945, NRC.

2 Oliver R. McCoy, "War Department Provisions for Malaria Control," in U.S. Army Medical Service, *Preventive Medicine in World War II*, vol. 6: *Communicable Diseases: Malaria* (Washington: GPO, 1963), 11–60, see 40.

3 E. C. Cushing, *History of Entomology in World War II* (Washington: Smithsonian Institution, 1957), 23.

4 Bureau of Entomology and Plant Quarantine, "Investigations on the Control of Insects and Other Arthropods of Importance to the Armed Forces Conducted by the Orlando, Fla., Research Laboratory, Apr., 1942 to October, 1945," National Research Council Insect Control Committee Report no. 158 (Final Report), Committees on Military Medicine, NRC (cited below as "Report 158"); Typhus Team, Rockefeller Foundation, Report 5: "Summary of Second Experiment with Louse-Killing Powders at Glencliff, N.H.," Sept. 1942, and Typhus Team, Rockefeller Foundation, Report 15: "Summary of Third Experiment with Louse-Killing Powders at Glencliff, N.H.," Nov. 1942, both in Insect Repellents – Reports, Committees on Military Medicine, Division of Medical Sciences, NRC; Fred L. Soper to Leon A. Fox, 8 Nov. 1943, USA Typhus Commission DDT General, USA Typhus Commission, RG 112.

5 Minutes, Conference on Insect Repellents, 14 July 1943, 1, Committees on Military Medicine, Division of Medical Sciences, NRC.

6 John H. Perkins, "Reshaping Technology in Wartime: The Effect of Military Goals on Entomological Research and Insect-Control Practices," *Technology and Culture* 19 (1978): 169–186, and Thomas R. Dunlap, *DDT: Scientists, Citizens, and Public Policy* (Princeton: Princeton University Press, 1981); Victor Froelicher, "The Story of DDT," *SSC* (July 1944): 115ff., see 117; R. C. Roark to P. N. Annand, 6 Jan. 1945, History of Developments – Bureau of Entomology and Plant Quarantine – World War 2 1945, History of Defense and War Activities, RG 7.

7 James S. Simmons, "How Magic Is DDT?" *Saturday Evening Post,* 6 Jan. 1945, 18 ff., see 19; James S. Simmons to Guy Denit, 7 Apr. 1944, 441 (DDT) July–Dec. 1944, Security Classified General Subject File, RG 112; Roark to Annand, 6 Jan. 1945; Froelicher, "Story of DDT," 117.

8 Simmons, "How Magic Is DDT?," 85; Pyrethrum Mission, "Summary 1, Neocid," 11 May 1943, HD725 Insect Control Malaria – Repellents and Insecticides 1943–1945, WW II Administrative Records, RG 112; James S. Simmons to D. T. Richardson, 12 May 1944, 441.-1, DDT, WW II Administrative Records, RG 112.

9 Pyrethrum Mission, "Summary 1, Neocid," 11 May 1943, and Pyrethrum Mission, "Supplementary Report, Summary 1, GNB (Neocid)," 8 June

1943, both in HD725 Insect Control Malaria – Repellents and Insecticides 1943–1945, WW II Administrative Records, RG 112.

10 Knipling, "Insect Control Investigations," 336.

11 Minutes, Conference on Insect Repellents, 14 July 1943, 4–6; Pyrethrum Mission, "Summary 1, Neocid," 11 May 1943; Pyrethrum Mission, "Supplementary Report, Summary 1, GNB (Neocid)," 8 June 1943; and Minutes, Conference on Insect Repellents, 14 July 1943, 4–6, all in Committees on Military Medicine, NRC; Herbert O. Calvery, "Bimonthly Progress Report No. 4, Toxicity of Insect Repellents and Lousicides," 31 Aug. 1943, USA Typhus Commission DDT-Reports (1943), USA Typhus Commission, RG 112; "Statement by Dr. H. O. Calvery Regarding the Toxicity of DDT, Tropical Diseases Report no. 19," 30 May 1944, attached to Clara L. Day to Clark Yeager, 27 Feb. 1945, 441. (DDT) Jan.–June 1945, General Subject File 1945–46, RG 112; "DDT Toxicity Studies," *SSC* (Dec. 1944): 147ff., see 149.

12 P. A. Neal, W. F. von Oettingen, W. W. Smith, R. B. Malmo, R. C. Dunn, H. E. Moran, T. R. Sweeney, D. W. Armstrong, and W. C. White, "Toxicity and Potential Dangers of Aerosols, Mists, and Dusting Powders Containing DDT," *Supplement No. 177 to the Public Health Reports* (Washington: GPO, 1944), 2; W. F. von Oettingen and Paul A. Neal, "Fourth Preliminary Report on the Toxicity and Potential Dangers of Gesarol Insecticides with Special Reference to their Toxicity by Inhalation," Aug. 1943, USA Typhus Commission Louse Power – MYL, USA Typhus Commission, RG 112; P. A. Neal, "Summary of Conclusions of the Report on the Toxicity and Potential Dangers of Gesarol," 28 Sept. 1943, Insect Repellents no. 3, Correspondence, Committees on Military Medicine, NRC; P. A. Neal, W. F. von Oettingen, W. W. Smith, R. B. Malmo, R. C. Dunn, H. E. Moran, T. R. Sweeney, D. W. Armstrong, and W. C. White, "Final Report on the Toxicity and Potential Dangers of Gesarol" [May-September 1943 handwritten], 49–50, USA Typhus Commission DDT-Toxicity, USA Typhus Commission, RG 112.

13 James S. Simmons to D. T. Richardson, 12 May 1944, 441.-1, DDT, WW II Administrative Records, RG 112.

Surviving documents do not state why the army relied on Neal's tests more than on Calvery's, but two reasons seem likely. First, medical doctors placed great weight on clinical experience. One of the army's key actors was General Stanhope Bayne-Jones. He received a memo saying: "Whether minute quantities of DDT ingested in this manner [from food] will prove harmful has not been determined." He wrote on the memo, "I should say that this *has* been determined – Major Wheeler and others [illegible] dusting whole and get into the mouth a considerable amount of powder (10% DDT)." Clarence Guyton to Stanhope Bayne-Jones, 17 July 1944, USA Typhus Commission DDT—Toxicity, USA Typhus Commission, RG 112.

Second, the conditions under which Neal tested animals more closely resembled the conditions under which the army would be using DDT. When Surgeon General Thomas Parran declared DDT safe, he specified the forms that Neal had tested ("a 1% to 5% solution of gesarol in 10% cyclohexanone with 89 to 85 per cent Freon as an aerosol, or in concentrations up to 10% in inert powders for dusting clothes, or the use of a 1% Gesarol-Deobase Mist"; Gesarol was an earlier name for DDT). Thomas Parran to L. H. Weed, 27 Oct. 1943, Insect Repellents no. 3, Correspondence, Committees on Military Medicine, NRC.

Neal later became even more convinced that his clinical studies showed DDT's safety. To collect data on the effects of DDT on humans, his team studied three men who had been exposed to "extremely great" amounts of DDT while working at the Orlando laboratory. In physical examinations spread over four days, they found that "none of them present definite findings that can be attributed to the toxic action of DDT." P. A. Neal, J. E. Dunn, S.S. Spicer, R. B. Malmo, W. W. Smith, H. L. Andrews, and E. C. Thompson, "Results of Examinations of Three Men Having Relatively Long Continued Occupational Exposure to DDT," 1 Aug. 1944, U. S. A. Typhus Commission DDT—Toxicity, USA Typhus Commission, RG 112.

[14] "Army Louse Powder," *SSC* 19 (July 1943): 101.

[15] P. H. Groggins, "Market Outlooks on Insecticide Materials," *SSC* 19 (July 1943): 94–96, see 94.

[16] "Army Louse Powder," 101.

[17] A German patent document dated 12 May 1943 appears, along with a French patent document (No. 870, 689) showing an application date of 7 March 1941, and an American patent (No. 2,329,074) showing application date of 4 March 1941 and issued 7 September 1943, in an official Geigy history: A. Buxtorf and M. Spindler, *Fifteen Years of Geigy Pest Control* (Basel, Switzerland: Buchdruckerei Karl Werner AG, 1954), 109.

Germany's knowledge of DDT, communication with Geigy, and adherence to the Geigy patent were described in allied intelligence reports prepared after the fall of Germany. Combined Intelligence Objectives Sub-Committee, "I.G. Farbenindustrie A.G. Plant Hoechst/Main," Item No. 22, File No. XX-II, 25 April 1945, 4, Library Projects File, RG 319; Combined Intelligence Objectives Sub-Committee, "The Leverkusen Works of I.G. Farben," Item No. 22, File No. XXIII-4, n. d., 4, Library Projects File, RG 319.

18 Knipling, "Insect Control Investigations," 335–337; James Phinney Baxter 3rd, *Scientists Against Time* (Boston: Little, Brown and Company, 1946), 369; "Report No. 158," 53.

19 Bayne-Jones paraphrased Eisenhower's radiogram in Stanhope Bayne-Jones to Records, 6 Dec. 1943, USA Typhus Commission—DDT—General, USA Typhus Commission, RG 112.

20 Dunlap, *DDT*, 61–62; Frederick C. Painton, "The Second Battle of Naples – Against Lice," *Reader's Digest,* June 1944, 21–22; Allen Raymond, "Now We Can Lick Typhus," *Saturday Evening Post,* 22 Apr. 1944, 14ff.

21 Frank Carey, "War Develops Powerful Attack Against Insects," *Mobile Press Register,* 12 Dec. 1943; Walter Adams, "DDT ... A Deadly New Bug Killer," *Better Homes and Gardens,* May 1944, 19ff.; "Coming: Freedom From Insect Pests," *Reader's Digest,* May 1944, 44; "DDT," *Time,* 12 June 1944, 66ff.; editorial, *Chicago Tribune,* reprinted in *SSC* (April 1944): 135.

22 David McCord, "Dusty Answer," *New Yorker,* 12 Aug. 1944, 48.

23 John W. Mountcastle, "Trial by Fire: United States Incendiary Weapons, 1918–1945" (Ph.D. diss., Duke Univ., 1979), 136–146; Brooks E. Kleber and Dale Birdsell, *The Chemical Warfare Service: Chemicals in Combat* (Washington: GPO, 1966), 621; Norman Polmar and Thomas B. Allen, *World War II: The Encyclopedia of the War Years 1941–1945* (New York: Random House, 1996), 29; "Hamburg in Ruins," *Life,* 23 Aug. 1943, 35; "Battle of Europe," *Time,* 16 Aug. 1943, 35; Wesley Frank Craven and James Lea Cate (eds.), *The Army Air Forces in World War II* (Chicago: University of Chicago Press, 1948–1958; reprint, Washington: Office of Air Force History, 1983), 1:591–593, 596–597.

24 W. N. Porter to Paul Pritchard, 28 Mar. 1945, 425, #228.01, HC-EA, quoted in Mountcastle, "Trial by Fire," 146.

25 Kleber and Birdsell, *Chemicals in Combat,* 622; Mountcastle, "Trial by Fire," 145.

26 On the controversial Dresden casualty figures, see Melden E. Smith, Jr., "The Bombing of Dresden Reconsidered: A Study in Wartime Decision Making" (Ph.D. diss., Boston University, 1971), 265–269; "Now Terror, Truly," *Newsweek,* 26 Feb. 1945, 34ff., see 36. For debates on British and American intentions, see Ronald Schaffer, "American Military Ethics in World War II: The Bombing of German Civilians," *Journal of American History* 67 (Sept. 1980): 318–334; Michael S. Sherry, *The Rise of American Air Power: The Creation of Armageddon* (New Haven, Conn.: Yale University Press, 1987), 162; Conrad C. Crane, "Evolution of U.S. Strategic Bombing of Urban Areas," *The Historian* 50 (Nov. 1987), 14–39.

27 United States Strategic Bombing Survey, *Over-all Report (European War)* (Washington: GPO, 1945), 92.

28 *Congressional Record,* Appendix 90 (Washington: GPO, 1944), A1217–A1218.

29 Robert L. Scott, Jr., *God Is My Co-Pilot* (New York: Charles Scribner's Sons, 1943), 138, 186, 209, 254; see also John W. Dower, *War Without Mercy: Race and Power in the Pacific War* (New York, 1986); "Rodent Exterminators," *Time,* 19 Mar. 1945, 32ff., see 34.

30 Herman Wouk, *The Caine Mutiny* (Garden City, N. Y.: Doubleday 1951), 240 (emphasis added). On the importance of Wouk's World War II experience for *Caine,* see Ken Ringle, "Fiction's Truest Voice," *Washington Post,* 16 May 1995.

31 Second Lieutenant Kermit Stewart, quoted in Annette Tapert (ed.), *Lines of Battle: Letters of American Servicemen, 1941–1945* (1987), 238, quoted in turn in Michael C. C. Adams, *The Best War Ever: America and World War II* (Baltimore: Johns Hopkins University Press, 1994), 113.

32 Knipling, "Insect Control Investigations," 338; P. A. Harper, E. T. Lisansky, and B. E. Sasse, "Malaria and Other Insect-Borne Diseases in the South Pacific Campaign," *American Journal of Tropical Medicine, Supplement,* 27 (no. 3, 1947): 1–67, see 36; O. R. McCoy in Minutes, Subcommittee on Dispersal, 18–19 Feb. 1946, 16, Committee on Insect Control (OSRD), Committees on Military Medicine, NRC.

33 James Simmons to Guy Denit, 7 Apr. 1944, HD 725 Insecticides (Airplane Spraying DDT) 1944–45, WWII Administrative Records, RG 112; Howard A. Jones et al., "Use of the Chemical Warfare Service M-10 Tank for Release of DDT Sprays," 15 Apr. 1944, 470.6 Bushnell Project, Miscellaneous Series Correspondence, RG 175.

34 "Report on Trip of Brig. General A. H. Waitt and Lt. Col. J. K. Javits to POA and SWPA, 24 Sep. 1944–21 Nov. 1944," 15 Dec. 1944, 35–36, box 43 (not in file), Miscellaneous Series Correspondence, RG 175.

35 Francisco J. Dy, "Report on Aircraft Spraying of DDT," n.d., HD 725 Insect Control (Airplane Spraying DDT) 1944–45, WWII Administrative Records, RG 112; MacArthur to Commanding Gen., Alamo Force, and Comdr., Allied Air Forces, 29 July 1944, HD 725 Insect Control (Airplane Spraying DDT) 1944–45, WWII Administrative Records, RG 112.

36 F. J. Dy to H. F. Smith, 3 Aug. 1944, HD 725 Insect Control (Airplane Spraying DDT) 1944–45, WWII Administrative Records, RG 112.

37 John M. Hutzel, "Insect Control for the Marines," *Scientific Monthly* 62 (May 1946): 417–420, see 420.

38 Frederick S. Philips, "Medical Division Report No. 13, A Review of the Biological Properties and Insecticidal Applications of DDT," 22 Nov.

1944, 2, USA Typhus Commission – DDT – General, USA Typhus Commission, RG 112; "destruction" from Minutes, Subcommittee on Dispersal, 18–19 Feb. 1946, 18, Committee on Insect Control (OSRD), Committees on Military Medicine, NRC; C. H. Curran, "DDT – The Atomic Bomb of the Insect World," *Natural History* 54 (Nov. 1945): 401ff., see 403.

39 Milton C. Winternitz, "Introduction," in E. C. Andrus et al. (eds.), *Advances in Military Medicine* (Boston: Little, Brown, 1948), 533–545, see 539, 542.

40 Members were M. Winternitz, R. Adams, A. Hastings, W. Kirner, W. Noyes, A. Waterman, and J. Wearn. V. Bush to W. Porter, 20 Sep. 1944, 710 Office of Scientific Research and Development, Miscellaneous Series Correspondence, RG 175.

41 William N. Porter to Vannevar Bush, 30 Sept. 1944, 710 OSRD, Miscellaneous Series Correspondence, RG 175.

42 Cornelius P. Rhoads for record, 17 Oct. 1944, 470.6 Chemical Warfare Service, Miscellaneous Series Correspondence, RG 175; see also M. M. Irvine to Chief, Chemical Warfare Service, 26 Oct. 1944, HD 438 Insect and Rodent Control, Insecticides, 1945, WW II Administrative Records, RG 112; Medical Research Laboratory, "Insecticide and Rodenticide Program," 1 Feb. 1945, attached to C. Rhoads to C. Stock, 15 Feb. 1945, 352 Massachusetts Institute of Technology 1945, Miscellaneous Series Correspondence, RG 175; Office of the Chief, CWS, "Report of Activities of the Technical Division During World War II," 1 Jan. 1946, 81, in envelope: History – World War II – Rough Draft, Assistant Chief for Materiel Technical Division General Administrative Series, RG 175. For a listing of projects, see "Chemical Warfare Service Project Program Summary, Fiscal Year 1945," revision 3, 2 Apr. 1945, Research and Development Project Program 1940–45, Assistant Chief for Materiel Technical Division General Administrative Series, RG 175.

43 Willard J. Slagle to Office of the Chief, CWS, 2 Mar. 1945, 352 MIT May 1945, Miscellaneous Series Correspondence, RG 175; Medical Research Laboratory, "Insecticide and Rodenticide Program," 1 Feb. 1945, attached to C. Rhoads to C. Stock, 15 Feb. 1945, 352 Massachusetts Institute of Technology 1945, Miscellaneous Series Correspondence, RG 175; W. A. Noyes, "Insecticide Dispersal," in W. A. Noyes, Jr., (ed.), *Chemistry: A History of the Chemistry Components of the National Defense Research Committee 1940–1946* (Boston: Little, Brown and Company, 1948), 333–341, see 339.

44 Joseph Dec, interview by A. L. Ahnfeldt, 6 Dec. 1944, USA Typhus Commission Mite Repellent no. 2, USA Typhus Commission, RG 112.

45 Cornelius P. Rhoads to W. B. Harrell, 20 Feb. 1945, and Harrell to Rhoads, 8 Mar. 1945, both in 161 University of Chicago, Station Series Security Classified, RG 175.

46 J. C. Troxel to M. F. Peake, 21 May 1945, 400.112 University of Chicago, Station Series Security Classified, RG 175.

47 William N. Porter and Boyden Sparkes, "Watch Our Smoke!" *Saturday Evening Post,* 20 Nov. 1943, 24ff., see 24; Brooks E. Kleber and Dale Birdsell, *The Chemical Warfare Service: Chemicals in Combat* (Washington: GPO, 1966), 322–324; "Notes from SOPAC Area on DDT," n.d., HD 725 Insecticides – Airplane Spraying DDT 1944–45, WWII Administrative Records, RG 112.

48 The Surgeon General's DDT Committee, "1st Interim Report," 3 Mar.–15 May 1944, 10, 441 DDT Through June 30, 1944, Security Classified General Subject File, RG 112.

49 Minutes, Subcommittee on Dispersal, 18–19 Feb. 1946, 17, Committee on Insect Control, OSRD, Committees on Military Medicine, NRC.

50 Georges F. Doriot to J. W. Mockabee, 29 Apr. 1944, 441 DDT Jan.–June 1944, General Subject File, RG 112.

51 Philip R. Faymonville to Chief, Chemical Warfare Service, 22 Jan. 1945, 441 DDT 1945–46, Security Classified General Subject File, RG 112.

52 Oliver R. McCoy, "War Department Provisions for Malaria Control," 46–47.

53 Vincent G. Dethier, telephone interview by author, 18 Sept. 1992.

54 "CWS Monthly Progress Report on Insect and Rodent Control, No. 2," Apr. 1945, 461 CWS, Miscellaneous Series Correspondence, RG 175.

55 George Fielding Eliot, "Should We Gas the Japs?" *Popular Science* 147 (Aug. 1945): 49–53.

56 Factors that scholars cite to explain restraint in the use of gas include deterrence (both sides feared retaliation in kind) and dislike of gas by military officers (who found it hard to control and use decisively). A number of reports charged that Japan used poison gas in China in the 1930s and 1940s. Frederic J. Brown, *Chemical Warfare: A Study in Restraints* (Westport, Conn.: Greenwood Press, 1968), 288–289; Robert Harris and Jeremy Paxman, *A Higher Form of Killing: The Secret Story of Chemical and Biological Warfare* (New York: Hill and Wang, 1982), 148–149; Jeffrey W. Legro, "Cooperation Within Conflict: Submarines, Strategic Bombing, Chemical Warfare and Restraint in World War II" (Ph.D. diss, University of California, Los Angeles, 1992); Stockholm International Peace Research Institute, *The Problem of Chemical and Biological Warfare,* vol. 1: *The Rise of CB Weapons* (New York: Humanities Press, 1971), 147–157; Richard M. Price, *The Chemical Weapons Taboo* (Ithaca: Cornell University Press,

1997); Edmund P. Russell III, "'Speaking of Annihilation': Mobilizing for War against Human and Insect Enemies, 1914–1945," *Journal of American History* 82 (Mar. 1996): 1505–1529.

57 Quoted in Barton J. Bernstein, "Why We Didn't Use Poison Gas in World War II," *American Heritage* 36 (no. 5, 1985), 40–45, see 43.

58 "Fire Blitz: Progress Report on the Incendiary Bombing of Japan," *Impact* (Aug. 1945): 18–39, see 19.

59 Craven and Cate, *Army Air Forces in World War II* 1:438–444; Leo P. Brophy, Wyndham D. Miles, and Rexmond C. Cochrane, *United States Army in World War II, The Chemical Warfare Service: From Laboratory to Field* (Washington: Office of the Chief of Military History, 1959), 174–175. For a critical examination of the Doolittle raid and its motives, see Sherry, *American Air Power*, 123–124.

60 *Congressional Record – House* 88 (Washington: GPO, 1942), 4075.

61 "Things to Cheer About," *New Republic*, 27 Apr. 1942, 555.

62 "Fire Blitz," *Impact* (Aug. 1945): 19.

63 "Record Air Attack," *NYT*, 10 Mar. 1945.

64 "Chemical Warfare Service Pays Tribute to Industry Leaders," *Chemical and Engineering News* 23 (10 Dec. 1945): 2206.

65 Stimson Diary, 6 May 1945 and 6 June 1945, reel 9, quoted in Crane, "Evolution of United States Strategic Bombing," 22.

66 "City's Heart Gone," *NYT*, 11 Mar. 1945.

67 "McNutt for Erasing Japanese," *NYT*, 6 Apr. 1945 (see also "M'Nutt Explains Speech," *NYT*, 10 Apr. 1945); Elliott Roosevelt quoted in John Morton Blum (ed.), *The Price of Vision: The Diary of Henry A. Wallace, 1942–1946* (New York: Houghton Mifflin, 1973), entry of 16 May 1945, 448.

68 Strategic Bombing Survey, *Summary Report (Pacific War)* (Washington: GPO, 1946), 12, 20–22.

69 Sherry, *American Air Power*, 277. For a careful discussion of the number of fatalities in the Tokyo raid of 9–10 Mar. 1945, with numerous citations, see Sherry, 406 n. 76; here Sherry shows the wide range of estimates, from 79,000 to 130,000. To Sherry, it is probable but not certain that more died in the Tokyo raid than at Hiroshima. See also Gordon Daniels, "The Great Tokyo Air Raid, 9–10 March 1945," in W. G. Beasely (ed.), *Modern Japan: Aspects of History, Literature and Society* (London: Allen and Unwin, 1975), 113–131, see 113, 129, 278 n. 1, 280 n. 60. According to an official history, "The official toll of casualties listed 83,793 dead and 40,918 wounded." Wesley Frank Craven and James Lea Cate (eds.), *The Army Air Forces in World War II*, vol. 5 (Washington: Office of Air Force History, 1983), 617.

[70] United States Strategic Bombing Survey, *Over-all Report (European War)* (Washington: GPO, 1945), 71–72; United States Strategic Bombing Survey, *Summary Report (Pacific War)*, 20.

[71] Martin Caidin, *A Torch to the Enemy* (New York: Ballantine Books, 1960), 22; United States Strategic Bombing Survey, *Summary Report (Pacific War)*, 23–24, W. H. Lawrence, "Nagasaki Flames Rage for Hours," *NYT*, 10 Aug. 1945; "New Age Ushered," *NYT*, 7 Aug. 1945. The literature on this event is huge. A sampling includes Sherry, *American Air Power*, 293–356; Gar Alperovitz, *The Decision to Use the Atomic Bomb and the Architecture of an American Myth* (New York: A. A. Knopf, 1995). The early reactions to the atomic bomb are spelled out beautifully in Paul Boyer, *By the Bomb's Early Light: American Thought and Culture at the Dawn of the Atomic Age* (Chapel Hill: University of North Carolina Press, 1994).

[72] "2d Big Aerial Blow," *NYT*, 9 Aug. 1945; "Japanese Reaction," *Washington Post*, 8 Aug. 1945; Lawrence, "Nagasaki Flames Rage"; "War News Summarized," *NYT*, 10 Aug. 1945; Barnet Nover, "The End in Sight," *Washington Post*, 11 Aug. 1945.

[73] "News of Weapon Electrifies Truman Ship," *NYT*, 7 Aug. 1945; Paul Fussell, "Thank God for the Atom Bomb," in Fussell, *Thank God for the Atom Bomb and Other Essays* (New York: Summit Books, 1988), 13–37; see also Patrick J. Dudley, interview by Peter Norton, tape recording, Charlottesville, Va., 8 Feb. 1998; "War without Quarter," *Washington Post*, 9 Aug. 1945.

[74] Leonie M. Cole to editor, *Milwaukee Journal*, 16 Aug. 1945. I thank Paul Boyer for bringing this letter to my attention.

[75] "A Decision for Mankind," *St. Louis Post-Dispatch*, 7 Aug. 1945, quoted in Boyer, *Early Light*, 5.

CHAPTER 8. PLANNING FOR PEACE AND WAR (1944–1945)

[1] Franklin Roosevelt to Vannevar Bush, 17 Nov. 1944, in Vannevar Bush, *Science: The Endless Frontier* (Washington: GPO, 1945), vii–viii, see vii.

[2] John Gimbel, *Science, Technology, and Reparations: Exploitation and Plunder in Postwar Germany* (Stanford: Stanford University Press, 1990), 4–8, see 8.

[3] British Intelligence Objectives Subcommittee, "Development of New Insecticides and Chemical Warfare Agents, Report No. 714," n. d.; and British Intelligence Objectives Subcommittee, "The Development of New Insecticides, Report No. 714 (Revised)," n. d., both in Library Projects File, RG 319.

[4] James S. Simmons to D. T. Richardson, 12 May 1944, 441.-1, DDT, Policy Documentation File, RG 179.

5 Pyrethrum Mission, "Summary 1, Neocid," 11 May 1943, HD725 Insect Control Malaria – Repellents and Insecticides 1943–1945, WWII Administrative Records, RG 112; Norman T. Kirk to Commanding General, Army Service Forces, 29 Dec. 1943, 441 (DDT) Thru June 30, 1944, Security Classified General Subject File, RG 112.

6 Melvin Goldberg to Walter G. Whitman, 21 Sep. 1943, 535.61142, Policy Documentation File, RG 179.

7 D. P. Morgan to G. N. McClusky, 26 Nov. 1943, attached to O. S. Anderson to C. E. Kohlhepp, 4 Dec. 1943, 535.611, Policy Documentation File, RG 179.

8 Program Adjustment Committee Meeting 137, 8 Dec. 1943, and J. A. Krug to Charles E. Wilson, 9 Dec. 1943, both in 535.611, Policy Documentation File, RG 179.

9 D. P. Morgan to G. N. McClusky, 30 Dec. 1943, 535.61142, Policy Documentation File, RG 179.

10 D. P. Morgan to L. R. Boulware, 14 Jan. 1944, 535.61141, Policy Documentation File, RG 179.

11 D. P. Morgan to G. N. McClusky, 30 Dec. 1943.

12 W. G. Whitman to Melvin Goldberg, 22 Dec. 1943, 535.61142, Policy Documentation File, RG 179.

13 J. A. Krug to L. R. Boulware, 15 Jan. 1944, 535.611, Policy Documentation File, RG 179.

14 J. W. Wizeman to J. C. Leppart, et al., 7 June 1944, 535.61142, Policy Documentation File, RG 179.

15 Davis Dyer and David B. Sicilia, *Labors of a Modern Hercules: The Evolution of a Chemical Company* (Boston: Harvard Business School Press, 1990), 247.

16 Melvin Goldberg to W. G. Whitman, 7 Jan. 1944, 535.61142, Policy Documentation File, RG 179; War Production Board, *War Production in 1944* (Washington: GPO, 1945), 29.

17 Walter G. Whitman to D. P. Morgan, 9 Nov. 1944, 535.61142, Policy Documentation File, RG 179.

18 Summary, DDT Producers Advisory Committee, 25 May 1944, 5, 535.61105, Policy Documentation File, RG 179.

19 Dyer and Sicilia, *Labors of a Modern Hercules,* 248.

20 Preston Peaker, "Over the Transom," *SSC* (July 1944):105.

21 D. P. Morgan to H. B. Boynton, 28 Jan. 1944, 535.61142, Policy Documentation File, RG 179.

22 Preston Peaker, "Over the Transom," *SSC* (July 1944): 105.

23 "Growing Strength of Synthetics Indicated at NAIDM Meeting," *Chemical Industries* 55 (July 1944): 66–68.

[24] Summary, DDT Producers Advisory Committee, 30 Mar. 1944, 3, 535.61105, Policy Documentation File, RG 179.

[25] Vannevar Bush to M. C. Winternitz, 1 Sep. 1944, 2, Committee on Insect Control, OSRD, NAS-NRC Central File, NAS.

[26] F. B. Jewett to R. G. Harrison, Isaiah Bowman, A. N. Richards, W. Mansfield Clark, G. B. Corner, E. B. Fred, Roger Adams, and A. Baird Hastings, 30 Oct. 1944, Committee on Insect Control, Executive Board, Administration, NRC Central File, NAS.

[27] Charles Brannan to V. Bush, 3 Nov. 1944, 1, Committee on Insect Control, Executive Board, Administration, NRC Central File, NAS.

[28] V. Bush to Charles Brannan, 15 Nov. 1944; Charles Brannan to V. Bush, 2 Dec. 1944; V. Bush to Charles Brannan, 7 Dec. 1944 (location of quotation), all in Committee on Insect Control, Executive Board, Administration, NRC Central File, NAS.

[29] V. Bush to W. Porter, 20 Sept. 1944, 710 Office of Scientific Research and Development, Subject Series Correspondence, RG 175; Milton C. Winternitz, "Introduction," in E. C. Andrus, D. W. Bronk, G. A. Carden, Jr., C. S. Keefer, J. S. Lockwood, J. T. Wearn, and M. C. Winternitz (eds.), *Advances in Military Medicine Made by American Investigators Working under the Sponsorship of the Committee on Medical Research* (Boston: Little, Brown and Company, 1948), 533–545, see 542.

[30] Preliminary Draft, Second Meeting of the OSRD Insect Control Committee, 27 Jan. 1945, 3–5, Committee on Insect Control, OSRD, Executive, Government, NAS-NRC Central File, NAS.

[31] Charles Brannan to F. Jewett, 13 Mar. 1945, Committee on Insect Control, Executive Board, NRC Central File, NAS.

[32] M. C. Winternitz to F. B. Jewett, 16 Mar. 1945, Committee on Insect Control, Executive Board, NRC Central File, NAS.

[33] James A. G. Rehn and Herbert Ross to F. Jewett, 10 July 1945, Committee on Insect Control, Executive Board, NRC Central File, NAS.

[34] D. L. Van Dine, "Involvements in Research in Present Day Economic Entomology," *Journal of Economic Entomology* 39 (1946): 1–5, see 2.

[35] F. Jewett to A. G. Rehn, 18 July 1945, Committee on Insect Control, Executive Board, NRC Central File, NAS.

[36] V. Everett Kinsey in Minutes, National Academy—Research Council Insect Control Committee and OSRD Insect Control Committee, 6 June 1945, 5; Walter R. Kirner to M. C. Winternitz, 13 Feb. 1946, 1; M. C. Winternitz to G. B. Darling, 2 Mar. 1946; M. C. Winternitz to F. Jewett, 31 May 1945; F. Jewett to M. C. Winternitz, 1 June 1945, all in Committee on Insect Control, Executive Board, Administration, NRC Central File, NAS.

[37] F. Jewett to A. G. Rehn, 18 July 1945, Committee on Insect Control, Executive Board, NRC Central File, NAS.

[38] James S. Simmons, "American Mobilization for the Conquest of Malaria in the United States," *Journal of the National Malaria Society* 3 (Mar. 1944): 7–10, see 10.

[39] H. G. Hanson to W. C. Kabrich, 30 Apr. 1945, 412 U. S. Public Health Service, Miscellaneous Series, RG 175.

[40] Margaret Humphreys, "Kicking a Dying Dog: DDT and the Demise of Malaria in the American South, 1942–1950," *Isis* 87 (Mar. 1996): 1–17, see 10–11.

[41] Information Branch, Office of the Chief of the Chemical Warfare Service, 1 June 1945, attached to George O. Gillingham to Commanding Officer, 17 Aug. 1945, 000.7 Chemical Warfare Service, Miscellaneous Series, RG 175.

[42] "Demonstrate Insecticide Mortar," *SSC* (May 1945):139.

[43] "Use of Big Guns Urged to Kill Jersey 'Skeeters,'" *NYT*, 31 Mar. 1945.

[44] "Battle-Smoke Maker May Find Peace Time Use in Bug Control," *Sales Management* 54 (15 June 1944): 110ff., see 110, 112.

[45] Clay Lyle, "Achievements and Possibilities in Pest Eradication," *Journal of Economic Entomology* 40 (Feb. 1947): 1–8, see 5.

[46] James S. Simmons, "How Magic Is DDT?" *Saturday Evening Post*, 6 Jan. 1945, 18.

[47] "Coming: Freedom from Insect Pests," *Reader's Digest*, May 1944, 44.

[48] "Our Next World War – Against Insects," *Popular Mechanics*, Apr. 1944, 66–70, see 66–67.

[49] "Sanitary Products," *SSC* 22 (Mar. 1946): 121.

[50] "Testing Thanite," *Hercules Mixer* 28 (Apr. 1946): 118.

[51] R. C. Roark indexed 174 publications on DDT published by June 1944, 418 in the second half of 1944, and 381 more in the first six months of 1945. R. C. Roark and N. E. McIndoo, *A Digest of the Literature on DDT Through April 30, 1944*, E-631 ([Washington]: Bureau of Entomology and Plant Quarantine, 1944), 4; R. C. Roark, *A List of Publications on 2,2-Bis(Parachlorophenyl)-1,1,1-Trichloroethane (Called DDT) from 1874 to April 30, 1944, Inclusive* ([Washington: Bureau of Entomology and Plant Quarantine], 1944); R. C. Roark, *A Second List of Publications on DDT*, E-660 ([Washington: Bureau of Entomology and Plant Quarantine], May 1945); R. C. Roark, *A Third List of Publications on DDT January Through June 1945*, E-674 ([Washington: Bureau of Entomology and Plant Quarantine], 1945).

[52] The minutes recorded statements but not identities of speakers. Minutes, DDT Producers Meeting, 18 July 1945, 7, 535.61105, Policy Documentation File, RG 179.

53 E. O. Essig, "An All Out Entomological Program," *Journal of Economic Entomology* 38 (Feb. 1945): 1–8, see 6, 8 (emphasis added).

54 "Total Insect War Urged," *Science News Letter* 47 (6 Jan. 1945): 5 (emphasis added).

55 "Report of Special Committee on DDT," *Journal of Economic Entomology* 38 (1945): 144.

56 "DDT Is Dynamite to Insects But Effect on Man Is Doubted," *Washington Post,* 10 July 1944; Roark and McIndoo, *A Digest of the Literature on DDT Through April 30, 1944, E-631.*

57 E. Bishop to O. R. McCoy, 13 Sept. 1944, 441 (DDT) July–Dec. 1944, General Subject File, RG 112; Frederick S. Philips, "Medical Division Report No. 13, A Review of the Biological Properties and Insecticidal Applications of DDT," 22 Nov. 1944, 2, USA Typhus Commission – DDT – General, USA Typhus Commission, RG 112; Summary, Joint Meeting of DDT Producers and Arsenical Producers Advisory Committee, 19 Oct. 1944, 9–10, 535.61105, Policy Documentation File, RG 179; John H. Perkins, *Insects, Experts, and the Insecticide Crisis: The Quest for New Pest Management Strategies* (New York: Plenum, 1982), 15–22, 40–44.

58 John H. Draize, Geoffrey Woodard, O. Garth Fitzhugh, Arthur A. Nelson, R. Blackwell Smith, Jr., and Herbert O. Calvery, "Summary of Toxicological Studies of the Insecticide DDT," *Chemical and Engineering News* 22 (1944): 1503–1504, see 1504; Arthur A. Nelson, John H. Draize, Geoffrey Woodard, O. Garth Fitzhugh, R. Blackwell Smith, Jr., and Herbert O. Calvery, "Histopathological Changes Following Administration of DDT to Several Species of Animals," *Public Health Reports* 59 (4 Aug. 1944): 1009–1020; Geoffrey Woodard, Ruth R. Ofner, and Charles M. Montgomery, "Accumulation of DDT in the Body Fat and Its Appearance in the Milk of Dogs," *Science* 102 (1945): 177–178.

59 R. D. Lillie and M. I. Smith, "Pathology of Experimental Poisoning in Cats, Rabbits, and Rats with 2,2 Bis-Parachlorophenyl-1,1,1 Trichlorethane," *Public Health Reports* 59 (28 July 1944): 979–984; M. I. Smith and E. F. Stohlman, "The Pharmacologic Action of 2,2 Bis(P-Chlorophenyl) 1,1,1 Trichlorethane and Its Estimation in the Tissues and Body Fluids," *Public Health Reports* 59 (28 July 1944): 984–993.

60 Jane Stafford, "Insect War May Backfire," *Science News Letter,* 5 Aug. 1944, 90–92, see 91; "DDT Warning," *Time,* 7 Aug. 1944, 66.

61 "DDT Outlook," *SSC* (June 1944): 127.

62 Norman T. Kirk and S. Bayne-Jones to Thomas Parran, 26 Aug. 1944, 441 (DDT) July–Dec. 1944, Security Classified General Subject File, RG 112.

63 Robert H. Williams, "Spray My Cares Away? I Don't Think So," *Washington Post,* 27 Oct. 1991.

64 "DDT Considered Safe for Insecticidal Use," *American Journal of Public Health* 34 (1944): 1312–1313.

65 In an influential study of environmentalism, Samuel P. Hays argued that government experts did not know about or look for ways that DDT might harm people or wildlife until the 1960s. Samuel P. Hays, *Beauty, Health, and Permanence: Environmental Politics in the United States, 1955–1985* (New York: Cambridge University Press, 1987), 3, 174. Angus A. MacIntyre stressed that during World War II, DDT's developers focused on "acute, short-term toxicity to persons directly exposed.... We simply did not understand the chronic adverse impacts of DDT." ["Why Pesticides Received Extensive Use in America: A Political Economy of Agricultural Pest Management to 1970," *Natural Resources Journal* 27 (1987): 533–578.]

66 H. H. Stage and C. F. W. Muesebeck, "Insects Killed by DDT Aerial Spraying in Panama," National Research Council Insect Control Committee Report No. 108, 1 July 1945, 1, Committees on Military Medicine, NRC; Minutes, Joint Meeting of the OSRD Insect Control Committee and the Army Committee for Insect and Rodent Control, 6 Apr. 1945, 3, Insect Control, Committees on Military Medicine, NRC.

67 Minutes, Joint Meeting of National Academy-Research Council Insect Control Committee and OSRD Insect Control Committee, 2 May 1945, 2, Committee on Insect Control, Executive Board, NRC.

68 Robert F. Griggs to M. C. Winternitz, 15 June 1945, Committee on Insect Control, OSRD, Office of Emergency Management, NRC.

69 Minutes, Joint Meeting of the Army Committee for Insect and Rodent Control and the Office of Scientific Research and Development Insect Control Committee, 12 Jan. 1945, 7, Committees on Military Medicine, NRC; Harriet Geer and Herbert Scoville, Jr., "Methods of Dispersal of DDT," 1 Mar. 1945, 2, Committee on Insect Control, OSRD, Office of Emergency Management, NRC.

70 Edwin Way Teale, "DDT," *Nature Magazine* 38 (Mar. 1945): 120.

71 "Use of DDT for Mosquito Control in the United States, A Joint Statement of Policy by the U. S. Army and the U. S. Public Health Service," attached to C. L. Williams to Surgeon General, U. S. Army, 20 Apr. 1945, 725.11 Prevention and Restriction 1945, General Subject File, RG 112; Humphreys, "Kicking a Dying Dog."

72 A. L. Ahnfeldt to Surgeon General, 7 July 1945; A. L. Ahnfeldt to P. H. Annand, 7 July 1945; A. L. Ahnfeldt to Ira N. Gabrielson, 7 July 1945; O. R. McCoy and Thomas A. Hart to Frederick C. Lincoln, 8 Aug. 1945, all in 334 (Committees) Jan.–June 1946 [discrepant dates in original], General Subject File, RG 112.

[73] "Use of DDT for Mosquito Control in the United States."

[74] J. Solon Mordell to George K. Hamill, 20 July 1945, 535.61105, Policy Documentation File, RG 179.

[75] J. Solon Mordell to George K. Hamill, 20 July 1945, 535.61105, Policy Documentation File, RG 179.

[76] Summary, DDT Producers Advisory Committee, 25 July 1945, 3–4, 535.61105, Policy Documentation File, RG 179.

[77] Sydney B. Self, "Chemists' Goal: Hold Wartime, Double Prewar Rate," *Barron's,* 7 Jan. 1946, 9.

[78] Thomas R. Dunlap, *DDT: Scientists, Citizens, and Public Policy* (Princeton: Princeton University Press, 1981), 63; James Whorton, *Before Silent Spring: Pesticides and Public Policy in Pre-DDT America* (Princeton: Princeton University Press, 1974).

[79] Summary, DDT Producers Advisory Committee, 25 July 1945, 4; John Rodda, "The Outlook for Insecticide Raw Materials," *SSC* (Oct. 1944): 109–110.

[80] Summary, DDT Producers Advisory Committee, 25 July 1945, 3–4.

[81] Summary, DDT Producers Advisory Committee, 25 July 1945.

[82] Summary, DDT Producers Advisory Committee, 25 July 1945, 3–4.

[83] Summary, DDT Producers Advisory Committee, 25 July 1945, 5.

CHAPTER 9. WAR COMES HOME (1945–1950)

[1] "War on Insects," *Time,* 27 Aug. 1945, 65.

[2] Advertisement for Rohm and Haas, *SSC* 22 (Aug. 1946): 134; advertisement for Velsicol, *AC* 1 (May 1946).

[3] Orlando Park, "'Unto One of the Least of These,'" *Science* 102 (19 Oct. 1945): 389–390, see 390.

[4] "Decries Atom Secrecy," *NYT,* 20 Sept. 1945.

[5] "Insecticides Play Vital Role in Human Affairs," *Scientific American,* June 1946, 268–269, see 268

[6] Quoted in Frank Graham, Jr., *Since Silent Spring* (Boston: Houghton Mifflin, 1970), 41.

[7] "WPB Lifts Restrictions on DDT," *SSC* (Aug. 1945): 125; "DDT Insecticides Rushed on Market," *SSC* 21 (Sept. 1945): 124A–124C, see 124A.

[8] O. T. Zimmerman and Irvin Lavine, *DDT: Killer of Killers* (Dover, N. H.: Industrial Research Service, 1946), 42–43.

[9] Hugh Benjamin, "Insecticide Dealer," *AC* 1 (Nov. 1946): 31ff., see 32.

[10] "Insect-Killing Bombs To Be Plentiful," *Science News Letter,* 2 Mar. 1946, 136.

11 Clay Lyle, "Achievements and Possibilities in Pest Eradication," *Journal of Economic Entomology* 40 (Feb. 1947): 1–8, see 6.

12 "By Fire and Fog," *Newsweek,* 15 Oct. 1945, 82–86, see 86.

13 Charles M. Reeves, "Next Year's Bug Blitz," *American City* 64 (Feb. 1949): 104–105.

14 William A. Lewis, "Growth, Importance and Problems of Agricultural Aviation," *AC* 15 (June 1960): 70ff.; William L. Popham, "Airplane Spraying of Insecticides," *AC* 1 (June 1946): 16; William L. Popham, "Airplane Spraying, Part II," *AC* 1 (July 1946): 19.

15 Industrial Management Corporation, "Insect-O-Blitz," *SSC* (Dec. 1946): 146; "Bug Bomb," *Modern Packaging* 18 (Oct. 1944): 98–102, see 98.

16 Earl C. Helfrick, "Mass Murder Introduces Sherwin-Williams' 'Pestroy,'" *Sales Management* (15 Oct. 1946): 60ff., see 62.

17 Advertisement by Industrial Management Corp., *SSC* 22 (May 1946): 138 (emphasis in original).

18 Helfrick, "Mass Murder"; "Newspaper Campaign Raises Insecticide Sales," *Printer's Ink* (16 Nov. 1945): 138–139; L. G. Gemmell, Charles L. Smith, Louis Pyenson, and Thomas Jefferson Miley, "Man's War upon Insect and Microbe Pests," Radio Business Forum presented by Commerce and Industry Association of New York, Inc., Station WMCA, 26 Md. 1946, in National Agricultural Library, Beltsville, Mary.

19 G. A. Campbell and T. F. West, *The Truth about DDT* (London: Findon Publications, Limited, [1945]); Zimmerman and Lavine, *DDT;* "Credit Policy Set for Surplus Sales," *NYT,* 12 July 1946.

20 "AIFA Holds 13th Annual Meeting at Spring Lake," *AC* 1 (Oct. 1946): 15–17.

21 "Insecticide Dealer," *AC* 1 (Nov. 1946): 31.

22 Lyle, "Achievements and Possibilities," 5.

23 Minutes, Committee on Sanitary Engineering and Environment, 15 Sept. 1948, 66, Division of Medical Sciences, NRC; Fred L. Soper, "Species Sanitation and Species Eradication for the Control of Mosquito-Borne Diseases," in Mark F. Boyd (ed.), *Malariology: A Comprehensive Survey of All Aspects of This Group of Diseases from a Global Standpoint* (Philadelphia: W. B. Saunders, 1949), 2:1167–1174.

24 "Why Put Up with Flies and Mosquitoes in Your Town?" *House Beautiful* 91 (June 1949): 195.

25 Paul F. Russell, *Man's Mastery of Malaria* (London: Oxford University Press, 1955), 158.

26 "DDT Can Wipe Out Plagues," *Science News Letter,* 8 Sept. 1945, 147.

27 Lyle, "Achievements and Possibilities," 6.

28 Lyle, "Achievements and Possibilities," 6.

29 "All-Out Anti-Fly Campaign June 1," *American City* 63 (May 1948): 5.

30 "'Toxaphene' for Cotton Pests," *AC* 2 (June 1947): 57.

31 "Insecticide List Growing," *Science News Letter,* 17 Jan. 1948, 45; "DDT Has New Competitor," *Science News Letter,* 2 Feb. 1946, 71; "New Insecticide Is Made," *NYT,* 23 Dec. 1946.

32 Advertisement for Commercial Solvents, *AC* 3 (Apr. 1948): 44; advertisement for Prentiss, *AC* 2 (June 1947): 30.

33 Robert L. Metcalf, "The Impact of Organophosphorous Insecticides upon Basic and Applied Science," *Bulletin of the Entomological Society of America* 5 (1959): 3–15; Lowell B. Kilgore, "New German Insecticides," *SSC* 21 (Dec. 1945): 138ff.; Lowell B. Kilgore, "German Insecticide Research," *SSC* 22 (Feb. 1946): 122–124; Lowell B. Kilgore, "German Insecticide Evaluation," *SSC* 22 (Mar. 1946): 122ff.; "German Pesticide Work Told in United States Reports," *Oil, Paint and Drug Reporter* 148 (10 Dec. 1948): 7ff.; "Release Data on German Insecticides," *SSC* 21 (Dec. 1945): 137ff.; Alvin J. Cox, "Comments," *AC* 2 (Apr. 1947): 47ff.; "Tale Ends," *AC* 2 (Sept. 1947): 82; "New Insecticide Announced," *AC* 2 (Mar. 1947): 51.

34 "Monsanto Unveils New Methyl Parathion Plant at Anniston, Alabama," *AC* 13 (Feb. 1958): 49ff.

35 S. A. Hall, and Martin Jacobson, "Chemical Assay of Tetraethyl Pyrophosphate," *AC* 3 (July 1948): 30–31.

36 Hanson W. Baldwin, "Chemistry of War Serves Peace, Too," *NYT,* 16 Feb. 1947.

37 Sam Matthews, "Gas Warfare on the Farm," *Science News Letter,* 9 Dec. 1950, 378–379, see 379.

38 Allen B. Lemmon, "Labeling Problems," *AC* 2 (June 1947): 29ff., see 31.

39 Telephone interview of Robert Metcalf by author, 3 Nov. 1992. American Cyanamid did not respond to my request for information.

40 "Nerve Gas vs. Insects," *Science News Letter,* 22 July 1950, 51.

41 Matthews, "Gas Warfare on the Farm," 378–379.

42 Bruce D. Gleissner, Frank Wilcoxon, and Edward H. Glass, "O,O-diethyl O-p-nitrophenyl thiophosphate ... A Promising New Insecticide," *AC* 2 (Oct. 1947): 61.

43 Alvin J. Cox, "New Insecticides," *AC* 3 (Aug. 1948): 35ff.

44 "German Insecticide Effective against Aphids," *Chemical and Engineering News,* 25 July 1946, 1954.

45 Stanley B. Freeborn, "How Experiment Stations Help Develop New Pesticides," *AC* 3 (Sept. 1948): 24ff.

46 "Outlook for DDT," *AC* 2 (Sept. 1947): 43ff., see 45.

47 The article did not set the editor's comments in quotation marks, so it may have paraphrased the original. "AIF Association Meeting," *AC* 2 (May

1947): 26ff., see 29. Dunlap and Perkins date the "triumph" of chemical insecticides over alternative methods of pest control differently. Dunlap dates it before 1920; Perkins dates it after World War II. Thomas R. Dunlap, "The Triumph of Chemical Pesticides in Insect Control, 1890–1920," *Environmental Review* 1 (no. 5, 1978): 38–47; John H. Perkins, *Insects, Experts, and the Insecticide Crisis: The Quest for New Pest Management Strategies* (New York: Plenum, 1982), 11–13.

48 P. N. Annand, "Patience Essential in Testing New Insecticides," *AC* 1 (Sept. 1946): 18ff., see 18, 65.

49 Minutes, Advisory Subcommittees on Germicides, Insecticides and Biologicals, Committee on Quartermaster Problems, 19 Dec. 1947, 3, Engineering and Industrial Research, NRC; Minutes, Conference on Insect and Rodent Control, 17 June 1948, 2, 5, 8–9, Division of Medical Sciences, NRC.

50 "Functional Chart of Research Projects Conducted for the Department of National Defense by the United States Department of Agriculture … Bureau of Entomology and Plant Quarantine," and "Organization Chart of Research Projects Conducted for the Department of National Defense by the … Bureau of Entomology and Plant Quarantine," both in 1948 Conference on Insect and Rodent Control, Division of Medical Sciences, NRC.

51 John J. Hayes to Comptroller of the Army, 7 Mar. 1951, 470.6, 67A4900, RG 175.

52 "Pine Bluff Arsenal," *AFCJ* 4 (Apr. 1951): 22–25, see 24.

53 Clarence B. Wiley, "History of the Rocky Mountain Arsenal," *AFCJ* 4 (Jan. 1951): 12ff., see 13, 15.

54 Quoted in draft of Truman to Attlee, 7 Mar. 1946, Box 155, Agriculture – Commercial, Cabinet, Subject File, President's Secretary's Files, Papers of Harry S. Truman, TL.

55 "Production Goals and Price Support Handbook," Box 16, Misc. Papers of Clinton P. Anderson, TL; P. N. Annand, "Insecticides," *AC* 2 (Oct. 1947): 34–39, see 34; Sherman E. Johnson, *Changes in American Farming, USDA Misc. Publication No. 707* (Washington: GPO, 1949), 11; "Outlook for DDT," *AC* 2 (Sept. 1947): 43ff., see 43.

56 "DDT Toxicity Discussed," *AC* 3 (Mar. 1948): 67.

57 Paul B. Dunbar, "The FDA Looks at Insecticides," *Food Drug Cosmetic Law Quarterly* 4 (Jun. 1949): 234–239.

58 "Conference on Toxicity of DDT to Man and Other Mammals and Hazards Involved in Agricultural Use," 1946, 2, Committee on Insect Control, Executive Board, NRC.

59 Horace S. Telford, "DDT Toxicity," *SSC* 21 (Dec. 1945): 161ff.

[60] H. J. Harris, E. J. Hansens, and C. C. Alexander, "Determination of DDT in Milk Produced in Barns Sprayed with DDT Insecticides," *AC* 5 (Jan. 1950): 51–52; Appendix A, Minutes, Committee on Sanitary Engineering and Environment, 20 Feb. 1950, 291–292, Division of Medical Sciences, NRC.

[61] "DDT Spray Called Injurious to Birds," *NYT,* 23 Oct. 1945.

[62] C. H. Curran, "DDT – The Atomic Bomb of the Insect World," *Natural History* 54 (Nov. 1945): 401ff., see 403.

[63] Graydon C. Essman to Chief, CWS, 7 Sept. 1945, 381, Dugway Proving Ground, Station Series Security Classified, RG 175; Porter to Patterson, 7 Sept. 1945, and Patterson to Porter, 11 Sept. 1945 both in 321: Secretary of War, Miscellaneous Series Correspondence, RG 175.

[64] Alden H. Waitt, "Why Germany Didn't Try Gas," *Saturday Evening Post* 218 (9 Mar. 1946): 17ff., see 138.

[65] George O. Gillingham to Commanding Officers, in turn to Public Relations Officers, 17 Aug. 1945, 000.7 Chemical Warfare Service, Miscellaneous Series Correspondence, RG 175.

[66] Leo P. Brophy, "The Issue of Gas Warfare," *AFCJ* 9 (no. 6, 1955): 20ff., see 34–35.

[67] Judging from the *New York Times Index, Industrial Arts Index,* and *Reader's Guide to Periodical Literature,* the change in name passed virtually without comment in the media.

[68] Patterson to Elbert D. Thomas, 25 June 1946, quoted in U.S. Congress, Senate, *Chemical Corps,* Report No. 1635, 79th Cong., 2d sess. (Washington: GPO, 1946); see also U. S. Congress, House, *Changing the Name of the Chemical Warfare Service,* Report No. 2602, 79th Cong., 2d sess. (Washington: GPO, 1946).

[69] P. L. 607, 79th Cong., 2 Aug. 1946, cited in Brophy, "The Issue of Gas Warfare," 35.

[70] "War of Nerves," *Time,* 1 May 1950, 44.

[71] Daniel P. Jones, "American Chemists and the Geneva Protocol," *Isis* 71 (Sept. 1980): 426–440, see 427.

[72] U.S. Army Chemical Corps, Office of the Chief, Historical Office, Feb. 1953, "Summary History of Chemical Corps Activities 9 September 1951 to 31 December 1952," 1, 18, U. S. Army Carlisle Barracks Library, Penn.

[73] M. F. Peake to A. Waitt, 12 Nov. 1946, 111C1946, 67A4900, RG 175; "New German Poison Gas Tested," *NYT,* 11 Apr. 1946.

[74] Hanson W. Baldwin, "War Gas Shield Sought," *NYT,* 14 Dec. 1948.

[75] Leigh E. Chadwick, "Mechanism of Entry and Action of Insecticidal Compounds," n. d., and Leigh E. Chadwick, "Determination of Toxicity of Insecticidal Compounds Relating to Studies of Mechanism of Action," n. d., both in 337 Chemical Corps Tech Committee, 67A4900, RG 175.

76 War Department, Bureau of Public Relations, Press Branch, "Outstanding German Scientists Being Brought to United States," 1 Oct. 1945, Committee on Post-War Treatment of German Research and Engineering, NAS.

77 William H. Greene to Chief, Chemical Corps, 20 May 1949, 161 Paperclip Project, 67A4900, RG 175.

78 Al Leggin, "Chemical Corps Research and Development," *Chemical and Engineering News* 24 (10 Dec. 1946): 3178ff.

79 Anthony C. McAuliffe, "The Role of the Chemical Corps in National Defense," *Chemical and Engineering News* 28 (8 May 1950): 1557–1560, see 1559.

80 E. Baker et al., "Post-War Policy on Research with Educational Institutions," 16 Oct. 1945, Policy and Procedures 1930–41 [discrepant date in original], Assistant Chief for Materiel, Technical Division, General Administrative Series, RG 175.

81 George H. Mangun, "Toxicity Laboratory, University of Chicago," *Chemical Corps Journal* 1 (Jan. 1947): 25ff., see 26.

82 Hanson W. Baldwin, "Chemistry of War Serves Peace, Too," *NYT*, 16 Feb. 1947.

83 William H. Summerson, "Progress in the Biochemical Treatment of Nerve Gas Poisoning," *AFCJ* 9 (no. 1, 1955): 24–26; John Kobler, "The Terrible Threat of Nerve Gas," *Saturday Evening Post* 230 (27 July 1957): 28ff.

84 Vincent G. Dethier, *Man's Plague? Insects and Agriculture* (Princeton, N. J.: Darwin Press, Inc., 1976), 118.

85 Interview of Vincent G. Dethier by author, 18 Sept. 1992; *American Men and Women of Science*.

86 A. Glenn Richards, "Studies on Insect Cuticle, Temperature, and Intracellular Bodies," 1, in Minutes (Appendix G: Review of Army Medical Service Research Program Relating to Entomology), 23 Feb. 1954, Subcommittee on Animal Reservoirs and Vectors of Disease, Committee on Sanitary Engineering and Environment, NAS.

87 "CWS Monthly Progress Report on Insect and Rodent Control," Aug. 1945, 461 CWS (CWS Monthly Progress Report on Insect and Rodent Control), Miscellaneous Series Correspondence, RG 175.

88 Minutes, Germicides, Insecticides, and Biologicals Subcommittee, Committee on Quartermaster Problems, 19 Dec. 1947, 3, Engineering and Industrial Research, NRC.

89 This version of the story is Reed's; I found no other records about the meeting. John W. Regan (as dictated by W. D. Reed) to File, 18 Apr. 1946, 334 (Committees) Jan.–June 1946, General Subject File, RG 112.

90 Appendix, Minutes, Executive Meeting of the Advisory Committee, NRC Chemical-Biological Coordination Center, 11 Nov. 1946, Executive Board, NRC.

91 Minutes, Executive Meeting, NRC Insect Control Committee, 10 July 1946, 8; "The National Research Council Insect Control Committee," 11 Feb. 1946, 2; Minutes, Executive Meeting, Advisory Committee, NRC Chemical-Biological Coordination Center, 21 Sept. 1946, 2, all in Executive Board, NRC; Robert L. Metcalf, *The Mode of Action of Organic Insecticides* (Washington: National Research Council, 1948).

92 Appendix, Minutes, Executive Meeting, Advisory Committee, NRC Chemical-Biological Coordination Center, 11 Nov. 1946, Executive Board, NRC.

93 Chemical-Biological Coordination Center, "Screening Agencies," 1 July 1949, Executive Board, NRC.

94 Agenda, NRC Chemical-Biological Coordination Center, Joint Meeting, Advisory Committee and Subcommittees, 9 Mar. 1947, Executive Board, NRC.

95 Minutes, Advisory Committee, Chemical-Biological Coordination Center, 13 June 1949, 4–5, Executive Board, NRC.

96 Minutes, Advisory Committee, Chemical-Biological Coordination Center, 8 Dec. 1949, 4, Executive Board, NRC.

97 Fearing that "commercial concerns would not be sufficiently disinterested" to provide "impartial testing," the advisory committee voted to use only nonprofit institutions as screening agencies. Minutes, Advisory Committee, Chemical-Biological Coordination Center, 10 July 1946, 3, Executive Board, NRC.

98 Minutes, Advisory Committee, Chemical-Biological Coordination Center, 11 Nov. 1946, 3, Executive Board, NRC.

99 Minutes, Advisory Committee, Chemical-Biological Coordination Center, 9 Mar. 1947, 3, and 7 Oct. 1947, 10, Executive Board, NRC.

100 Minutes, Advisory Committee, Chemical-Biological Coordination Center, 21 Sept. 1946, 5, Executive Board, NRC.

101 C. C. Stock to G. B. Darling, 14 Feb. 1946, General, Committee on Insect Control, Executive Board, NRC.

102 N. E. Dodd to F. B. Jewett, 3 May 1946, and Surgeon General of USPHS to F. B. Jewett, 1 May 1946, both in General, Committee on Insect Control, Executive Board, NRC.

103 Walter Kirner to Detlev Bronk, 22 Aug. 1947, General, Chemical-Biological Coordination Center, Executive Board, NRC.

104 Jerry Greene, "'Invited to Quiz, May Reveals He's Told All," *New York Sunday News,* 7 July 1946, reprinted in U.S. Congress, Senate, Special Committee Investigating the National Defense Program, *Investigation of the National Defense Program,* Part 34, *War Contracts, Erie Basin Metal Products, Inc.* 79th Congr., 2d sess. (Washington: GPO, 1946),

18502–18504; U.S. Congress, Senate, Special Committee Investigating the National Defense Program, *Investigation of the National Defense Program*, Part 35, *War Contracts, Erie Basin Metal Products, Inc.* 79th Congr. 2d sess. (Washington: GPO, 1947).

105 John G. Norris, "Navy Was Satisfied with Garsson Deal – Company Performed Creditably in Filling Order for $1,042,500 in Shells, Officers Say," *Washington Post*, 25 July 1946, reprinted in U.S. Senate, *National Defense*, Part 35, 19445.

106 Congressional Quarterly, *Congress and the Nation 1945–1964: A Review of Government and Politics in the Postwar Years* (Washington: Congressional Quarterly Service, 1965), 1689.

107 U.S. Congress, Senate, Investigations Subcommittee of the Committee on Expenditures in the Executive Departments, *Influence in Government Procurement*, 81st Congr., 1st sess. (Washington: GPO, 1949), 20–21, 155, 157, 165–170, 257–258.

CHAPTER 10. ARMS RACES IN THE COLD WAR (1950–1958)

1 Daniel Yergin, *Shattered Peace: The Origins of the Cold War and the National Security State* (Boston: Houghton Mifflin, 1977), 174–178.

2 Frank S. Adams, "Churchill Gets Columbia Degree; Stresses Chance to Serve World," *NYT*, 19 Mar. 1946.

3 Melvyn P. Leffler, *The Specter of Communism: The United States and the Origin of the Cold War, 1917–1953* (New York: Hill and Wang, 1994), 97–111.

4 H. A. Kuhn, "The Chemical Industry and National Defense," *AFCJ* 6 (July 1952): 34–38.

5 "AAEE Elects Roy E. Campbell; Discusses Toxicological Problems of Insecticides," *AC* 6 (Jan. 1951): 51ff., see 84–85.

6 U.S. Department of Agriculture, *Insects* (Washington: GPO, 1952), 197 (emphasis in original).

7 Churchill's comments set off a burst of interest in ants and communism. The Book of Proverbs, the *New York Times* pointed out, contradicted the "totalitarian notion" of ants because the ant "having no guide, overseer, or ruler, Provideth her meat in the summer, and gathereth her food in the harvest." "Topics of the Times," *NYT*, 20 Mar. 1946.

8 Maynard Nichols, "White Ant World," *New York Times Magazine*, 31 Mar. 1946, 15.

9 "Chemical Pesticides Discussed at AAEE & APS Meetings," *AC* 3 (Jan. 1948): 30ff., see 30.

10 "The Enemy," *Time*, 11 Dec. 1950, 29–34.

[11] F. C. Bishopp, "Insecticide Use Seen Essential to American Agriculture," *AC* 5 (Feb. 1950): 23ff., see 87–88.

[12] Advertisement for Julius Hyman, *AC* 6 (June 1951): [p. illegible].

[13] U.S. Congress, Senate, Committee on Agriculture and Forestry, *Hearings on Supply and Demand for Fertilizer, Farm Machinery, and Pesticides,* 82nd Congr., 1st sess. (Washington: GPO, 1951), 380.

[14] "I Heartily Agree," *AFCJ* 4 (Apr. 1951): 55; see also Charles E. Loucks, "Science in Modern Warfare," *AFCJ* 5 (Apr. 1952): 21–24, see 22; Arthur G. Trudeau, "The Banquet Speech," *AFCJ* 12 (July–Aug. 1958): 12ff., see 13.

[15] Victor C. Searle, "Military Procurement Today," *Proceedings of the American Association of Textile Chemists and Colorists* (30 Apr. 1951): 283; U.S. Army Chemical Corps, Office of the Chief, Historical Office, "Summary History of Chemical Corps Activities 9 September 1951 to 31 December 1952," Feb. 1953, 26–27, U.S. Army War College Library, Carlisle Barracks, Pa.

North Korea and China charged that the United States waged chemical and biological warfare against North Korea, including the releasing of insects that transmitted diseases. The United States hotly denied the charges and called for an impartial investigation. That proposal was rejected. The controversy continued to swirl for a couple years after the war, but neither side changed its position and the issue faded. Stockholm International Peace Research Institute, *The Problem of Chemical and Biological Warfare,* vol. 4: *CB Disarmament Negotiations, 1920–1970* (New York: Humanities Press, 1971), 196–223; Stockholm International Peace Research Institute, *The Problem of Chemical and Biological Warfare,* vol. 5: *The Prevention of CBW* (New York: Humanities Press, 1971), 238–258.

[16] "A Time of Horror," *Christian Century* 69 (14 May 1952): 581–582, see 581.

[17] Cornelius Ryan, "A New Weapon of Chilling Terror: G-Gas, We Have It – So Does Russia," *Collier's,* 27 Nov. 1953, 88–95, see 94–95 (emphasis added).

[18] P. H. Groggins, "Research Basis for Continued Advancement in Development of Agricultural Chemicals," *AC* 6 (Oct. 1951): 49ff., see 51, 101, 103.

[19] U.S. Congress, Senate, Committee on Agriculture and Forestry, *Hearings on Supply and Demand for Fertilizer, Farm Machinery, and Pesticides,* 82nd Congr., 1st sess. (Washington: GPO, 1951), 47, 153.

[20] Quoted in *Agriculture in National Defense,* 1 Feb. 1952, Office of Information, RG 16.

21 Advertisement for Niagara, *AC* 6 (Sept. 1951): 22.

22 Charles Brannan to Harry Truman, 23 Apr. 1951, Box 155, Agriculture – Commercial, Cabinet, Subject File, President's Secretary's Files, Papers of Harry S. Truman, TL.

23 U.S. Senate Committee on Agriculture and Forestry, *Supply and Demand for Fertilizer,* 36, 156; *Agriculture in National Defense,* 27 June 1951, 1 Mar. 1951, 28 Nov. 1951, 1 Nov. 1951, 1 Aug. 1951, 19 Sept. 1951, 26 Sept. 1951, 3 Oct. 1951, 18 Jan. 1952, 28 May 1952, 10 July 1952, Office of Information, RG 16.

24 Centennial Commemoration Committee, *Insect Facts* (n.c.: n.p., n.d.) National Agricultural Library, Beltsville, Mary.

25 William M. Creasy, "General Creasy Addresses New York and Boston Meetings," *AFCJ* 9 (Jan.–Feb. 1955): 5–9, see 8.

26 William M. Creasy, "What the Chemical Corps Is Doing," *AFCJ* 9 (July–Aug. 1955): 12–16, see 15.

27 Alfred C. Benson, "Procurement of Research and Development by the Army Chemical Corps," *AFCJ* 10 (Jan.–Feb. 1956): 28–31, see 28–29.

28 "Expert Fears Use of Toxic Weapons," *NYT,* 10 Apr. 1957; R. Macy, "The Chemical Corps Search for Chemical Warfare Agents," *AFCJ* 10 (no. 6, 1956): 22–24, see 23; U.S. Army Chemical Center, *Industrial Liaison Program of the United States Army Chemical Warfare Laboratories* ([Edgewood, Md.: Army Chemical Center, 1957]), Walter Reed Army Medical Center Library, Washington, D.C.; "Give and Take," *Chemical and Engineering News* 36 (21 July 1958): 54–55, see 55.

29 Minutes, Subcommittee on Animal Reservoirs and Vectors of Disease, 10 Mar. 1953, 84, Committee on Sanitary Engineering and Environment, Division of Medical Sciences, NRC.

30 The center's status within the National Academy of Sciences had always been ambiguous, its punch card system had not yielded hoped-for insights, some believed the center had been mismanaged, the center's scope may have been too broad, funding was uncertain, and the Chemical Corps and industry had been reluctant to share data lest others find out the "general class of compounds in which the group is interested." Richard Martin Dougherty, "The Scope and Operating Efficiency of Information Centers as Illustrated by the Chemical-Biological Coordination Center of the National Research Council" (Ph.D. diss., Rutgers University, 1963), 13–17; O. M. Ray to Milton C. Winternitz, 13 Mar. 1953, Chemical-Biological Coordination Center, Executive Board, NRC; "Distribution of CBCC Information and Related Materials within NAS-NRC," [1959], Chemical-Biological Coordination Center, Governing Board, NRC.

[31] Kenneth D. Roeder, "Insects as Experimental Material," *Science* 115 (14 Mar. 1952): 275–279, see 275, 279.

[32] Kenneth D. Roeder (ed.), *Insect Physiology* (New York: Wiley, 1953).

[33] "Nerve War Gas Tried," *Science News Letter,* 25 Apr. 1953, 271.

[34] Charles E. Loucks, "Science in Modern Warfare," *AFCJ* 5 (Apr. 1952): 21–24, see 23.

[35] Anthony C. McAuliffe, "The Role of the Chemical Corps in National Defense," *Chemical and Engineering News* 28 (8 May 1950): 1557–1560, see 1560.

[36] U.S. Senate Committee on Agriculture and Forestry, *Supply and Demand for Fertilizer,* 364.

[37] "Agricultural Experiment Station," *AC* 6 (June 1951): 89ff, see 91.

[38] "Tale Ends," *AC* 16 (Feb. 1961): 106.

[39] H. A. Kuhn, "The Chemical Industry and National Defense," *AFCJ* 6 (July 1952): 34–38, see 35; Howard R. Huston, "Minutemen of Mobilization – The Chemical Industry," *AFCJ* 7 (no. 1, 1953): 20–25, see 22; Harry A. Kuhn, "Chemical Industry and National Defense," *AFCJ* 14 (Mar.–Apr. 1960): 6–8, see 8.

[40] Carl A. Steidtmann to ACofS, G-4, 30 Oct. 1951, Cross References Commercial 1951, 67A4900, RG 175.

[41] C. J. Merrill to Commanding General, Chemical Corps Material Command, 29 Apr. 1952 (emphasis in original); Robert L. Silber to the Division Engineer, 13 Feb. 1952; Claude Pepper to Frank Pace, Jr., n.d.; Claude Pepper to Frank Pace, 19 Jan. 1952; Chief, Facilities Branch for the record, 21 Feb. 1952, all in 161 Julius Hyman Co., 67A4900, RG 175.

[42] Advertisement for Shell, *AFCJ* 7 (no. 2, 1953): 25.

[43] Victor C. Searle to Chief Chemical Officer, 26 July 1952, 161 Shell Chemical Co. 1952, 67A4900, RG 175.

[44] U.S. Army Chemical Corps, Office of the Chief, Historical Office, "Summary History of Chemical Corps Activities 9 September 1951 to 31 December 1952," Feb. 1953, 6, U.S. Army Carlisle Barracks Library, Pa.

[45] C. S. Cronan, "Army Permits Peek at Nerve Gas Facilities," *Chemical Engineering* 65 (22 Sept. 1958): 74; Serge Tonetti, "Chemical Corps Phosphate Development Works," *AFCJ* 10 (Sept.–Oct. 1956): 32ff.; "Toxicological Shell Program," 23 June 1954, 470–1954; "Service Test Items, FY 1954 Budget Items," n.d., 400.112–1953; Ward H. Maris, "Requirements for GB-Filled Munitions," 22 Jan. 1952, 470.6; Ward H. Maris to Chief of Staff, United States Air Force, 26 Feb. 1952, 470.6; "Difficulties Encountered in Construction of GB Facilities," 11 Feb. 1954, 470.6—1954, last five sources all in 67A4900, RG 175.

[46] "Denver Calmed on War Gas Fear," *NYT,* 28 Mar. 1954.

47 Anthony C. McAuliffe, "The Role of the Chemical Corps in National Defense," *Chemical and Engineering News* 28 (8 May 1950): 1557–1560, see 1557.

48 "War of Nerves," *Time*, 1 May 1950, 44.

49 "United States Turning Out New Deadly Gas," *NYT*, 21 Mar. 1954.

50 Hanson W. Baldwin, "Race for New Weapons: The Score as It Stands Today" *NYT*, 7 May 1950; Watson Davis, "Madness Gases Rival A-Bomb," *Science Digest,* June 1951, 77–79, see 77.

51 "Army, Industry in Close Liaison," *NYT*, 7 Sept. 1951, 14.

52 William M. Creasy, "The Forward Look in the Army Chemical Corps," *AFCJ* 11 (July–Aug. 1957): 26ff., see 26.

53 "Now, an Argument over Gas Warfare," *U.S. News and World Report,* 4 May 1964, 8.

54 Arthur G. Trudeau, "Catalyst for the Future," *AFCJ* 13 (Nov.–Dec. 1959): 45–47, see 46–47.

55 Robert L. Metcalf, "Insects v. Insecticides," *Scientific American* 187 (Oct. 1952): 21–25, see 22; John J. Pratt, Jr., and Frank H. Babers, "Cross Tolerances in Resistant Houseflies," *Science* 112 (4 Aug. 1950): 141–142; Frank H. Babers, *Development of Insect Resistance to Insecticides, E-776* ([Washington]: USDA Bureau of Entomology and Plant Quarantine, May 1949), 1–2; Minutes, Subcommittee on Animal Reservoirs and Vectors of Disease, 2 June 1952, 28, Committee on Sanitary Engineering and Environment, Division of Medical Sciences, NRC; Von R. Wiesmann, "Untersuchungen Über Das Physiologische Verhalten Von *Musca domestica* L. verschiedener Provenienzen," *Mitteilungen Der Schweizerischen Entomologischen Gesellschaft* 20 (1947): 484–504.

56 Minutes, Subcommittee on Animal Reservoirs and Vectors of Disease, 2 June 1952, 28, Committee on Sanitary Engineering and Environment, Division of Medical Sciences, NRC.

57 Metcalf, "Insects v. Insecticides," 22; Pratt and Babers, "Cross Tolerances."

58 Minutes, Committee on Sanitary Engineering and Environment, 20 Sept. 1951, 526, Division of Medical Sciences, NRC.

59 Metcalf, "Insects v. Insecticides," 21–25.

60 Ralph Bunn, Appendix C: Armed Forces Problems in Insecticide Resistance, 1, of Minutes, Subcommittee on Animal Reservoirs and Vectors of Disease, 1 Dec. 1953, Committee on Sanitary Engineering and Environment, Division of Medical Sciences, NRC.

61 Dixie Leppert, "Has the Fly Got Us Licked?" *Popular Science* 160 (Jun. 1952): 113ff., see 113.

62 Henry W. Pierce, "The Insect War," *Science News Letter,* 28 Apr. 1956, 266–267, see 266.

[63] "The Editor Comments," *AC* 8 (Jan. 1953): 29.

[64] Roy Hansberry, "Role of Chemicals in the Future of Insect Control," *AC* 9 (Apr. 1954): 42ff., see 43.

[65] Advertisement for American Cyanamid, *AC* 9 (Apr. 1954): 32.

[66] J. Keiding, "Resistance to Organic Phosphorous Insecticides of the Housefly," *Science* 123 (29 June 1956): 1173–1174; "Bugs Shrugging Off Phosphate Poisons," *Farm Journal* 80 (July 1956): 26.

[67] Robert L. Metcalf, "Carbamate Insecticides," *AC* 16 (June 1961): 20ff.

[68] "What's New in Pesticides?" *AC* 13 (Apr. 1958): 30ff., see 33, 114.

[69] Metcalf, "Carbamate Insecticides," 20.

[70] R. D. O'Brien and J. G. Matthysse, "Carbamate Insecticides in the United States and Abroad," *AC* 16 (Nov. 1961): 27ff., see 28.

[71] Stockholm International Peace Research Institute, *The Problem of Chemical and Biological Warfare,* vol. 1: *The Rise of CB Weapons* (New York: Humanities Press, 1971), 74–75.

[72] T. J. Marnane to Distribution, 7 Jan. 1957, catalogued as U.S. Army, *V Agents,* Army War College Library, Carlisle Barracks, Pa.

[73] "Military Construction, Army," 1st qtr. FY 1959, Quarterly Reviews, General Correspondence, Subject Series, RG 175.

[74] Minutes, Subcommittee on Animal Reservoirs and Vectors of Disease, 15 Sept. 1952, 39, Committee on Sanitary Engineering and Environment, Division of Medical Sciences, NRC; Herbert S. Hurlburt, Robert M. Altman, and Carlyle Nibley Jr., "DDT Resistance in Korean Body Lice," *Science* 115 (4 Jan. 1952): 11–12; Gaines W. Eddy, "A Report on the Effectiveness of Certain Insecticides Against DDT-Resistant Body Lice in Korea," (Orlando, Fla.: Bureau of Entomology and Plant Quarantine, 6 Nov. 1951), in National Library of Medicine, Bethesda, Mary.

[75] Minutes, Subcommittee on Animal Reservoirs and Vectors of Disease, 10 Mar. 1953, 83, and 9 Dec. 1952, 57, Committee on Sanitary Engineering and Environment, Division of Medical Sciences, NRC.

[76] The report credits the National Military Establishment with funding the study, but it does not specify which part of the armed forces. The A-bomb argument appears in the 1951 review as a quotation from entomologist A. E. Haarer. Frank H. Babers, *Development of Insect Resistance,* 21; Frank H. Babers and John J. Pratt, Jr., *Development of Insect Resistance to Insecticides – II: A Critical Review of the Literature up to 1951, E-818* (Washington: USDA Bureau of Entomology and Plant Quarantine, May 1951), 1, 28.

[77] Ralph W. Sherman, "Are We Winning the War on Insects?" *Rotarian* 87 (Sept. 1955): 26–28, see 27.

[78] Herbert N. Gardner to M. C. Winternitz, 28 Sept. 1951, Conference on Insect Physiology, Division of Medical Sciences, NRC.

79 Minutes, Committee on Sanitary Engineering and Environment, 11 Jan. 1952, 545, Division of Medical Sciences, NRC.

80 Minutes, Subcommittee on Animal Reservoirs and Vectors of Disease, 2 June 1952, 28; minutes, Committee on Sanitary Engineering and Environment, 3 June 1952, 578; minutes of Joint Meeting, Subcommittee on Animal Reservoirs and Vectors of Disease and Army Committee for Insect and Rodent Control, 23 Feb. 1954, 139, all in Division of Medical Sciences, NRC; National Academy of Sciences, *Conference on Insecticide Resistance and Insect Physiology* (Washington: National Academy of Sciences, 1952), 12.

81 Minutes, Committee on Sanitary Engineering and Environment, 13 Mar. 1956, Appendix C, 934, Division of Medical Sciences, NRC.

82 Minutes, Committee on Sanitary Engineering and Environment, 13 Mar. 1956, 934, Division of Medical Sciences, NRC.

83 National Academy of Sciences, *Conference on Insecticide Resistance and Insect Physiology,* 86.

84 "Editorials," *AC* 16 (July 1961): 13ff., see 13.

85 Minutes, Subcommittee on Animal Reservoirs and Vectors of Disease, 1 Dec. 1953, 107–108, Committee on Sanitary Engineering and Environment, Division of Medical Sciences, NRC; Rosmarie von Rumker, "Inter-Relations Between Basic and Applied Research in the Development of Modern Insecticides," *AC* 10 (Dec. 1955): 40ff.

86 National Academy of Sciences, *Conference on Insecticide Resistance and Insect Physiology,* 54.

87 Minutes, Committee on Sanitary Engineering and Environment, 13 Mar. 1956, Appendix C, 930–931, Division of Medical Sciences, NRC.

88 Minutes, Committee on Sanitary Engineering and Environment, 13 Mar. 1956, Appendix C, 937–938, Division of Medical Sciences, NRC.

89 "More Entomological Research Called for by Speakers at Insect Resistance Symposium," *AC* 14 (Nov. 1959): 34–35, see 34.

90 "More Entomological Research Called For," 35.

91 Quoted in Macon Reed, Jr., "Atomic War on Insects," *Science Digest* 34 (Aug. 1953): 73–75; John H. Perkins, *Insects, Experts, and the Insecticide Crisis: The Quest for New Pest Management Strategies* (New York: Plenum Press, 1982).

92 Gale Hanson, "Certification of the Aerial Applicator Industry," *AC* 13 (May 1958): 57ff.; William A. Lewis, "Growth, Importance and Problems of Agricultural Aviation," *AC* 15 (June 1960): 70ff., see 111, 113; "Aerial Agriculture," *AC* 13 (Sept. 1958): 41ff.

93 Dusting cost $2.25 per hour by air, versus $3.02 by ground; spraying cost $1.33 by air versus $1.99 by ground. "NATA Discusses Insurance and Efficient Pest Control and Operation," *AC* 14 (Jan. 1959): 53ff., see 55.

[94] Ernest Hart, "Pesticide Industry," *AC* 6 (Sept. 1951): 38–40, see 38.

[95] Howard R. Huston, "Minutemen of Mobilization," 20.

CHAPTER 11. BACKFIRES (1958–1962)

[1] Warner Bros. Inc., *Them!* (1954; Burbank, Calif.: Warner Home Video, 1994).

[2] Thomas R. Dunlap, *DDT: Scientists, Citizens, and Public Policy* (Princeton: Princeton University Press, 1981), 103–105; Ralph H. Lutts, "Chemical Fallout: Rachel Carson's *Silent Spring*, Radioactive Fallout, and the Environmental Movement," *Environmental Review* 9 (Fall 1985): 210–225.

[3] Ernest Lehman, *North by Northwest* (New York: Viking, 1959), 74–76.

[4] "Brucker Presses Germ War Plans," *NYT*, 7 Nov. 1955.

[5] Jack Raymond, "Pentagon Spurs Chemical Arms," *NYT*, 9 Aug. 1959; see also Herbert J. Coleman, "Army Presses Nerve Gas Development," *Aviation Week*, 5 Sept. 1960, 32–33, see 33; "Army Conducts Nerve Gas Tests," *NYT*, 28 Aug. 1960.

[6] Walter Schneir, "The Campaign to Make Chemical Warfare Respectable," *The Reporter* 21 (1 Oct. 1959): 24–28, see 24–25.

[7] J. H. Rothschild, "Germs and Gas: The Weapons Nobody Dares Talk About," *Harper's* 218 (June 1959): 29–34, see 29, 31, 34.

[8] John C. MacArthur, "'Psycho-Chemical Warfare' and the Case of the Discombobulated Cat," *AFCJ* 13 (Jan.–Feb. 1959): 4–7, see 4; "CBR – United States Programs Need Money, Motivation," *Chemical and Engineering News* 37 (17 Aug. 1959): 21.

[9] "Ordeal by Mice for a Mouser," *Life*, 15 Dec. 1958, 83–84, see 83.

[10] MacArthur, "'Psycho-Chemical Warfare' and the Case of the Discombobulated Cat," 4.

[11] Raymond, "Pentagon Spurs Chemical Arms"; "Victory through Goof-off," *Newsweek*, 30 Nov. 1959, 28–29.

[12] Jack Raymond, "Army for Using Chemical Arms," *NYT*, 10 Nov. 1959; see also Alden P. Armagnac, "Can 'Loony Gas' Win Wars Without Bloodshed?" *Popular Science*, Jan. 1960, 85ff, see 224.

[13] Schneir, "The Campaign to Make Chemical Warfare Respectable," 27. Valerie Adams says that the "change in policy away from retaliatory use only was not publicly confirmed until some 20 years later, when it had been reversed" in *Chemical Warfare, Chemical Disarmament* (Bloomington: Indiana University Press, 1990), 146.

[14] Raymond, "Army for Using Chemical Arms."

[15] "Army May Expand Gas Warfare Plans," *NYT*, 30 Jan. 1962.

[16] Richard Fryklund, "Dr. York Seeks Full Knowledge of Chemical Weapon Potentials," *AFCJ* 14 (July–Aug. 1960): 37.

17 "New Worry for World?" *U.S. News and World Report,* 30 May 1958, 39–44, see 39, 42.

18 "Chemical Warfare Dangers," *Science News Letter,* 16 April 1960, 243; "Experts Blast Public Apathy Toward CW, BW," *Chemical and Engineering News* 38 (18 April 1960): 37–40.

19 Charles L. Ruttenberg, "Political Behavior of American Scientists: The Movement against Chemical and Biological Warfare" (Ph.D. diss., New York University, 1972), 133–136.

20 Norman Cousins, *In Place of Folly* (New York: Harper, 1961), 10, 55, 78, 202–203.

21 "Eisenhower's Farewell Sees Threat to Liberties in Vast Defense Machine," *NYT,* 18 Jan. 1961.

22 "Home Garden Market," *AC* 8 (Nov. 1953): 38ff, see 38.

23 "Eveready: A New Home Garden Line," *AC* 13 (Mar. 1958): 28ff., see 125.

24 "Editorials," *AC* 13 (Jan. 1958): 27ff., see 27, 103.

25 "More Products for the Home Garden Market," *AC* 9 (Mar. 1954): 45ff.; "Home Garden Market," *AC* 8 (Nov. 1953): 38ff., see 135; "Point-of-Sale Merchandising Key to Eveready Sales Program," *AC* 15 (Nov. 1960): 40ff, see 41.

26 John Burnham, "How the Discovery of Accidental Childhood Poisoning Contributed to the Development of Environmentalism in the United States," *Environmental History Review* 19 (fall 1995): 57–81, see 69.

27 "California Group Studies Problems," *AC* 14 (Feb. 1959): 57ff., see 57.

28 L. F. Curl, "Aerial Application in Eradication Program," *AC* 13 (Apr. 1958): 42–43.

29 J. I. Rodale to editor, *AC* 13 (May 1958): 38.

30 E. D. Burgess, "Let's Look at the Gypsy Moth Problem," *AC* 12 (Nov. 1957): 33ff., see 34–35.

31 "Fire Ant Control," *AC* 13 (Feb. 1958): 51; Pete Daniel, "A Rogue Bureaucracy: The USDA Fire Ant Campaign of the Late 1950s," *Agricultural History* 64 (1990): 99–114.

32 "Aerial Spray Projects – Subject of Panel at Garden Club Meeting," *AC* 13 (Apr. 1958): 43.

33 "The National Audubon Society Comments on the Pesticide Problem," *AC* 13 (Mar. 1958): 34ff., see 34.

34 Quoted in "Cure Worse than the Disease," *Audubon* 60 (July–Aug. 1958): 151.

35 Durward L. Allen, "Poison from the Air," *Field and Stream* 63 (Feb. 1959): 49ff., see 49–50 (emphasis in original).

36 Editorial, *NYT,* 8 Jan. 1958, reprinted in *AC* 13 (Feb. 1958): 131.

37 Robert S. Strother, "Backfire in the War Against Insects," *Reader's Digest* 74 (June 1959): 64–69, see 69.

[38] Quoted in "Pesticides Are Good Friends, but Can Be Dangerous Enemies If Used by Zealots," *AC* 16 (Oct. 1961): 34.

[39] "Editorials," *AC* 16 (Dec. 1961): 15.

[40] "Editorials," *AC* 17 (July 1962): 13.

[41] "*Sports Illustrated* Joins Anti-Pesticide Publications," *AC* 15 (June 1960): 86.

[42] Burgess, "Let's Look at the Gypsy Moth Problem," 35, 109.

[43] "The Editor Comments," *AC* 6 (Feb. 1951): 29.

[44] "The Editor Comments," *AC* 5 (Apr. 1950): 29.

[45] "Politics, or Ignorance?" *AC* (Aug. 1951): 30ff.

[46] "Delaney Committee Submits Report," *AC* 7 (Jul. 1952): [n.p.].

[47] Watson Davis, "Madness Gases Rival A-Bomb," *Science Digest,* June 1951, 77–79, see 79; John Kobler, "The Terrible Threat of Nerve Gas," *Saturday Evening Post* 230 (27 July 1957): 28ff., see 76.

[48] "Nerve War Gas Tried," *Science News Letter,* 25 Apr. 1953, 271.

[49] Advertisement for Victor, *AC* 14 (June 1959): n. p.

[50] Quoted in "*Reader's Digest* Replies to *Agricultural Chemicals,*" *AC* 14 (Aug. 1959): 45ff., see 45.

[51] Alfred G. Etter, "A Protest against Spraying," *Audubon* 61 (July–Aug. 1959): 153ff., see 153, 181.

[52] J. I. Rodale to editor, *AC* 13 (May 1958): 38.

[53] Wilhelmine Kirby Waller, "Poison on the Land," *Audubon* 60 (Mar.–Apr. 1958): 68–70, see 68, 70.

[54] "Aerial Spraying," *AC* 13 (Jan. 1958): 42ff.

[55] Advertisement for Diamond Chemicals, *AC* 13 (Feb. 1958): 25.

[56] R. E. Monroe, "Can Agricultural Aviation Survive?" *AC* 13 (June 1958): 49ff., see 119.

[57] "Toxicologist Testifies to No Ill Effects by DDT at Trial," *AC* 13 (Mar. 1958): 69ff., "Case 17609 ... Relating to Gypsy Moth Spraying," *AC* 13 (Apr. 1958): 28–29.

[58] "Court Upholds Mass Spraying of DDT," *AC* 13 (Aug. 1958): 87ff., see 94.

[59] "Systemic Pesticides, Cattle Grub and Lygus Bug Control Among Highlights of ESA Discussions," *AC* 13 (Aug. 1958): 83–85, see 83.

[60] "Fire Ant Control," *AC* 13 (Feb. 1958): 51.

[61] Daniel, "Rogue Bureaucracy," 108.

[62] Donald Lerch, "Washington Report," *AC* 12 (July 1957): 62ff., see 65.

[63] Quoted in "*Reader's Digest* Replies to *Agricultural Chemicals,*" 45.

[64] "Editorials," *AC* 13 (Apr. 1958): 27ff., see 27.

[65] "Editorials," *AC* 12 (Sept. 1957): 35.

[66] "Editorials," *AC* 12 (Sept. 1957): 35.

[67] Martha Freeman (ed.), *Always, Rachel: The Letters of Rachel Carson and Dorothy Freeman, 1952–1964* (Boston: Beacon, 1995), 380; see also Linda J. Lear, *Rachel Carson: Witness for Nature* (New York: Henry Holt, 1997).

68 Stephen Fox, *The American Conservation Movement: John Muir and His Legacy* (Madison: University of Wisconsin Press, 1981), 292.

69 "The Desolate Year," *Monsanto Magazine* 42 (Oct. 1962): 4–7; H. Davidson to editor, *New Yorker,* 20 and 27 Feb. 1995, 18.

70 Jeffrey Ellis and Stephen Fox stimulated my thinking about Carson and the Cold War (Fox, *The American Conservation Movement,* 297).

71 Some commenters at the time felt their way toward, but did not quite reach, identifying similarities between *Silent Spring* and Eisenhower's critique of the military-industrial complex. *Consumer Reports* wrote in 1963, "Until *Silent Spring* was published, however, the mounting concern over the way pesticides were being used in the United States was uneasily contained within the ranks of a particular business-scientific-government community. Miss Carson's book opened up that circle and brought to the general public an awareness of the nature and seriousness of the problems involved." "Pesticides: Attack and Counterattack," *Consumer Reports* 28 (Jan. 1963): 37–39, see 37.

72 Rachel Carson, *Silent Spring* (New York: Fawcett Crest, 1962), front cover, 16, 19, 22–23, 217–231.

73 Carson, *Silent Spring,* 21, 25, 70, 73, 85, 91, 94, 141, 143.

74 Carson, *Silent Spring,* 245.

75 Barton J. Bernstein, "America's Biological Warfare Program in the Second World War," *Journal of Strategic Studies* 11 (1988): 292–317; Merck quoted in Gale E. Peterson, "The Discovery and Development of 2,4-D," *Agricultural History* 44 (1967): 243–253, see 247–248.

76 "Report on Trip of Brig. General A. H. Waitt and Lt. Col. J. K. Javits to POA and SWPA, 24 Sept. 1944–21 Nov. 1944," 15 Dec. 1944, 35–36, box 43 (not in file), Miscellaneous Series, RG 175.

77 "A Time of Horror," *Christian Century* 69 (14 May 1952): 581–582, see 581.

78 "Tale Ends," *AC* 17 (Feb. 1962): 116; "Tale Ends, *AC* 17 (Mar. 1962): 120; Thomas Whiteside, *The Withering Rain: America's Herbicidal Folly* (New York: E. P. Dutton & Co., 1971); Arthur Westing (ed.), *Herbicides in War: The Long-Term Ecological and Human Consequences* (London: Taylor & Francis, 1984); John Lewallen, *Ecology of Devastation: Indochina* (Baltimore: Penguin Books, 1971), Stockholm International Peace Research Institute, *Ecological Consequences of the Second Indochina War* (Stockholm: Almqvist & Wiksell International, 1976).

79 "Tale Ends," *AC* 17 (Feb. 1962): 116.

80 "Tale Ends, *AC* 17 (Mar. 1962): 120.

81 "Tale Ends, *AC* 17 (Mar. 1962): 120.

82 "One Man's Meat," *New Republic,* 23 Mar. 1963, 5–6, see 5.

83 Bertrand Russell to editor, *Nation,* 6 July 1963, n. p.

[84] Anthony Harrigan, "The Case for Gas Warfare," *New Republic,* 9 Apr. 1963, 283ff., see 283.

[85] "Eisenhower's Farewell Sees Threat to Liberties in Vast Defense Machine."

[86] "Eisenhower's Farewell Sees Threat to Liberties in Vast Defense Machine."

[87] Carson, *Silent Spring,* 18.

CHAPTER 12. EPILOGUE

[1] Debra Rosenthal, *At the Heart of the Bomb: The Dangerous Allure of Weapons Work* (Reading, Mass.: Addison-Wesley, 1990), 72.

[2] Thomas R. Dunlap, *DDT: Scientists, Citizens, and Public Policy* (Princeton: Princeton University Press, 1981); Lawrence E. McCray, "Mouse Livers, Cutworms, and Public Policy: EPA Decision Making for the Pesticides Aldrin and Dieldrin," in National Research Council, *Decision Making in the Environmental Protection Agency: Case Studies* (Washington: National Academy of Sciences, 1977), 58–118; Edmund P. Russell, "'Lost Among the Parts Per Billion': Ecological Protection at the United States Environmental Protection Agency, 1970–1993," *Environmental History* 2 (Jan. 1997): 29–51.

[3] Marcos Kogan (ed.), *Ecological Theory and Integrated Pest Management Practice* (New York: Wiley, 1986); Edmund Russell, "Enemies Hypothesis: A Review of the Effect of Vegetational Diversity on Insect Predators and Parasitoids," *Environmental Entomology* 18 (1989): 590–599; C. Ronald Carroll, John H. Vandermeer, Peter Rosset (eds.), *Agroecology* (New York: McGraw-Hill, 1990); John Vandermeer, *The Ecology of Intercropping* (New York: Cambridge University Press, 1989); National Research Council, *Alternative Agriculture* (Washington: National Academy of Sciences, 1989).

[4] Peter Matthiessen, "Rachel Carson," *Time,* 29 Mar. 1999, cover, 187–191.

[5] National Research Council, *Pesticide Resistance: Strategies and Tactics for Management* (Washington: National Academy Press, 1986), 16–17.

[6] "Antibiotics Raise Concerns," *Washington Post,* 18 Jan. 1995; "'Wonder Drugs' Losing Healing Aura," *Washington Post,* 26 June 1995.

[7] Richard Nixon, "Remarks Announcing Decisions on Chemical and Biological Defense Policies and Programs, 25 Nov. 1969," in *Public Papers of Richard Nixon 1969* (Washington: GPO, 1971), 969–970.

[8] Gerald Ford, "Remarks upon Signing Instruments of Ratification of the Geneva Protocol of 1925 and the Biological Weapons Convention, 22 Jan. 1975," in *Public Papers of Gerald R. Ford 1975* (Washington: GPO), 1:72–73.

[9] Michael Heylin, "Chemical Arms Pact Ratified," *Chemical and Engineering News,* 28 April 1997 (online at acs.org).

[10] "Pentagon's Cleanup Bill Is Escalating," *Washington Post,* 27 Mar. 1995.

[11] "Global Warming Treaty Has Pentagon Loophole," Charlottesville, Va. *Daily Progress,* 1 Jan. 1998.

[12] "US Raises Estimate of Troops Near Iraqi Chemical Arms," *Washington Post,* 27 June 1997.

[13] Author's recollection.

[14] CNN, "Survey: Tokyo Sarin Attack Survivors Still Suffer," 29 Jan. 1999 (http://cnn.com?WORLD/asiapcf/9901/28/BC-JAPAN-SARIN.reut/ion-dex.html).

[15] "US Pushes NATO on Arms Threat," *Washington Post,* 17 Dec. 1997.

[16] "New Arms Race Taking Shape," *Richmond (Va.) Times-Dispatch,* 26 Nov. 1997.

[17] Frank C. Conahan, *Human Experimentation: An Overview on Cold War Era Programs* (Washington: General Accounting Office, 28 Sept. 1994), 5, 7, 10.

[18] U. S. Entomological Commission, *First Annual Report of the United States Entomological Commission for the Year 1877 Relating to the Rocky Mountain Locust* (Washington: GPO, 1878), 115.

[19] *Oxford English Dictionary.*

[20] James Phinney Baxter, 3rd, *Scientists Against Time* (Boston: Little, Brown, 1946), 370.

[21] William N. Porter to Vannevar Bush, 30 Sept. 1944, 710 Office of Scientific Development and Research, Miscellaneous Series, RG 175.

[22] Brian Shannon, "Arsenal Base Clean-Up," Case 38, Trade and Environment Database (http://ausolaris1.american.edu/projects/mandala/TED/ice/ARS ENAL.HTM), Summer 1997, viewed 12 Oct. 1999; United States Government Accounting Office, *Environmental Cleanup: Inadequate Army Oversight of Rocky Mountain Arsenal Shared Costs* (Washington: General Accounting Office, Jan. 1997), 1.

[23] "Nature Abounds in Shadow of Lethality," *Washington Post,* 9 Oct. 1996.

[24] "New Rallying Cry: Save the DMZ!" *Washington Post,* 8 Oct. 1997.

[25] "Demilitarized Zone," *Washington Post,* 21 Mar. 1997.

Index